The Novel and the
Globalization
of Culture

MICHAEL VALDEZ MOSES

The Novel and the Globalization of Culture

New York   Oxford
OXFORD UNIVERSITY PRESS
1995

Oxford University Press

Oxford   New York
Athens   Auckland   Bangkok   Bombay
Calcutta   Cape Town   Dar es Salaam   Delhi
Florence   Hong Kong   Istanbul   Karachi
Kuala Lumpur   Madras   Madrid   Melbourne
Mexico City   Nairobi   Paris   Singapore
Taipei   Tokyo   Toronto

and associated companies in
Berlin   Ibadan

Copyright © 1995 Michael Valdez Moses

Published by Oxford University Press, Inc.,
200 Madison Avenue, New York, New York 10016

Oxford is a registered trademark of Oxford University Press

Library of Congress Cataloging-in-Publication Data
Moses, Michael Valdez, 1957–
The novel and the globalization of culture / Michael Valdez Moses.
p. cm.   Includes bibliographical references and index.
ISBN 0–19–508951–0
ISBN 0–19–508952–9 (pbk.)
1. English fiction—History and criticism.
2. Cultural relations in literature.
3. Hardy, Thomas, 1840–1928.   Mayor of Casterbridge.
4. Conrad, Joseph, 1857–1924.   Lord Jim.
5. Achebe, Chinua—Political and social views.
6. Vargas Llosa, Mario, 1936–   La guerra del fin del mundo.
7. Culture conflict in literature.
8. World history in literature.
9. Literature and anthropology.   I. Title.
PR830.C84M67   1995   809.3'9355—dc20   94–19639

1 3 5 7 9 8 6 4 2

Printed in the United States of America
on acid-free paper

For
Margarita Valdez, Pedro Salas,
and Carmen Salas,
in this world

and for
Margarita Salas y Bañuelos,
Espiridión S. Valdez, Jr.,
Consuelo Falcone, and Ettore Falcone
in the next

Our cultural crisis, for perhaps the first time in history, is the same as the crisis of our species. . . . It is not Western culture that is in danger of being destroyed tomorrow, as the cultures of the Greeks and the Arabs, the Aztecs and the Egyptians were destroyed in the past: it is man himself. The old plurality of cultures, postulating various and contrary ideals, and offering various and contrary views of the future, has been replaced by a single civilization and a single future. Until recently, history was a meditation on the many truths proposed by many cultures, and a verification of the radical heterogeneity of every society and archetype. . . . All of today's civilizations derive from that of the Western world, which has assimilated or crushed its rivals. . . . World history has become everyone's task, and our own labyrinth is the labyrinth of all mankind.

Octavio Paz, *The Labyrinth of Solitude*

Preface

Among the most vivid memories of my childhood are the long warm afternoons I spent in my grandparents' home in Los Angeles, listening to my great-grandmother and her children tell stories of the Mexican Revolution. Under the avocado trees that vaulted over the stone patio next to the house, with its whitewashed walls and Spanish tile roof, I sat while my great-aunt, Carmen Salas, recalled the day in 1914 when, as a young girl, she watched helplessly as her father was assassinated on the streets of Valparaíso, Zacatecas, stabbed and shot by Pancho Villa's men. I heard my great-grandmother, Margarita Salas y Bañuelos, bitterly recall how her husband's body was brought home over the back of a horse, how she had also lost her father, three brothers, and a first cousin in the revolution, how her hacienda had been burned to the ground. I listened to my grandmother, Margarita Valdez, and her brother and sister, Consuelo and Pedro, remember the day and night they spent as children, without food or water, hiding between the inner and outer walls of an abandoned adobe house, on the run from the *villistas* who were hunting down the *hacendados*. They recollected their struggle to keep still—almost a half century later they could still feel the ants crawling over their skin in the dark.

The security and middle-class pleasures that I enjoyed growing up in Los Angeles in the 1960s and 1970s—trips to the beach, to the mountains, to Disneyland—seemed utterly remote from the violent world my elderly Mexican relatives had known firsthand, a world of political bloodshed and revolution, civil war and exile. (Even today it is sometimes hard for me to believe that my grandparents and I grew up in the same century, on the same continent, in cities only hundreds of miles apart from each other). Of course, I did not realize then that I was already living in what many would later regard as the world's first postmodern city, nor did I recognize that the destruction of my great-grandparents' semifeudal way of life in Mexico in the early part of this century was a chapter in a vast historical narrative of global modernization. I could not have understood then that the drama of their lives, marked by the convulsive transition from a traditional to a modern society, was a typical story of the twentieth century. It has been left to me as an adult to make such observations, and to try to make sense of the story of my own family and that of hundreds of millions of other families who have made the tragic journey into modernity.

For the story of my great-grandparents and their children has been told over and over again, with major and minor variations, by many of the most significant writers of the past two centuries. That which I regarded as a boy with proprietary family interest has turned out to be the common inheritance of authors from around the world who have dramatized the historical process that we call modernization. The novels of Carlos Fuentes, Rudolfo Anaya, Gabriel García Márquez, and Mario Vargas Llosa have resonated in an especially powerful way for me, but I have also often felt that same sense of excitement, wonder, and recognition when reading the works of Joseph Conrad and Jean Rhys, Walter Scott and Chinua Achebe, André Malraux and Tayeb Salih, Elizabeth Bowen and Salman Rushdie, William Faulkner and Ruth Prawer Jhabvala. The political revolutions and tragic historical events that constitute either the background or the explicit subject matter of their writing, for all their differences, collectively comprise an overarching cosmopolitan narrative, a story that encompasses the whole globe, a tale related by the distinctive and individual voices of a large extended family.

I would venture that we have witnessed over the last two centuries the emergence of a world literature, the existence of which implies the concurrent establishment of a world that in some important respects can be spoken of as a meaningful whole. In the following pages I attempt to describe what I understand as the development of a truly global culture, in which the customary boundaries between different national literatures and distinct literary traditions are being steadily eroded. In addition to the authors I treat in this book, I think of the lives and works of many modern writers as suggestive of this global hybridization: Salman Rushdie, born in Bombay of Muslim parents, given a secular education in England, where he has become a citizen, devotee of García Márquez and Günter Grass, a novelist who writes about the modernization of India in *Midnight's Children*, Pakistan in *Shame*, Nicaragua in *The Jaguar Smile*, Argentina, England, India, Saudi Arabia, and Iran in *The Satanic Verses*. Rushdie's Japanese counterpart might be the celebrated novelist, Shusaku Endo, a Catholic convert educated in France and the author of *The Samurai*, which chronicles the historical voyage of Hasekura Rokuemon, whose circumnavigation of the globe in the seventeenth century, in an attempt to open up Japan to the Christian West, took him to *Nueva España* and Europe. Endo, in turn, calls to mind Brian Moore, born in Belfast, claiming Canadian citizenship, resident in the United States and France, whose novel *Black Robe* tells the story of a seventeenth-century French Jesuit traveling in the wilderness of North America among the Iroquois in order to convert the Hurons to Christianity. Taken to be a sorcerer by the native tribes, Moore's hero succeeds in destroying the Huron culture for the sake of a religion in which he gradually loses faith. And I think of Tahar Ben Jelloun, a Moroccan writer living in Paris, whose novel *L'enfant de sable* (*The Sand Child*), a parable of the transition from colonial to postcolonial existence, culminates in a fantastic scene in present-day Marrakech, in which the frequently interrupted story of his protagonist is resumed by an enigmatic figure known as the Blind Troubadour. Conjuring up visions of the lost Almoravid and Almohad kingdoms in medieval Spain, in which Muslims, Christians, and Jews together produced a remarkable hybrid culture, the Blind Troubadour speaks to the Berber and Arabic crowd who congregate in the city square and gradually reveals himself to be Jorge Luis Borges, an Argentine author fascinated by Arabic culture and especially *The Thousand and One Nights*, which is one of Ben Jelloun's own narrative models. The modern cosmopolitan character of the literature these writers have produced has neither required the emergence of a universal language such as Esperanto nor the homogenization of all literary forms. However, the collective works of this international set of writers, for all their differences in form and content, reflect a common concern with how a multitude of distinct traditional societies have had the same historical destiny forced upon them, a fate necessarily marked by the tragic destruction of what are retrospectively understood as "premodern" ways of life. The emergence of a global literature signals a decisive world-historical turn: the prospect that modernity is not merely a transient or provincial Western phenomenon, but instead has become the universal and perhaps permanent condition of humanity and therefore the inevitable subject of any literature that would represent contemporary existence. In short, the very process of global modernization that has made a world literature possible has itself become a principal subject of that literature.

In rethinking the history of modern literature—very broadly defined as works produced since the French Revolution—I have therefore attempted to investigate the interplay among the self-consciousness we call modernity, the narrative practices we call modernism, and the social, political, and economic process we call modernization. I am aware that such an endeavor runs the risk of slighting what is distinctive about an individual work or national literature, and worse yet, that it may be misperceived as an unwarranted return to a Eurocentric conception of cultural history. But if my thesis has merit, then the very existence of a single and hegemonic Eurocentric conception of literature is rendered obsolete, insofar as Western literature itself becomes part of a larger body of work that is truly global, hybrid, and cosmopolitan. I regard my effort as one of the many contemporary enterprises that attempt to broaden our sense of literary heritage and to give much greater critical attention to non-Western and noncanonical literatures. But I do not conceive of it as a hostile assault on "classical" or canonical texts and have resisted the temptation to erect a new Berlin Wall between Western and non-Western literatures. In fact by bringing together two of the most firmly established authors in the English literary canon, Thomas Hardy and Joseph Conrad, with two of the most significant authors who have emerged from the Third World, Chinua Achebe and Mario Vargas Llosa, I hope to show that traditional and nontraditional works can mutually illuminate each other: *Lord Jim* takes on new meaning when viewed in the context of the postcolonial novels it anticipates and *Things Fall Apart,* as its title from Yeats suggests, emerges as a telling critique of the Western literary and cultural tradition it self-consciously invokes.

In the past, it was at least arguable that literatures written in different languages at different times by different peoples ought to be studied in isolation from one another; to do otherwise would risk effacing the historically distinctive and culturally unique characters of these various literatures. At the present moment, however, when the global interpenetration of different literary and cultural traditions proceeds at an ever-increasing pace, it seems both provincial and futile to subdivide contemporary world literature into warring camps or to reinstate a new cultural Manicheanism, especially if we aim at promoting greater political tolerance and cultural diversity. The most sophisticated and ardent objections to universalist theoretical approaches cannot halt, much less roll back, a sociopolitical development that has been at least two centuries in the making and that has profoundly altered life everywhere on the planet. As I see it, contemporary postcolonial and Third World literatures are not radical alternatives to global modernity but distinctive and extremely significant reflections of its rise and diffusion.[1]

Attempts to conceptualize the globalization of culture in the modern era have taken many forms, most recently and suggestively in the debate over the so-called "end of history." Sparked by an article and then a book by Francis Fukuyama, this controversy has seemed to many to be concerned solely with a particular historical moment at the close of the twentieth century: the collapse of Soviet communism, the end of the Cold War, and the apparent triumph of liberal democracy. But before assigning a limited partisan meaning to Fukuyama's claims, it is well to remember that he derived the idea of the end of history from the work of a Russian emigré, the French philosopher Alexandre Kojève, a Marxist who was elaborating his thesis in the late 1940s and 1950s—that is, precisely at the height of the Cold War. And Kojève in turn developed his ideas in the form of a commentary on *The Phenomenology of Spirit,* a work by Hegel, whose philosophy of history emerged from a meditation on the end of the last vestiges of the Holy Roman Empire at the battle of Jena—that is, in the aftermath of the French Revolution and Napoleon's efforts to spread its principles throughout Europe.[2] The complicated genealogy of "the end of history" suggests that, although recent events clearly have lent a certain timeliness to Fukuyama's thesis and contributed to its impact, the issues he raises are broader and have greater historical scope than many of his critics grant. Despite my many reservations about "the end of history," I have found this philosophic thesis a useful way of framing the issues I wish to investigate in this book: modernization and the globalization of culture. Contemporary critics are understandably skeptical of the teleology implicit in "the end of history," but they ought to be aware that Kojève's talk of posthistorical existence is only another way of formulating the idea of the postmodern condition that the majority of intellectuals today recognize as their common fate.

No doubt some may feel that my reliance upon the thinking of Hegel and Kojève as a way of conceptualizing the emergence of a global literature reveals an insidious Eurocentric bias, especially since their work tends to embody the thesis that the West is where the future happens first. But I would respond that one cannot simultaneously fault the West for imposing its way of life upon the rest of the world and insist with equal fervor that its historical and cultural centrality has been greatly overstated. To the degree that Third World literature continues to offer a trenchant critique of modernity, it does so by preserving in some way the heterogeneous premodern forms of life that are often incompatible with the ethical and political virtues adumbrated by the phrases "multiculturalism," "political tolerance," and "democratic pluralism." What Ghanaian philosopher Kwasi Wiredu has said with respect to contemporary postcolonial African society seems generally applicable to all cultures seeking to redefine themselves in a new global context:

> The quest for development, then, should be viewed as a continuing world historical process in which all peoples, Western and non-Western alike, are engaged. . . . [I]t becomes possible to see the movement towards modernization in Africa not as essentially a process in which Africans are unthinkingly jettisoning their own heritage of thought in the pursuit of Western ways of life, but rather as one in which Africans in common with all other peoples seek to attain a specifically *human* destiny.[3]

If I have endeavored here to find some common ground among a diverse set of writers, to explore the underlying historical and political developments that have linked together the modern global novel, I have also tried to honor what is local and unique in the works of individual authors. By attending closely to the specific historical contexts and tragic texture of novels written by Hardy, Conrad, Achebe, and Vargas Llosa, I hope to suggest my own considerable reservations about the grandiose and Olympian philosophic historicism of Hegel and Kojève. As uncompromising defenders of the historical process that culminates in modernity, they are not inclined to dwell in any detail on the tragic events that constitute the substance of history, nor are they likely to pause for very long to consider the immense human suffering that makes "progress" possible. As opposed to the philosophic detachment that characterizes their synoptic view of human destiny, the novelists I have treated here express a much deeper and richer appreciation of the personal and social cataclysms that are too easily lost sight of from a philosophic vantage point at "the end of history." In bringing together the study of philosophy and the study of literature in this book, I am guided by the fact that, although philosophical thinking can help us uncover and formulate the issues raised by literature, literature can help us correct the distortions of abstract philosophical theory, especially of the German Idealist variety represented by Hegel.

Inevitably the limitations of a single book restrict the scope of a critical enterprise. These constraints have seemed to me all the more problematic given the wide-ranging and synthetic aims of this project. Thus, I need not have restricted myself to an analysis of the modern novel and might, for example, have profitably included in this study a consideration of modern drama and poetry. Plays such as Wole Soyinka's *Death and the King's Horseman* or Brian Friel's *Translations* deal directly with the political and social disruptions caused by modernization. The works of such poets as Yeats and Neruda frequently explore the same territory. But I have chosen to concentrate on the novel because, given the distinctive nature of the genre, it provides the fullest representation of society and hence of the issues I wish to analyze. In this regard, I follow Lukács, who characterizes the novel as an artistic form intended to represent the "totality of objects" in society:

> The novel has the task of evoking directly the full span of life, the complexity and intricacy of its developments, the incommensurability of its detail. . . . This whole includes not simply the dead objects through which men's social life manifests itself, but also the various customs, institutions, habits, usages etc. characteristic of a certain phase of human society and of the direction it is taking. Society is the principal subject of the novel, that is, man's social life in its ceaseless interaction with surrounding nature, which forms the basis of social activity, and with the different social institutions or customs which mediate the relations between individuals in social life.[4]

In short, the novel, with its density of detail, ideally provides a condensation or crystallization of social life that registers both the objective conditions of society and the particular subjective reactions of individuals to those conditions during decisive moments of historical change.

Having decided to focus on the novel, I found it necessary to limit the number of novels treated in this study. There are many more works of fiction I would like to have discussed, including Thomas Mann's *Doctor Faustus,* Malraux's *Man's Fate,* Faulkner's *Absalom,*

Absalom!, Solzhenitsyn's *The Red Wheel,* Ngugi wa Thiong'o's *A Grain of Wheat,* Salman Rushdie's *Midnight's Children,* and Alejo Carpentier's *Explosion in a Cathedral.* I especially regret that I have not had the opportunity to discuss at any length the important roles played by both fascism and Marxian socialism in the historical process of modernization, and the way in which these two political movements have been represented in some of the most significant fiction written in this century. The subject deserves an entire book to itself. Within the limits of my present study, I have endeavored to capture at least a sense of broad historical and geographical sweep, focusing on nineteenth- and twentieth-century novels, "First" and "Third World" authors. In an effort to represent the way in which modernity has imposed itself upon the world as a whole, the novels on which I focus are variously set in Europe (*The Mayor of Casterbridge*), Asia (*Lord Jim*), Africa (*Things Fall Apart* and *No Longer at Ease*), and Latin America (*The War of the End of the World*). The varied backgrounds of their authors—Hardy, Conrad, Achebe, and Vargas Llosa—reflect a similar geographic and ethnic heterogeneity, especially if one remembers that Conrad was an Eastern European Pole.

These disparate novels share a common concern with isolated and archaic communities facing the prospect of subversion and even annihilation under the onslaught of modernity. Casterbridge, Patusan, Igboland, and Canudos are all historical anachronisms, political backwaters in which remnants of premodern and traditional ways of life maintain their precarious hold.[5] And yet despite the relative poverty and lack of sophistication that characterize these societies, each community stands as a distinct, legitimate, and in many ways inviting alternative to modern society. Not that any of these novels presents traditional communities in an idealized fashion, for Hardy, Conrad, Achebe, and Vargas Llosa all insist on revealing the shortcomings and injustices that characterize these diverse premodern societies. Nevertheless, each novelist attempts to recover in fictional form the heterogeneous possibilities for human life lost and nearly forgotten as a consequence of the victory of modernity. Though all these novelists admit the benefits that progress brings, they are nonetheless concerned that the possible ways of organizing human society, of gratifying individual desires and ambitions, of being-in-the-world have been considerably narrowed in the course of history. For a brief moment in each of the novels, a world comes to life populated by human beings whose beliefs, mores, and values are radically different from those that have come to prevail in the twentieth century, and in that moment the limitations of modernity are also illuminated.

Above all, by dramatizing the violent and destructive process by which these archaic societies are transformed by and incorporated into the modern world, these four novelists testify to the havoc wreaked upon individual human lives in the name of progress. The novelists I discuss are all citizens and beneficiaries of the modern world, but they nonetheless feel compelled to record for posterity the great costs, paid in blood and pain, that peoples around the world have rendered to settle accounts with history. Hegel recognized that "History" is "a slaughter-bench," but it has been left to imaginative writers such as Hardy, Conrad, Achebe, and Vargas Llosa to present the tragic nature of the conflict between traditional and progressive societies in dramatic fashion and riveting detail. In contrast to the philosophic abstractions that characterize Hegel's and Kojève's formulation of universal history, the novels I treat never lose touch with how that history looks from the perspective of an individual human actor struggling against its overpowering flow. It is particularly their concern for individual human tragedy, a concern I first felt when listening to my Mexican elders recall their own personal histories, that has drawn me to this study.

Durham, N.C.; Canberra, ACT.   M. V. M.
July 1994

Acknowledgments

The progress and the unexpected turns of my personal history are evident in the debts I owe to others. My teachers at Harvard, New College, Oxford, and the University of Virginia have given generously of themselves; and I feel especially grateful for the help and encouragement of Douglas Day, Patrick Glynn, E. D. Hirsch, Robert Langbaum, Paul Cantor, Michael Levenson, Harvey Mansfield, David Perkins, and Walter Sokel.

In recent years, my friends and colleagues at Duke University have provided me a vibrant intellectual community and real home. Both on and off the court, Stanley Fish has given me a key role on his team, and urged me to take the open shot. Frank Lentricchia early on expressed his enthusiasm for my work; more importantly, he has been for me a model of uncompromising intellectual integrity. Jane Tompkins, Lee Patterson, and Annabel Patterson have offered a rare combination of professional advice and personal confidence. George Gopen, Thomas Pfau, Olga Valbuena, Melissa Malouf, Sara Beckwith, and John Twyning have collectively provided an ideal place to think and live. I consider myself especially fortunate to have met Thomas Ferraro and Beth Eastlick some years ago. Tom has read the manuscript in its entirety and contributed directly to its clarity and tone; Beth has generously given her expert editorial advice. Together Tom and Beth have extended to me the constancy and support of family.

I should like to thank the many other readers of this manuscript (some of them anonymous), including Kevin Taylor, Farley Kern, Lisa Mulman, Paul Kelleher, and my research assistant, Joshua Esty, all of whom offered valuable suggestions. Lucía Suárez was kind enough to check my translations of Spanish and Portuguese texts. Liz Maguire, at Oxford University Press, has been the most indulgent and enthusiastic of editors.

Much appreciated financial support for the writing of this book has been provided by the Woodrow Wilson Foundation, which granted me a Charlotte Newcombe Fellowship; by Hillel Fradkin, who arranged a postdoctoral fellowship from the Bradley Foundation; and by the Duke University Research Council, which made available a summer research grant. Finally, I should like to thank Graeme Clark and Iain McCalman of the Humanities Research Centre at the Australian National University in Canberra; a Visiting Fellowship at the HRC in 1994 provided me the opportunity to make the final revisions of this book.

An earlier and substantially different version of the Hardy chapter appeared as "Agon in the Marketplace: *The Mayor of Casterbridge* as Bourgeois Tragedy," *South Atlantic Quarterly* 87 (Spring 1988): 219–51.

Contents

The Novel and the
Globalization
of Culture

Introduction: Hegel, Stendhal, and Posthistorical Existence

> If we look at the life of the thirteenth century, passing from Chartres to Borobudur and from Venice to the Mayas, from Constantinople to Peking and from Kublai Khan to Dante, from the house of Maimonides at Cordoba to Nara, and from the *Magna Carta* to the Byzantine monks copying Aristotle; compare this extraordinary diversity with the present state of the world, where countries are not really different from each other in terms of their present—which, as such, is everywhere *the same*—but only in terms of their past. *That* is what the developed world *is*.
>
> Cornelius Castoriadis, "Reflections on 'Rationality' and Development"

I

To speak seriously of the end of history is generally to invite incredulity or even derision. The idea that history has a discernible telos or that it has in some fundamental sense already come to an end strikes most people as absurd. And yet, when asked whether they can seriously envision a return to monarchic or aristocratic government, a reestablishment of slavery or of serfdom, or a complete abandonment of modern science, industry, and technology, these same people would be unanimous in insisting that such developments are unthinkable, or at any rate, undesirable. What their reaction suggests is that almost all citizens in the developed world, and especially the intelligentsia of modern nations, tacitly accept the thesis, first articulated in a rigorously systematic philosophical manner by Hegel, that history does indeed have a *direction* and an *end*.

I am fully aware that most academicians, and particularly those

3

working in the humanities, regard themselves as post-Nietzscheans, who reject the "totalizing" and absolutist claims to historical knowledge associated with Hegelian philosophy. Whether they call themselves poststructuralist, neopragmatist, or postaxiological critics, all agree that our view of history is partial, prejudiced, interested, constructed, and ideologically bound by the epistemological limits and social contingencies of the present moment. But this position is itself derivative from Hegel's thought, though it forms only a part rather than the whole of his philosophy of history. For Hegel insists that the insight that all human knowledge has hitherto been historically limited can only be arrived at once history has been completed. All nonteleological forms of historicism are for Hegel logically inconsistent. Only because he understands himself to be no longer subject to the process of history itself and therefore in possession of absolute knowledge concerning the completed course of historical human development can Hegel make the assertion that all previous ideologies were only the partial or relative truths of their times, ideologies that are subsequently synthesized in and completed by Hegel's universal philosophy of history.

Unlike most contemporary theorists, Hegel is undaunted by the magnitude and immodesty of his claim that history has come to an end and that he is the first to understand and to articulate the meaning of this singular event. Many contemporary intellectuals have eschewed Hegel's grandiose pretensions, preferring to face the logical aporia that confronts any form of nonteleological historicism: why is the truth of historicism itself not merely an historically conditioned "truth"? It is not my purpose here to discuss the various and in my view unsatisfactory answers that have been given to this question. It is enough to note that Hegel and his twentieth-century interpreter and advocate, the French philosopher Alexandre Kojève, avoid this impasse by insisting that history is at an end, or what amounts to the same thing, that for the first time the end of history can now be known.[1] For both thinkers, human history can only be understood as the basis of truth when it has been completed; for both, the philosophical understanding of the whole of human history marks a final stage in the historical emergence of truth.

Although it is difficult to overstate the vehemence of contemporary theoretical hostility to the Hegelian thesis, it is nevertheless the case that it has continued to exert a strong if often subterranean influence upon current thinking. Francis Fukuyama in *The End of History and the Last Man* has recently offered a sophisticated defense of the

Hegel-Kojève thesis on the basis of a comparative analysis of geo-political developments in the post–Cold War world. In *Freedom: Freedom in the Making of Western Culture,* sociologist Orlando Patterson has rewritten and revised the central narrative thread of Hegel's *The Philosophy of History,* his argument that the historical development of humanity in the West culminates in the universal recognition of human freedom. These recent works take their place within a historicist philosophic tradition that has often been attacked and occasionally dismissed, but nevertheless winds along a tortuous route from Hegel and Comte through Feuerbach and Marx to Weber, Lukács, Kojève, Merleau-Ponty, Sartre, Adorno, and Habermas.[2]

The enduring and pervasive influence of the Hegelian thesis in our own time becomes evident when we consider just how common and even routine is our use of words like "modernization" and "development." We speak easily and confidently of "modernizing" industrial plants and entire nations, just as we talk of the tasks of economic and political "development" in the newly liberated states of Eastern Europe, the impoverished nations of the Third World, and the most depressed sectors of Western industrialized societies. In much the same way, the terms "progressive" and "reactionary" serve as the common coin of political exchange. Both words imply that one can classify political positions, individuals, parties, movements, ideologies, and regimes according to whether they advance or retard some ill-defined but unidirectional process of historical evolution. The widespread and unproblematic use of these terms does not in itself validate the Hegelian thesis, but it does point to the implicit acceptance of a progressive linear conception of human history on the part of a vast majority of those who live in both the "developed" and "developing" worlds. In fact, a whole range of phenomena that occupy the attention of cultural critics and social scientists—the globalization of culture, the campaign for international human rights, the historical formation of a "world system," the spread of "cultural imperialism," the creation of a media-centered "global village," the sudden collapse of many autocratic and totalitarian governments throughout the world, the emergence of independent postcolonial nations, the struggle of ethnic minorities and subjugated peoples for self-determination, the resilience and widespread appeal of liberal democratic principles, the rapid development of an interdependent global market—all can be understood as particular manifestations of what Kojève calls "posthistorical" society or the "universal and homogeneous state."[3]

A less controversial way of stating that history has come to an end is to suggest that a homogenizing worldwide process of modernization has become irreversible. All human communities are gradually but inexorably coming to resemble one another, exhibiting the same salient characteristics of a modern society. While serious and significant disagreements remain concerning the origins, historical development, and unitary character of modernity, a loose consensus exists as to some of its principal constitutive features. A modern society accepts and exploits the technological achievements of modern natural science. As such, it is based upon the (sometimes unacknowledged) premise that humanity need not conform to a natural or divinely sanctioned order; collectively human beings possess the power and authority to command nature, to dominate and order the cosmos according to their own needs and desires. Modern society is consequently one that at least implicitly embraces the secularization of human society.[4] While lip service may still be paid to a divine order and a variety of faiths tolerated, even celebrated, the underlying reality of modernity is the rational and scientific demystification of the world, the autonomy of human authority, and the flight of the gods. Intimately connected to the spread of modern science and the secularization of society is the simultaneous advance of trade and commerce. The market economy, especially the advantages it produces from the division of labor, leads to an ever-increasing accumulation of capital. And this accumulation makes possible the development and widespread application of new technologies that are the fruit of modern science. Based on the primacy of material progress and the care of the body, the market economy thus further weakens the hold of religions that traditionally devoted themselves to spiritual concerns.

If modern natural science, secularization, and the market economy collectively constitute one of the essential bases of the modern project, a second is provided by what Kojève, following and to some degree modifying Hegel, calls the "struggle" for "universal recognition."[5] As interpreted by Kojève, Hegel tells a philosophical tale in which human history begins with a violent struggle for pure prestige between two human beings. The victor willingly risks his life in order to force his foe to acknowledge his humanity. The vanquished submits to the will of his adversary rather than face death. This is the origin of the distinction between master and slave. The master demonstrates his humanity by forcing the slave to recognize him; he proves his distinctively human potential by virtue of his insistence on placing greater importance on the recognition of his human dignity than on his purely physical existence. By contrast, for the sake of his brute physical survival, the slave relinquishes all claims to have his humanity recognized by another. The victory of the master is, however, both provisional and incomplete. He faces a tragic paradox that he never overcomes; he wins recognition from a creature that he in turn does not and cannot recognize as fully human. The victory the master gains over his slave is therefore in a fundamental sense unsatisfying.

Hegel suggests that the master remains at this impasse until he vanishes from history. He cannot escape his tragic historical fate, since to repudiate his mastery would be to repudiate the very thing on which his humanity rests. Consequently, the future development of human history depends on the activities of the slave. The latter works for the master, whom he supplies with a wealth of things meant for consumption. Whereas the master never works and essentially remains static throughout the rest of history, the slave gradually develops as a result of the work he performs for the master. Through his work, the slave produces the objects and technologies that help to drive human history forward and that transform the world in which he and his master live. Moreover, the slave begins to recognize himself in the objects he creates for the pleasure of the master. His initial self-recognition takes the form of seeing himself as a free and independent creator of his own works and as a master of the natural materials that he uses in his labor. But the recognition that work provides the slave is not equivalent to that enjoyed by the master; although the slave recognizes himself, he cannot force others to do so.

The resolution of the master–slave dialectic requires that the incipient self-recognition of the slave culminate in a revolt against the master. Only through an act of violent rebellion does the slave finally overcome the fear of death that initially condemned him to inhuman servitude. Violent revolution is necessary for the slave to assert his human dignity and to win for himself the recognition he hitherto lacked. Through this violent action the slave ceases to be a slave, but he does not thereby become a master. For in that violent rebellion the old master is destroyed. The liberated slave is neither master nor slave, but a synthesis of the two, a bourgeois. His rebellion, which Kojève and Hegel identify with the French Revolution, establishes at least in principle the mutual recognition of all human beings by all other human beings. The historical struggle for recognition ends with a new and universal acknowledgment of the humanity of each and every individual. The distinction between master and slave is definitively and permanently overcome; in its place comes the Declaration of the Rights of Man, the universal establishment of human freedom, and the dawning of posthistorical society.

Such a philosophical tale, however interesting, may seem unconvincing when presented in this simple skeletal form. The explanatory power of this philosophic account makes itself felt only in Hegel's comprehensive account of human history, which reiterates and elaborates this abstract narrative in encyclopedic detail. Hegel's *Philosophy of History, Aesthetics, History of Philosophy, Philosophy of Religion,* and *Philosophy of Right* collectively provide a detailed working out of his thesis with regard to the development of politics, philosophy, art, and religion throughout the whole of human history. This is not the place to rehearse Hegel's gargantuan narrative. It is enough to suggest that the conclusion at which Hegel arrives, that history culminates in the universal recognition of human freedom, is implicit within the political ideology that has come to dominate the modern world. Although many governments continue to violate human rights, they customarily deny that such abuses take place within their borders; few regimes are willing to reject openly the existence or legitimacy of those rights, internationally recognized and codified in such documents as the United Nations Charter. Even tyrannical regimes typically insist that the legitimacy of their government rests upon the sovereign will of the people; the most authoritarian and oppressive rulers routinely attempt to demonstrate to the world that despite appearances they in fact truly represent and serve the interests of those they rule. It is crucial that we understand that for Hegel and Kojève the end of history is not the moment when all people on earth have in practice secured their rights as free human beings, but only that moment when, with the overthrow of all aristocratic bases of rule, such rights have in principle been recognized.

Thus the validity of the Hegel-Kojève thesis does not depend on the fact that the cessation of all human struggle and the end of all war and political conflict have already occurred. As Kojève notes, when Hegel finished *The Phenomenology of Spirit* shortly after the Battle of Jena in 1806, the process of global modernization was far from complete. Nonetheless, in 1948 Kojève could insist that all historical events that followed in the wake of this decisive military and political event, in which the French forces under Napoleon defeated the last remnants of the Holy Roman Empire (monarchist and aristocratic Prussia), had merely confirmed the essential validity of Hegel's insight that the definitive end of human political evolution was already discernible in 1806:

> Observing what was taking place around me and reflecting on what had taken place in the world since the Battle of Jena, I understood that Hegel was right to see in this battle the end of History properly so-called. In and by this battle the vanguard of humanity virtually attained the limit and the aim, that is, the *end,* of Man's historical evolution. What has happened since then was but an extension in space of the universal revolutionary force actualized in France by Robespierre-Napoleon. From the authentically historical point of view, the two world wars with their retinue of large and small revolutions had only the effect of bringing the backward civilizations of the peripheral provinces into line with the most advanced (real or virtual) European historical positions. If the sovietization of Russia and the communization of China are anything more than or different from the democratization of imperial Germany (by way of Hitlerism) or the accession of Togoland to independence, nay, the self-determination of the Papuans, it is only because the Sino-Soviet actualization of Robespierrian Bonapartism obliges post-Napoleonic Europe to speed up the elimination of the numerous more or less anachronistic sequels to its pre-revolutionary past. Already, moreover, this process of elimination is more advanced in the North American extensions of Europe than in Europe itself. One can even say that, from a certain point of view, the United States has already attained the final stage of Marxist "communism" seeing that, practically, all the members of a "classless society" can from now on appropriate for themselves everything that seems good to them, without thereby working any more than their heart dictates.[6]

For Kojève, the most fundamental human question, that is the basic historical question concerning the sole legitimate form of government, was already decided, at least in principle, by 1806. All events following the French Revolution and the Napoleonic wars merely served to confirm and to actualize on a global scale that earlier and definitive historical decision.

Only one who comfortably occupies an Olympian position can view two world wars, the liberation of the Third World from European and Asiatic imperialism, and the rise and fall of communism and fascism as little more than "mopping up" operations that follow the end of history. For those who fought, suffered, and died in those events, the wars and revolutions of the twentieth century were tragic affairs of immense significance. Kojève's apparent calm and equanimity when reflecting on these events, his studied disinterestedness in conflicts among the United States, China, and the Soviet Union throughout the Cold War, his godlike detachment from the cataclysmic political crises of his time, all derive ultimately from an insight central to the Hegelian philosophy of history. For Hegel, the dialectical progression of history proceeds by way of great tragic conflicts. While the ultimate resolution of human history brings about what Kant called "perpetual peace," the means by which mankind arrives at the end of history are inherently tumultuous, violent, and tragic. It is for this reason that Hegel makes reference in the famous introduction to *The Philosophy of History* to history itself as a "slaughter-bench."[7]

Hegel's theory of the tragic dialectic of human development provides a crucial link between his philosophy of history and his philosophy of art, and begins to suggest the relevance of his thought to understanding the modern global novel. Hegel's theory of tragedy is arguably the most insightful ever offered, though still less well-known than Aristotle's. For Hegel, tragedy, as opposed to what we would call melodrama, does not consist in the conflict between good and evil. Melodramatic conflict, if resolved in favor of the principle of virtue leaves the audience edified, and if in favor of vice, depressed or outraged. But in neither case does it provoke the emotions peculiar to a genuinely tragic conflict. The latter, according to Hegel, requires a collision between two moral principles or "ethical substantives," both of which command the respect of an audience. In short, tragedy consists of the irresolvable conflict between two incompatible moral "goods" or ethical systems. In his *Aesthetics,* Hegel offers the tragic conflict of *Antigone* as the prototype of his theory: Antigone must choose between loyalty to the gods of the family and the gods of the city. If she buries her brother, who has been a traitor to Thebes, she violates the law of the city; but if she leaves him unburied, she violates her obligations to her family. The moral good of the family comes into irreconcilable conflict with the ethical good of the political community.

Strictly speaking, Hegel's theory of tragedy describes an aesthetic form and is only indirectly related to his theory of history. Nevertheless, the importance to Hegel of moments of historical crisis supplies a link between his aesthetics and his philosophy of history. In Hegel's view, historical change involves fundamental clashes between old ways of life and new, thus creating the kinds of tragic choices between two ethical substantives that he sees portrayed in drama. Indeed, although Hegel may seem to offer an abstract and universal theory of tragedy, he always locates tragic conflict at specific moments of historical crisis.[8] In the case of *Antigone,* the play reflects the shift from the family-based tribal organization of archaic Greece to the more "modern" organization of the polis, which attempts to suppress and transcend family loyalties. In that sense, the prototypical and recurrent tragedy in Hegel *is* the tragedy of "modernization," the conflict between traditional ways of life that have become ingrained and the modes and orders that try to displace and supersede them. This link between Hegel's theory of tragedy and his philosophy of history has provided me with the conceptual basis for analyzing literary representations of modernization in the fully contemporary sense of the term.

Thus Hegel does not understand history per se as tragic, but instead understands tragedy as the principal engine of historical development. Retrospectively, Hegel looks back at the most violent political conflicts, turbulent religious and ethical controversies, and bloody collisions of peoples and individuals as forming a linear pattern of human development that ultimately resolves itself in a final ideal synthesis at the end of history. The wars of Greece against Persia, the conquests of Alexander the Great, the imperial victories of Rome, the persecution of Christianity and its eventual triumph, the destruction of Rome by barbarians, the military triumphs of Islam, the crusades of the Middle Ages, the violent subjugation of the New World, the great European religious wars of the seventeenth century, the French Revolution and the Napoleonic Wars, all are simultaneously tragic historical events and chapters in the progressive realization of freedom. For Hegel, the worst and most inhumane abuses of history—the slave trade of Africa, the tyrannical rule of the Caesars, the torture and crucifixion of Christians, the chattel existence of women and children under Mandarin rule, the degradation of the *chandala* in India, the exploitative treatment of European serfs, the religious violence of Catholic and Protestant sectarians, the Terror of the French Revolution—ultimately assume a necessary role in a historical progression that dialectically overcomes and cancels out all of these horrific practices. Humanity creates and liberates itself *through* history, but its birth and development occur only through tragic violence *in* history.

Whether a violent political or religious conflict appears as a tragedy or a reassuring chapter in the history of human evolution thus depends upon one's historical perspective. It is only because Hegel and Kojève understand themselves to come at the end of history that they can remain sanguine in the face of immeasurable human suffering and unspeakable cruelty. For the participants in such political and social upheavals, these events—whether they point toward or merely confirm the end of history—remain tragic, particularly since they generally demand the destruction of many, if not most, of those involved. The difference in perspective between those who participate in world-historical events and those like Hegel and Kojève who presume to come at the end of history reflects a distinction between those who remain fundamentally ignorant of their role in human development and those who know themselves to be the fully self-conscious products of the end of history. Hegel refers to the "cunning of reason" or the "ruse of reason" in history, by which he means that the rationality of completed history is produced by and out of the irrational (or incompletely rational) actions of historical actors.[9] Tocqueville refers to the same paradox of historical development when he argues:

> Everywhere the diverse happenings in the lives of peoples have turned to democracy's profit; all men's efforts have aided it, both those who intended this and those who had no such intention, those who fought for democracy and those who were the declared enemies thereof; all have been driven pell-mell along the same road, and all have worked together, some against their will and some unconsciously.[10]

Regardless of the particular intentions or ideologies of historical participants, individually and collectively their actions, which take the form of tragic conflict, eventuate in the realization of what Tocqueville called equality or democracy, Hegel universal human freedom, and Kojève posthistorical society or the universal and homogenous state.

II

For Hegel, the end of history means the end of tragedy. Tragic conflicts are the motive forces of history, but at the end of history all tragedies are resolved in a higher synthesis of opposing forces. One consequence of the democratizing influence of the French Revolution is therefore a decisive turn in the history of literature; no longer can authors—at least those who live in a postrevolutionary world—look to their own age as a suitable subject for tragic treatment. The central figure of traditional tragedy, the master or aristocrat, and the tragic drama itself, regarded at least since Aristotle as one of the highest and most prestigious literary forms, appear to have become historical anachronisms. A postrevolutionary age requires a new literature if it is to reflect the new democratic character of society. As a direct participant in the Napoleonic revolution of Europe, Stendhal is one of the first, and one of the most profound, authors to confront the problem posed for both literature and society by the Hegelian end of history (even though he was undoubtedly unaware of Hegel's precise philosophical formulation of the issue.) Both in his critical and fictional works and most especially in his novel *The Red and the Black,* Stendhal attempts to come to terms with what Kojève calls posthistorical existence. Unwilling to concede that comedy is the only appropriate artistic form for his age, and unhappy with a postrevolutionary society in which, as one of his characters says, "everything ends with a song," Stendhal seeks to reveal the subterrannean discontents and diagnose the psychological maladies that beset post-Napoleonic France. In so doing, Stendhal anticipates the critical and sometimes openly hostile view of modernized Europe that was to characterize later novelists, a view that led many of them to consider some alternative to modernity.

In Stendhal one finds a European novelist who seriously entertains and effectively dramatizes the prospect that all truly significant and fundamental political struggle is at an end, that the "history" of postrevolutionary and post-Napoleonic Europe at most marks only a coda to or reprise of what has gone before. Though not a philosophical historian like Hegel, Stendhal did write about history, and often in quasi-Hegelian terms. In his *A Life of Napoleon,* Stendhal argues that civilization passes through three distinct stages. The first is primitive democracy or despotism, the second aristocracy under one or more rulers, and the third (and presumably final) one is representative government. Napoleon represents for Stendhal the last grand figure in the second stage of history, the nineteenth-century tyrant who paradoxically brings about the third phase of civilization (LN, p. 181). Although as emperor, Napoleon had striven to create a new aristocracy, reestablish the religious authority of the Catholic Church, and found a new monarchic dynasty, in Stendhal's view his lasting contribution to civilization is to have actualized and spread the revolutionary doctrines of the French Revolution beyond the political boundaries of France. His fall from power, ostensibly brought about by the Grand Alliance, actually grows out of his failure to adhere steadfastly to the republican principles animating him at the time of those early military victories that made him the Savior of the Revolution and the Liberator of Italy (LN, pp. 114, 124–25).

His increasingly despotic character gradually corrupts the once virtuous republican armies, rendering them vulnerable to their traditional antirepublican enemies. Stendhal insists that had Bonaparte
replaced the monarchies of Europe, which he had defeated by 1806,
with a federation of republics naturally allied with revolutionary
France, his success would have been assured (LN, pp. 61, 136). In any
case, despite his defeats at Moscow, Leipzig, and Waterloo,
Napoleon over the course of his entire career sowed the seeds of
European modernity and served to accelerate the democratization of
the continent. Napoleon is thus, for Stendhal, a "great tragic actor,"
who embodies both the radical republicanism of his youth and the
despotic ambitions of his later years. His life represents an ethical and
historical struggle that is objectified in the wars, both civil and foreign, waged first under the Directory and later under Napoleon's own
regime (LN, p. 139).[11] The individual tragedy of Napoleon's life is
thus the tragedy of France and implicitly that of Europe as a whole.
For Napoleon makes impossible the subsequent emergence of any
figure of comparable heroic stature. He is at the same time the
quintessential representative of the second phase of civilization and
its destroyer, a despot antithetical to the republicanism of the final
phase of history, and yet its creator.

Stendhal realized the implications of these historical developments
for literature; in particular, they made the successful literary representation of heroic figures extremely problematic. While still a young
man, Stendhal had aspired to write dramatic tragedies and went so
far as to sketch out a number of tragic plays that he subsequently
abandoned, including one tentatively entitled *The Return from Elba:
A Prose Tragedy in Five Acts*.[12] But the collapse of the Restoration
and the fall of the last of the Bourbons confirmed Stendhal's suspicion that the possibilities of French drama had been played out, and
that only a popular bourgeois literary genre, the novel, offered him a
real future.[13] His decision to turn to the novel reflected his conviction
that between 1780 and 1823 the French public had undergone a
fundamental change in their morals and tastes, a change as rapid and
complete as any in previous history.[14] The relatively stable aristocratic tastes of the court of Louis XIV had given way to the ever-
shifting democratic tastes of a new reading public, the bourgeoisie.[15]
In the post-Napoleonic age, both the hero of literature and the audience for literature were therefore to be of a new democratic type.
Moreover, the dramatic conflicts that characterized the lives of Stendhal's new heroes and heroines would consequently also take a new

form; they would be internalized or subjective struggles chiefly concerned with nuances of feeling and shifts in psychological states.[16]

Stendhal's efforts at novelistic "bourgeois tragedy" thus reflect his desire to respond to and record the new social conditions of post-Napoleonic France.[17] We might say that *Le rouge et le noir: Chronique de 1830* emerges from Stendhal's ambition to write a subjective tragedy in a posthistorical age. But if Hegel and Kojève are correct in assuming that the end of history means the end of tragedy, then a posthistorical tragedy would seem to be a contradiction in terms. For Hegel, even subjective tragedy—for example, the drama of Shakespeare—reflects decisive shifts in the historical consciousness of characters. Modern subjective tragedy, though different from classical objective tragedy by virtue of its interiorization of ethical conflict, nevertheless represents a substantive collision that occurs *within* history, albeit rather late in the unfolding of human self-consciousness. By contrast, *The Red and the Black* appears to be Stendhal's attempt to write a tragedy about characters who live after the work of history has already been completed, that is after the possibility of tragedy would seem to have been historically exhausted. Stendhal's highly self-conscious narrative voice, his insistent ironic deflation of his hero, Julien Sorel, and the exaggerated theatricality of his principal characters all speak to the historical paradox that confronts the most advanced elements within Western European society in the post-revolutionary age. In Stendhal's novel tragedy appears only in the form of historical anachronism or as the highly self-conscious theatrics of characters whose psychological disturbances and personal frustrations masquerade as political conflicts.

Julien tells himself that had he "lived twenty years ago, a life of heroic action would have" been his (RB, p. 159). If not the new Napoleon, Julien would have been at the very least a second Danton or Robespierre, or another Marshal Ney. But his misfortune is to be a Napoleonic imitator who lives in a post-Napoleonic age.[18] His own epoch frustrates his every effort to rise in the world by virtue of military heroism or revolutionary activity. The France of the Bourbon Restoration cannot provide Stendhal's hero with the historical field on which to play out a second time Napoleon's or Robespierre's tragic destiny.

Superficially, Restoration France under Louis XVIII and Charles X seems a hierarchical regime in which the monarchy, nobility, and clergy are once again in the ascendant. The victory of reactionary forces, while making it more difficult for a petit bourgeois like Julien to rise in society, would seem to have made republican and revolutionary change once again necessary and desirable. But as René Girard points out in *Deceit, Desire, and the Novel,* below its surface Restoration France is in fact already a profoundly egalitarian society. The "return" to a prerevolutionary stage is merely formal, masking an underlying continuity in the body politic of postrevolutionary France. The nobility and bourgeoisie have in fact become mirror images of one another, the aristocrats assuming the financial interests of middle-class businessmen, the bourgeoisie the affectations and tastes of their erstwhile superiors.[19] Even before the revolution of 1830, in which the "citizen-King" Louis-Phillipe came to the throne (passing his idle moments speculating on the stock exchange), the French monarch, Louis XVIII, had granted the citizens a *chartre,* a written constitution guaranteeing a number of important economic and political rights and establishing a bicameral legislature. By 1830, the *Code Napoléon* has helped to guarantee a certain equality under the law and the divine right of Kings has lost its legitimacy. Even the Catholic Church enjoys renewed prestige and influence primarily because it has become a virtual bureaucratic agency of the state whose secular interests it serves; in the world of *The Red and the Black,* the Church functions principally as a clearing house for ambitious young men eager for material success and social advancement, rather than as an autonomous spiritual community devoted to otherwordly concerns and the salvation of souls. Although political parties vie for power within Restoration France, the differences between liberals and ultras (conservatives) turn out to be negligible. Partisans such as Monsieur Valenod and Monsieur de Rênal exchange party affiliations without in any way altering their habits, mores, interests, or mutual antagonisms.[20]

Julien Sorel is not the only character within this "Chronicle of 1830" who discovers that his heroic ambitions are frustrated by his historical belatedness and by the fundamental ineffectuality and triviality of politics within Restoration society. Stendhal's most important aristocratic characters recognize that the Restoration of the Bourbons has not actually led to a recovery of their feudal privileges or political powers. Modeling herself on Queen Marguerite of Navarre and Catherine de Medici, Mathilde de la Mole vainly longs for a return to the "heroic days" of Henri III or Charles IX (the late sixteenth century), or for the chance to lead a new counterrevolutionary campaign in the Vendée whereby she and Julien will restore the *ancien régime* (RB, pp. 251, 265, 281).[21] Even the most genuinely aristocratic figure in the novel, the Marquis de la Mole, a man born prior to the revolution of 1789, suffers from a crippling sense of historical dislocation. In the midst of a "restoration," the marquis vainly attempts to enlist Julien and the peasantry in a violent ultraist counterrevolution that will provoke the intervention of a foreign monarchic power. But his address to his aristocratic conspirators reveals a deep historical anxiety brought on by his anticipation of Europe's egalitarian future:

> Either you become businessmen, peasants, or you take up your guns. Be weak, if you want, but don't be stupid; open your eyes. *Form your battalions,* I say to you, in the words of the Jacobin song. . . . In fifty years nothing will be left in Europe but presidents of republics, not a single king. And with those four letters, K-I-N-G, away go the priests and the gentlemen. I see in the future nothing but *candidates* making up to slimy *majorities.* (RB, Pp. 308–9)

The fact that he must resort to the words of a Jacobin song in order to rekindle the feudal honor of his fellow aristocrats strikingly reveals the historical bankruptcy of the marquis and his class; even in their attempt to turn back the revolutionary tide, the ultras must mimic their erstwhile republican enemies.

The Red and the Black amply reflects the total vitiation of the *ancien régime.* Mathilde's contempt for the overly mannered, enervated, and characterless nobles of her class stems in part from her understanding that nobility has itself become merely a commodity openly traded in the new bourgeois order. Those who can afford them may purchase the titles of baron and viscount, the increasing commonness of these honorifics suggesting a form of "inflation" that rapidly devalues their social worth. Despite his humble origins as the son of a provincial carpenter, Julien successfully "passes" in the most exclusive salons of Paris, openly imitating the tastes, dress, manners, and pastimes of an aristocracy that has lost its political raison d'être. His social mimicry extends as far as the aristocratic custom of dueling, which under the Restoration has become a frivolous game played by feckless nobles. Sorel's ridiculous and inconsequential duel with the doll-like chevalier de Beauvoisis, who wounds Julien and then politely escorts him home in a carriage, lacks the mortal seriousness or political consequences of the Hegelian struggle for recognition. The duel between "noble" and "commoner" eventuates neither in the subjugation of the slave by the master, nor in the decisive revolt of the slave who makes himself free. Instead, Stendhal's postrevolutionary characters stage a meaningless performance of anachronistic and stylized gestures, in which the ostensible loser paradoxically gains more than the victor. Since Julien is only a commoner, Beauvoisis must spread false rumors of Sorel's (fictitious) aristocratic parentage in order for the chevalier to save face among his social peers; he cannot admit to dueling with a social inferior. Thus these lies have the effect of raising Julien's status in the fluid social landscape of an increasingly egalitarian France.

The gratuitous, theatrical, and apolitical nature of this potentially mortal conflict calls to mind Kojève's analysis of the defining feature of posthistorical society in Japan: *"Snobbery* in its pure form."[22] According to Kojève:

> [T]he peaks (equalled nowhere else) of specifically Japanese snobbery—the Noh Theater, the ceremony of tea, and the art of bouquets of flowers—were and still remain the exclusive prerogative of the nobles and the rich. But in spite of persistent economic and political inequalities, all Japanese without exception are currently in a position to live according to totally *formalized* values—that is, values completely empty of all "human" content in the "historical" sense. Thus, in the extreme, every Japanese is in principle capable of committing, from pure snobbery, a perfectly "gratuitous" *suicide* (the classical épée of the samurai can be replaced by an airplane or a torpedo), which has nothing to do with the *risk* of life in a Fight waged for the sake of "historical" values that have social or political content.[23]

Similarly, dueling in Restoration France embodies life lived according to "purely formalized values," snobbery in its pure form (RB, p. 265).

Julien's career as perhaps the most famous parvenu in modern European literature comes into clear focus once we understand the posthistorical condition of the society in which he finds himself marooned. All of his noblest and most heroic ambitions, his deepest aggressive drives and erotic desires, his highest intellectual aspirations and spiritual longings are continually diverted into and transformed by formalized acts of social snobbery. As a priest and scholar, Julien is not concerned with the salvation of his soul or with that of others, nor is he interested in the worship of God or understanding the moral teachings of Christianity. The Church simply serves as the most convenient and surest means by which Julien can rapidly improve his social standing. Similarly, as a lover of first Madame de Rênal and then Mathilde de la Mole, Sorel generally seeks not erotic satisfaction, but principally a gratification of social ambition. Denied the opportunity to act as a true revolutionary on the model of Robespierre and Danton, Julien expresses his lingering *ressentiment* by seducing women of a higher class; he thereby achieves a mediated victory over them, as well as over Monsieur de Rênal and the Marquis de Croisnois (his socially superior rivals for their affections).[24] Coming too late to make his name on the battlefields of Europe during the Napoleonic wars, Julien seeks to become a conqueror in the salons and bedrooms of Restoration France.

Julien's snobbery is only the most obvious manifestation of the artificiality and inauthenticity of his posthistorical existence. His religious and moral hypocrisy, his inconstancy in affairs of the heart, his mercurial swings in mood, his shifting political convictions and affiliations, his frequent changes in dress, vocation, and intellectual pursuits, his ephemeral friendships, all evidence a personality that seems perfectly fluid, without defining character. Stendhal's protean hero fascinates us; he seems so complex and multifaceted, with something of the enigmatic celebrity about him. Surely there must be psychological depth to this figure, who can alternately appear as a closet Jacobin and a secret agent for the ultras, a pious and learned priest and a passionate lover, a petit bourgeois parvenu and a dandified chevalier. And to be fair to Julien, what distinguishes him from other citizens of the Bourbon Restoration is his historically anachronistic desire to be *great,* to become another Danton or Napoleon. Julien exhibits what Nietzsche calls the "pathos of distance"—the desire to be recognized not merely as the equal, but as the superior of other human beings.[25] Unfortunately for Julien, as a posthistorical man he has no way to objectify that desire; or at any rate, all the concrete objects of his ambition turn out to be ephemeral and insubstantial. His conviction that he possesses the great soul of a Napoleon cannot be historically substantiated; it depends finally on nothing more than his purely subjective estimation of his true worth.

Julien Sorel desires to be a world-historical actor, a man who can fundamentally alter human society. But in the posthistorical world of *The Red and the Black* he must settle for becoming merely an actor in the most theatrical sense of the word, a man who succeeds only in assuming the masks or outward demeanor of prior historical figures. Julien and Mathilde are drawn to one another in large part because their relationship enables them to stage a series of private historical costume dramas, wherein they can play the parts of their favorite characters from times past: Napoleon, Boniface de la Mole, Robespierre, Catherine de Medici, and Queen Marguerite of Navarre.

Their greatest, most convincing, and final performance is the public staging of Julien's "tragic" death.

The crime for which Julien is executed is his attempted murder of Madame de Rênal in the Church at Verrières. Whatever Julien's immediate motives for shooting an unarmed and kneeling woman in the back—jealousy, love, frustrated ambition, greed, vengeance, temporary insanity—the objective act itself lacks heroic grandeur or political significance. Julien's real fear is not his impending trial and punishment, but the prospect that the public will view him as simply a "vulgar murderer" (RB, p. 365). He might easily avoid the fatal consequences of his precipitous action, but instead frustrates all schemes to save his life. He refuses to allow Madame de Rênal (whose wound proves as superficial as the one Julien suffers at the hands of the chevalier de Beauvoisis) to seek a royal pardon, rejects the advice of his lawyer, who wishes to play on the sympathy of his jurors, and contemptuously dismisses the possibility of bribing his jailor. At his trial, Julien only needs to appear contrite, humble, and to say little in his defense in order to be acquitted. Mathilde has used her wealth and influence to mould the composition of the jury in her lover's favor. Julien's youth, charm, and beauty, combined with the public belief that his crime reveals a grand passion, dispose the jurors to pity him. But Julien understands that, in a posthistorical age, only by self-consciously playing the dramatic *role* of a tragic hero in a public forum can he give his life the outward semblance of political seriousness and historical importance.

He thus seizes upon his trial as an opportunity to create for himself a public image suited to his Napoleonic ambition. Employing every rhetorical stratagem and histrionic gesture at his command, Julien attempts to transform his petty crime into a politically revolutionary action:

> Gentlemen, I have not the honor to belong to your social class, you see in me a peasant in open revolt against his humble station. . . . Mme. de Rênal had been like a mother to me. My crime is atrocious, and it was *premeditated*. I have therefore deserved the death sentence. . . . But even if I were less guilty than I am, I see before me men who . . . are determined to punish in me and discourage forever a certain class of young men—those who, born to a lower social order, and buried by poverty, are lucky enough to get a good education and bold enough to mingle with what the arrogant rich call good society. . . . I am not being judged by my peers. I do not see in the seats of the jury a single rich peasant, only outraged *bourgeois*. (RB, Pp. 387–88)

After the jurors obligingly hand Julien a death sentence, his ally, the Abbé de Frilair, astutely notes that Julien's speech seemed deliberately calculated to offend the political interests and social prejudices of his jurors; Sorel's death will be "a kind of *suicide*" (RB, p. 397).

Here we have what Kojève describes as the gratuitous suicide of posthistorical man, an act of social snobbery by which Julien demonstrates his superiority to his fellow *bourgeois*. Objectively Julien is nothing more or less than a petit bourgeois, but his carefully meditated speech suddenly recasts him in the role of a peasant in revolt. As Julien represents himself, he is initially lower, but by virtue of his crime, ultimately higher than those who pass judgment upon him. The brilliance of Julien's rhetorical performance appears to transform a petty act of violence with no political purpose or historical importance into a heinous action befitting a classical tragedy, replete with overtones of matricide and incest, and carried out by an ardent political revolutionary who threatens the very foundations of the existing social order.

In retrospect, the entire period from Julien's assault on Madame de Rênal to his funeral appears as a succession of staged events forming an elaborate public performance, a self-consciously constructed "tragedy." Julien becomes a celebrity in Besançon: the young women of the town peer at him through telescopes as he takes his daily walk on the battlements of the prison; street vendors hawk his portrait to devoted admirers. Though reduced to the cringing and tearful condition of a complete "coward" in the privacy of his cell, on the day of his death, Julien trusts to "the public eye" as his "spur to glory" (RB, p. 398). At the dramatic climax of his performance, which he brings off without a hint of affectation, Julien successfully conveys the impression of a great public figure who, with his head high and his gaze steady, strolls bravely and unflinchingly to the guillotine to meet a spectacular death, an end conveniently reminiscent of Danton's and Robespierre's. Even while striving to save her lover, Mathilde eagerly collaborates in Julien's theatrical performance, making a great public show of her grief on the streets and in the courtroom of Besançon. Her final dramatic coup is stage-managing Julien's spectacular public funeral, which rivals that of Mathilde's ancestor, Boniface de la Mole. Amidst great pomp, she lays Julien's head and decapitated body to rest in a "savage grotto" "adorned with marbles sculptured at great expense in Italy" (RB, p. 408). Stendhal's posthistorical world offers not political tragedy but its simulacrum.

III

In his later novels, such as *The Charterhouse of Parma* (1839), the posthistorical condition of Stendhal's characters becomes ever more pronounced. The source for *The Charterhouse* is not, as in the case of *The Red and the Black,* contemporary newspaper accounts of minor criminals (Antoine Berthet and Lafargue), but a sixteenth-century Italian manuscript chronicling the life of a young nobleman, Alessandro Farnese, whose violent and heroic exploits climaxed with his becoming Pope Paul III in 1534. *The Charterhouse* is not a historical novel, but rather a kind of postmodern pastiche, the events of sixteenth-century Italy transposed to and intermingled with those of post-Napoleonic Europe. Stendhal's stated aim was imaginatively to escape the stultifying atmosphere of France under Louis-Phillipe, "where everything ends in a song or in a year or two's imprisonment," and to turn his attention to those violent, dangerous, and more primitive southern lands such as Corsica, Sicily, and Italy, which still produced great men like Napoleon and where one was "surrounded by tragic events."[26]

Stendhal's hero, a disinherited aristocrat, republican partisan, and admirer of Bonaparte, quite literally arrives too late and too inebriated to take an active and meaningful part in the final great action of modern history, the battle of Waterloo. His horse stolen from under him, the disoriented Fabrizio del Dongo is never sure whether he has actually caught a glimpse of the last great-souled man of France, the Emperor Napoleon. In the aftermath of Bonaparte's defeat, Fabrizio sets out for a backwater of Europe, the historically anachronistic enclave of Parma ruled by Ernesto IV and his minister, Conte Mosca, where he hopes to fulfill the heroic ambitions that no longer have an outlet elsewhere on the continent. But Stendhal cannot long sustain this limited heroic fiction; his representation of a more exotic and less modernized Parma gradually proves little more than his personal fantasy. Over the course of the novel, the artificial character of Stendhal's historical pastiche becomes increasingly evident; Parma gradually modulates from a sixteenth-century Italian city into a mere parody or miniature of Bourbon France.

Accordingly, the tragic destiny of the aristocratic hero also degenerates into a pathetic farce. Barred from active political life even in Parma, Fabrizio pines away in the Farnese tower, smitten by love for the virginal Clelia. Eventually she grants him her favors, but à la Boccaccio, only in complete darkness. When she dies in childbirth, partly out of remorse for having broken her vow of chastity to the Madonna, Fabrizio retires like a monk to the Charterhouse of Parma, where he mercifully expires of grief. Stendhal's narrative response to modernity, which rather easily breaks through the hastily erected defenses of the fantastical Parma, is finally resignation and askesis. Thus Stendhal offers no real escape from the end of history, only a rich variety of possible aesthetic strategies for representing and responding to the posthistorical condition. Perhaps what is most suggestive in Stendhal's great novels—and even so anticlimactic a work as *The Charterhouse* shares in this virtue—is their detailed and penetrating analysis of the dissatisfaction that the end of history engenders, particularly in those like Julien, Mathilde, and Fabrizio who admire and wish to exhibit greatness of soul. For Hegel and Kojève, the end of history is coterminous with the process of human self-creation, the long struggle for universal recognition, and the development of an ideal and specifically human form of freedom. Human beings at the end of history should be *satisfied*. But as Kojève occasionally and darkly hinted, and as Stendhal's fiction dramatically attests, the triumph of modernity leaves certain human types, perhaps even the most interesting types, profoundly dissatisfied.[27]

In the chapters that follow, I have attempted to analyze a variety of novelistic responses to the prospect of posthistorical society. From the outset, I grant that not all of the novelists I discuss are convinced that the end of history has arrived, and more significantly, not all are persuaded that modernity necessarily guarantees the universal satisfaction of human desire. In fact, the novelists I discuss register, at one time or another, and for many different and even incompatible reasons, suspicion of and even resistance to the modernization of human society. Nevertheless, I believe that they are united as writers if only by the fact that they are responding to the same unitary global phenomenon. Since the French Revolution, modernization has assumed many different guises and created different historical and political conflicts, whose features vary significantly according to the specific traditional society affected. I hope that I have managed to capture the particular nature of these conflicts and the individual novelistic responses they have inspired, while still preserving a sense of how these seemingly disparate and unrelated political collisions and tragic novels nevertheless deal with a single fundamental, though multifaceted development in world history.

The first half of this study deals with the specific responses of European novelists to the advent of modernity. The chapter on *The*

Mayor of Casterbridge focuses on Hardy's archaeological endeavor to uncover social anachronisms within an already modernized England. After the rapid industrial development of the nineteenth century, brought about by economic liberalization and the continuing extension of the franchise to ever greater numbers of British citizens, Hardy's regionalism seems a deliberate effort to recapture the premodern elements that managed to survive in the least advanced regions of England. His nostalgia for traditional communities notwithstanding, Hardy seems interested in digging up the premodern practices of Casterbridge only in order to demonstrate that their historical extinction was inevitable. The archaic appears attractive only when (and perhaps because) it ceases to exist. By contrast, Conrad's *Lord Jim* illustrates a bolder and more daring response to the modernization of Europe, the turn to non-Western and premodern communities as a kind of historical refuge. Inevitably, however, the discontented modern European hero—Jim—brings to Patusan those very elements of modernity that he hoped to escape. *Lord Jim,* usually considered a kind of imperialist fantasy, upon reconsideration appears as a prototype of the postcolonial novel, in which Jim, assuming the role of the leader of a newly independent Third World country, tries unsuccessfully to harmonize the contrary demands of a traditional non-Western society and Western modernity.

In the second half of this study, I turn my attention to authors who write not from the center of modern Western society but from its periphery, the so-called Third World. The chapter on Achebe considers not merely the technological or economic threat that modernity poses for a traditional African society, but also the more profound ideological challenge it offers. In *Things Fall Apart,* Christianity appears not merely as one among many religions, but, as in Hegel's philosophy and Weber's sociology, the prototype of Western rationalization and the vehicle of political democratization. In *No Longer at Ease* and *Anthills of the Savannah* Achebe dramatizes the often tragic possibilities inherent in modernizing a postcolonial African nation while endeavoring to preserve what is best in a premodern African society. He presents the political corruption and brutal dictatorships of postcolonial Africa as dangerous hybrid growths, the result of an unsuccessful synthesis of modern European and traditional African cultures. In a similar vein, in his epic novel, *The War of the End of the World,* Vargas Llosa examines the explosive potential for counterrevolutionary violence within Latin America. Acknowledging the formidable power of radical alternatives to liberal democratic society—theocracy, oligarchic feudalism, utopian socialism or anarchism, military dictatorship—Vargas Llosa dramatizes the precarious triumph of modernity in Brazil at the turn of the century. The novel illustrates not only that modernization can produce powerful antimodern reactions, but also that modernity itself may be divided among warring factions. Vargas Llosa expresses his faith in the long-term prospects for stable and prosperous liberal democracies in Latin America chiefly through the formal structure of his work, especially the manipulation of point of view. Modernity triumphs in the course of a great conflagration in which the political alternatives to liberal democratic society cancel out each other. A pluralistic liberal vision of history, implicit in the modernist form and radical perspectivism of the novel, is all that survives the war of the end of the world.

I

THE CENTER
CANNOT HOLD

1

Hardy: The Archaeology of a Vanishing Life

I

When *The Mayor of Casterbridge* was first published complete in 1886, England was widely regarded as the most fully modernized nation on earth. To the Igbo villagers of Chinua Achebe's *Things Fall Apart,* the British missionaries who arrived in Umuofia and Mbanta (at approximately the same time Hardy was completing the final major revision of his novel) were *the* representatives of Western European modernity.[1] The greatest military and industrial power in the world, the global leader in science and commerce with one of the most fully democratized governments, late Victorian England epitomized the future of Europe that Stendhal's Marquis de la Mole both prophesied and abhorred.

When the nineteenth century began, a landed aristocracy still dominated English political and economic life by means of bribery, patronage, and a system of "rotten boroughs" that insured that a small number of families retained control of Parliament. But by the time *The Mayor of Casterbridge* appeared, the democratization of British political institutions was very far advanced. The Reform Bills of 1832, 1867, and 1884 had abolished the rotten boroughs and extended suffrage to middle and working class men throughout Great Britain. The financial power of the landed gentry had been dealt a further blow by a liberalization of the British economy that progressively eliminated most of the mercantilist and protectionist measures that had given these families economic advantages at the expense of the new manufacturing interests and the mass of British workers and

29

consumers, who paid artificially high prices particularly for agricultural products. The repeal of the Corn Laws in 1846 marked a decisive turn in the economic fortunes of the landed gentry, who for the first time were forced to compete for business in an increasingly integrated world market. By the 1870s the profitability of their estates was in rapid and permanent decline as a result of foreign competition from America. Before Hardy had completed his final major revision of *The Mayor of Casterbridge* in 1912, the British Parliament had established popularly elected assemblies in the rural counties and municipalities (a legislative process that had also begun in the mid-1830s), thereby extinguishing one of the last vestiges of aristocratic political authority in Great Britain.[2]

Thus, for a late Victorian writer such as Hardy, the economic and political modernization of Great Britain was largely a fait accompli. To be sure, the process of political and social democratization had not reached its end; for example, women over thirty were not enfranchised until 1918, and those over twenty-one only in 1928. Nevertheless, by the late nineteenth century the process of modernization would have seemed irreversible to most Victorians. The future task of England at the height of its imperial success in the mid-1880s seemed to far-sighted liberals and conservatives alike to lie primarily in its "civilizing mission" abroad, in remote imperial domains in the undeveloped world. Thus, when it first appeared in print, *The Mayor of Casterbridge* typically struck Hardy's contemporary readers as willfully anachronistic and nostalgic, a work that evoked a world remote from the everyday realities of most British citizens, who increasingly lived in the urban centers where trade and manufacturing were concentrated.[3] In creating the fictional town of Casterbridge, Hardy looked back to the Dorchester of sixty years earlier, a provincial and agricultural community as it existed between the mid-1820s and the late 1840s—that is, before the repeal of the Corn Laws, and before the full effects of political democratization and economic modernization made themselves felt in the more remote rural areas of Britain. Casterbridge is, in Hardy's striking phrase, a community "untouched by the faintest sprinkle of modernism" (p. 59).

Hardy's literary regionalism is usually conceived of in geographic terms, as representing a particular place. But I would like to suggest that Hardy's regionalism, and in fact regionalism in general, might be better understood in temporal terms, as the fictional presentation of a premodern historical epoch that has effectively come to an end in the relatively recent past. Hardy's regionalism eulogizes a society whose distinctive features are gradually being effaced by the homogenizing influence of modernity.[4] Like Scott's Scottish Highlands, Faulkner's Yoknapatawpha County, Achebe's Igboland, and García Márquez's Macondo, Hardy's Wessex embodies a lost world that must be archaeologically uncovered for the contemporary reader:

> [I]f these country customs and vocations, obsolete and obsolescent, had been detailed wrongly, nobody would have discovered such errors to the end of Time. Yet I have instituted inquiries to correct tricks of memory, and striven against temptations to exaggerate, in order to preserve for my own satisfaction a fairly true record of a vanishing life.[5]

Only through this archaeological process is a way of life temporally remote and distinctively premodern preserved and made available to the contemporary reader.[6] Whether or not Hardy ultimately approves of modernization, his regionalism carries a conservative or antimodern charge; it functions as an imaginative bulwark against the globalizing and homogenizing tendencies of modernity, even while it acknowledges the inevitability of its spread.

Hardy goes to some lengths to heighten and even exaggerate the historical remoteness of his fictional world. He resurrects a geographical entity—Wessex—that had not existed as a distinct unit since the heptarchy of Anglo-Saxon times. Moreover, Hardy suggestively associates Wessex with ancient Greece as it appeared in Attic drama:

> I would state that the geographical limits of the stage here trodden were not absolutely forced upon the writer by circumstances; he forced them upon himself from judgment. I considered that the magnificent heritage from the Greeks in dramatic literature found sufficient room for a large proportion of its action in an extent of their country not much larger than the half-dozen counties here reunited under the old name of Wessex. . . . So far was I possessed by this idea that I kept within the frontiers when it would have been easier to overleap them and give more cosmopolitan features to the narrative.[7]

By insisting upon a connection between the fictional world of Wessex and that of Attic drama, Hardy intimates that the heroic tenor and tragic grandeur of an earlier historical period might once again be invoked. Hardy offers an escape from the placid character of modern bourgeois existence and a generic swerve away from the domestic preoccupations of the typical late Victorian realistic novel by way of the deep and disturbing connections among the regional, the archaic, and the tragic. In *The Mayor of Casterbridge*, Hardy's success as a tragic novelist depended on his realizing that he could imaginatively reconstruct a remote corner of Victorian England, whose premodern features seemed to offer the sort of dramatic possibilities that the advent of modernity had foreclosed. Michael Henchard's story requires the peculiarly archaic characteristics of Casterbridge to lend a tragic ambience to what might otherwise remain a typical novelistic tale of modern bourgeois life.

As Stendhal's attempt to resurrect the prerevolutionary world in *The Charterhouse of Parma* suggests, the effort to exhume a premodern world often leads to bizarre reconstructions, which fail to observe distinctions between prior historical periods. Hardy's Casterbridge contains various fragments of a heavily sedimented history dating as far back as the age of Hadrian and the Roman Empire, if not to an even more primitive Neolithic epoch. This imprecise sense of local history is given comic expression by a minor folk character who offers a grotesque but suggestive lecture on this provincial town:

> Casterbridge is a old, hoary place o' wickedness, by all account. 'Tis recorded in history that we rebelled against the King one or two hundred years ago, in the time of the Romans, and that lots of us was hanged on Gallows Hill, and quartered, and our different jints sent about the country like butcher's meat; and for my part I can well believe it. (P. 83)

Buzzford's account of Monmouth's Rebellion and the "Bloody Assize" that followed its suppression in 1685 manages to conflate the period just prior to the Glorious Revolution with that of Roman imperial rule of Britain many centuries earlier. His unscholarly rendering of the past might illustrate merely the historical ignorance of an uneducated provincial were it not that Hardy himself frequently resorts to the same sort of historical pastiche. Thus, in *Tess of the d'Urbervilles,* Hardy's nineteenth-century provincial heroine, a distant and impoverished heir of a virtually extinct aristocratic family dating back to the Norman invasion, suffers the indignities and hardships of the first wave of modern industrialism, only to find herself at the conclusion of the novel at the Neolithic ruin of Stonehenge, where she offers herself up as a symbolic ritual sacrifice to the Aeschylean gods of ancient Greece. In *The Mayor of Casterbridge,* Hardy casts Henchard in a succession of figurative roles (without regard to historical chronology) drawn from discrete epochs and literary periods. He is compared to classical Greek heroes such as Achilles, Bellerophon, and Oedipus; Roman historical figures such as Brutus and Caesar; Biblical characters such as Cain, Joseph, Samson, Saul, and

David; Shakespearean tragic heroes such as Macbeth and Lear; exemplars of the Renaissance and early modern eras such as Faust; and finally to that harbinger of political modernity, Napoleon.

Like Casterbridge itself, Hardy's novel is a kind of heavily stratified archaeological dig or historical palimpsest, in which various and distinct forms of premodern life are superimposed one on top of another, as if the "posthistorical" or modern perspective Hardy occupies is at such a great remove from all earlier forms of premodern existence that they appear as equally and uniformly archaic—and therefore tinged with the threat of violence and tragedy. Thus, when Hardy recounts the local history of the Roman amphitheatre located just outside Casterbridge—based on the Maumbury Ring near Dorchester, which, as it turned out, was itself built upon even earlier Neolithic ruins—we get an ominous chronicle of seemingly perpetual violence that neatly condenses events occurring over millennia: Roman gladiatorial contests from the second century A.D., spectacular public tortures and executions from the early eighteenth century, sanguinary bare-knuckle boxing bouts and sinister crimes of the early nineteenth century.

It would be unfair to Hardy to suggest that his penchant for historical pastiche is simply the consequence of his being an autodidact; as a practicing architect who spent many years restoring old English churches, he was acutely sensitive to subtle shifts in architectural style throughout Western history.[8] In fact, Hardy's archaeological method enables him simultaneously to render the almost organic process by which the accretions of history constitute the provincial character of Wessex and to isolate a given stratum of regional history whenever it serves his dramatic purpose. In *The Mayor of Casterbridge* Hardy often seems particularly anxious to highlight the antique Roman heritage of the city; its earlier incarnation as a kind of ancient polis[9] provides him with a suitable setting in which to play out a highly mediated and exceedingly belated version of classical tragedy. As I hope to suggest, this classical element is by no means the only important historical stratum that Hardy evokes in his novel. He seems equally interested in the quasi-feudal and late mercantilist character of Casterbridge's political, economic, and social institutions. Nevertheless, Hardy often insists upon depicting the advent of modernity in Casterbridge against its "classical" background as a way of heightening the dramatic sense of historical rupture and political change that ultimately overtakes this community.

II

Thinking of Casterbridge as a polis allows us to consider one particularly important premodern form of community, one that can help sharpen our sense of what is distinctive about modern political organization. In the classical world, the polis formed the fundamental and comprehensive basis of all human relationships and all human activities. We misunderstand "polis" as long as we translate the word as "state" or "city-state," as if the polis were merely a diminutive form of the kinds of modern community prevalent today. In fact, the polis and the state are fundamentally different forms of community. "State" implies a modern set of distinctions: between state and society, state and individual, and state and church.[10] By contrast, the classical "polis" was an all-inclusive community that assimilated all other possible communities and that was not included in any other whole or community. The polis did not separate civil and religious authority; in fact authority in all matters of law and custom rested with the city. The welfare of the citizens, whether material or spiritual, was the concern of the regime. Moreover, this ancient form of political life was not conceived of as contractual, as is the modern state in the theories of Hobbes, Locke, and Rousseau. All citizens of the polis were thought to be part of a larger organic whole and not autonomous agents who agreed to form some larger legal collective entity out of their individual wills. The idea of a realm of activity— "society" or "culture"—which can be conceived of apart from the city was foreign to the classical understanding of politics.

In practical terms, the polis had to be limited in size. In terms of number of inhabitants, the ancient city would be dwarfed by modern urban centers such as London and Paris.[11] Accordingly, political relationships in the ancient city were still coextensive with what we would call personal relationships. Moreover, these ancient cities remained autonomous, self-sufficient, and independent regimes for much of their history. They were not parts of some larger nation-state, in the way that New York and Los Angeles are subsumed by the United States. The economy of the ancient polis was agricultural rather than industrial and governed largely by local considerations and conditions. Though each city had its own peculiar set of communal institutions, in general they were hierarchically ordered. Distinctions between aristocrats and plebeians, masters and slaves, citizens and foreigners were important, but the inhabitants of the city were nevertheless politically and economically interdependent, forming together one larger, comprehensive human whole.

Casterbridge descends directly from a Roman polis and still retains many of its ancient architectural features and even ghostly traces of its violent historical spirit:

> Casterbridge announced old Rome in every street, alley, and precinct. It looked Roman, bespoke the art of Rome, concealed dead men of Rome. It was impossible to dig more than a foot or two deep about the town fields and gardens without coming upon some tall soldier or other of the Empire, who had lain there in his silent unobtrusive rest for a space of fifteen hundred years. . . . Some old people said that at certain moments in the summer time, in broad daylight, persons sitting with a book or dozing in the [amphitheatre] had, on lifting their eyes, beheld the slopes lined with a gazing legion of Hadrian's soldiery as if watching the gladiatorial combat. (Pp. 100–101)

Most striking to the visitor first setting eyes upon Casterbridge, the community remains bounded by its ancient square of defensive walls, transformed into treelined walks (pp. 59–60). Though they no longer serve a military function, these defenses fix a precise limit to the size of a community that completely lacks modern suburbs.

The city's diminutive scale offers Henchard a restricted public sphere in which his everyday activities assume a genuine communal significance. For Hardy as for Stendhal, the hero's actions gain in public importance as the range of his movements becomes more narrowly circumscribed. Provincial Casterbridge offers Henchard what modern London cannot, just as Besançon provides Julien Sorel with something that Paris denies him: notoriety and civic stature. In Casterbridge as in Besançon, the provincial courtroom provides an especially important public venue, in which the revelations of the hero's past transgressions, the attack on an old lover or the sale of a wife and child, though motivated by essentially private, psychological, and domestic concerns, momentarily assume the force of a politically explosive revelation, producing the classical *anagnorisis* of traditional tragic drama. The specific equivalent of the agora or public square in Casterbridge is the carrefour, where the business of the community is transacted. Hardy compares the market square to "the regulation Open Place in spectacular dramas, where the incidents that occur always happen to bear on the lives of the adjoining residents" (p. 192).

The assimilation of Casterbridge's physical organization to that of the classical stage suggests an underlying correspondence between the public quality of life in the ancient polis and that in Hardy's provincial city. Compared to most nineteenth-century European novels, *The Mayor of Casterbridge* seems remarkable for its preoccupation with the public rather than the private aspects of modern middle-class life.[12] This tendency is evident in the preponderance of pivotal scenes that take place in public. Henchard's sale of his wife and child, his successful effort to persuade Farfrae to accept employment, his initial conflict with his manager over the treatment of Abel Whittle, his competitive staging of municipal entertainments, his commercial rivalry with his former employee, his confession in the courtroom, his bankruptcy proceedings, his disgrace before the "Royal Personage"—all are conducted in a public manner, frequently in full view of the entire community and quite often in the open air. Moreover, the action of the novel turns upon the fact that a series of private relationships, secret agreements, and intimate discussions ultimately becomes public knowledge. In a town as small as Casterbridge, Henchard's original "secret" marriage to Susan, Elizabeth-Jane's true parentage, Lucetta's clandestine affair with Henchard in Jersey, and even Elizabeth-Jane's temporary service in the Three Mariners cannot long remain private matters.

The Mayor of Casterbridge thus departs from the modern bourgeois novelistic tradition Watt has described:

> The world of the novel is essentially the world of the modern city; both present a picture of life in which the individual is immersed in private and personal relationships because a larger communion with nature or society is no longer available. . . . [The novel] tells of an intimate world of which no one speaks out loud in ordinary life, a world which had previously found utterance only in the diary, the confession or the familiar letter.[13]

Hardy's "man of character" defines himself by means of public actions and speeches, rather than by private correspondence or self-reflective moments to which the reader is privy.[14]

Henchard thus fits Bakhtin's model of the public man of classical biography, who lives his life in the agora, always before the eyes of his fellow citizens:

> The square in earlier (ancient) times itself constituted a state. . . . [I]t was the highest court . . . [T]he entire people participated in it. . . . [Within it] the laying bare and examination of a citizen's whole life was accomplished, and received its public and civic stamp of ap-

proval. . . . Here the individual is open on all sides, he is all surface, there is in him nothing that exists "for his sake alone," nothing that could not be subject to public or state control and evaluation. Everything here, down to the last detail, is entirely public.[15]

According to Bakhtin, the novel's preoccupation with the representation of inner life and the purely private realm of experience developed only after the collapse of the polis and the emergence of new forms of political organization, which lacked the comprehensive and unified communal character of the ancient city.[16] By contrast, Henchard lives his life without regard to a distinction between the public and the private realms of experience, or to sharp divisions among civic responsibilities, religious duties, economic activities, and domestic obligations.[17] Henchard is not only the mayor of the city, but simultaneously its principal businessman, chief magistrate, churchwarden, outstanding patron of the poor, and most notable domestic patriarch. If Farfrae is to be his business partner, then he must also become his trusted friend (pp. 94–95); if Henchard is to marry Susan or Lucetta, it is with an eye toward his social reputation and financial status within the community (pp. 112, 175, 200); if he is to serve as Elizabeth-Jane's father, it is primarily out of a sense of public duty and social propriety (pp. 156–60).

The relevance of Henchard's actions to the community is assured not only by the limited size and public character of Casterbridge, but also by the town's virtual political, economic, and social autonomy. To be sure, nineteenth-century Casterbridge, like Roman Casterbridge, is officially part of an immense worldwide empire. But just as the remoteness of Roman Casterbridge from the imperial capital gave its administrators a de facto autonomy, the extent and power of imperial Britain paradoxically makes possible the relative independence of its provincial agricultural townships. Though not at liberty to pursue an independent foreign policy, Casterbridge can safely ignore political matters beyond its local horizons. Unlike ancient Athens or republican Rome, it has no need to defend itself against hostile powers. In certain respects, then, Casterbridge is more autonomous and absorbed in its local affairs than any ancient polis could afford to be. Consequently, the people of Casterbridge think of themselves first and foremost as citizens of their *city*. Their sense of belonging to the larger community of British subjects who live outside the narrow confines of the city walls often seems weak and attenuated, as if their status as English citizens were more an abstract idea than an immediate living reality. A full hundred years after the last vestiges of independent clan power were suppressed in the Scottish Highlands, the common folk of Casterbridge, who no longer have to fear an invasion from the north as in 1715 or 1745, can still greet Farfrae as an exotic foreigner from a distant "country" (p. 83).

The local autonomy of an English provincial town such as Casterbridge was especially pronounced before the late nineteenth century, when the ministries in Whitehall began to centralize governmental control and assume a much more intrusive role in the political and economic life of rural municipalities. Accordingly, the presence of the central government in London makes itself felt only once in *The Mayor of Casterbridge,* during the largely ceremonial visit of a "Royal Personage" to Casterbridge. Hardy mentions the landed gentry in the outlying areas only in passing, and then only to note that the interests of the Corporation and chief burghers and those of the aristocracy are not felt to be opposed to one another by the citizenry (p. 92). Hardy thus memorializes the provincial life of Casterbridge during an age when almost all political and economic matters of concern to the citizenry were addressed by the leading men of the local town council. Under such circumstances, a mayor, member of the Corporation, chief local magistrate, and church warden such as Henchard possesses more genuine political power, economic clout, and civic responsibility than any other individual with whom a citizen of Casterbridge would ordinarily come into contact. They feel, perhaps rather naively, that their communal existence depends upon the economic fortunes and political decisions of their local civic leaders, rather than on the actions and decisions of a distant imperial government in London.

The agricultural basis of life in Casterbridge further contributes to the city's nearly autonomous character. In the days before the repeal of the Corn Laws, the existence of high tariffs on imported grain effectively localized the English grain markets. As a consequence, an agricultural community such as Casterbridge largely depended upon its own harvests and local weather conditions for its economic livelihood (p. 209). Unaffected by fluctuations in the international grain market, the prosperity of the community turns on the fortunes of a few prominent farmers and merchants. Henchard's sale of bad grain early in the story adversely affects the daily diet of the entire community. His scheme to drive Farfrae out of business by means of competitive bidding and selling similarly depends on the existence of an essentially local grain market subject to the manipulation of a single powerful trader. Since the repeal of the Corn Laws in 1846 neutralized the impact that any one merchant could have on the availability and price of grain, their elimination at an earlier date would have made Henchard's plan to ruin Farfrae inconceivable and thus forestalled the tragic conclusion to the hero's career.

Ostensibly a city that excludes monarchs, nobles, and patricians, as well as slaves, serfs, and plebeians, Casterbridge nevertheless generates its own rather archaic social distinctions. One may, for example, roughly determine the status of a Casterbridge citizen according to which of the town's three inns he frequents: The King's Arms, The Three Mariners, or Peter's Finger.[18] The preeminent citizen in Casterbridge is of course the mayor, who belongs to "an elective dynasty dating back to the days of Charles I" (p. 268). Directly beneath him are the "Peerage of burghers" (p. 162)—the aldermen and members of the Corporation—followed in turn by the other chief businessmen and professionals, then the small shopkeepers and skilled tradesmen, and finally the unskilled laborers and menials. From a broad historical perspective, the social distinction between a corn factor and a skilled tradesman might seem relatively fine. But the diminutive size and insularity of Casterbridge magnify the smallest differences in social status, thereby producing a stratified regime out of a seemingly homogeneous society and lending this community something of the hierarchical character of an ancient polis (p. 71).

At times Hardy seems nostalgic for the semifeudal interdependence of social classes that follows from the economically undeveloped character of Casterbridge. The relatively static nature of its agrarian economy—mutual dependence on a single industry—makes necessary a historical form of social cooperation that becomes increasingly obsolete with the advanced division of labor under capitalism. The populace retains "the primitive habit of helping one another" in the face of a potentially disastrous harvest (p. 219). While this precapitalist form of "organic" interdependence issues in an attractive version of communal harmony, it comes at the cost of individual economic freedom and empowerment. Since they have relatively few opportunities for alternative employment and by the terms of their leaseholds have little incentive to seek work in other parts of the country, the poorest laborers of Casterbridge remain largely dependent upon the financial patronage and personal largesse of a few wealthy farmers and merchants.[19]

The working relationship between Henchard and Abel Whittle is instructive in this regard; it remains personal, direct, and subject to Henchard's mercurial temperament, unmediated by the fixed terms of bureaucratic procedures, governmental statutes, union contracts, or corporate regulations. Rather than summarily dismiss a perpetually tardy workman or dock his pay as a modern corporate officer might do, Henchard personally humiliates Abel Whittle before his coworkers and fellow townsfolk in order to teach him a lesson and reform his work habits.[20] Henchard secretly compensates for his severity by supplying Whittle's indigent elderly mother with coals and potatoes during the winter. For his part, Whittle seems reluctant to face life as a fully autonomous individual, endowed with economic rights and a human dignity incompatible with perpetual servitude. Voluntarily accompanying his old master into self-imposed exile on Egdon Heath, the humble and devoted Whittle clings to their anachronistic relationship long after the society that gave birth to it has been modernized. Hardy's archaeology here seems directed towards resurrecting an archaic set of moral virtues and social obligations that once inhered in the unequal relationships of a socially stratified premodern community. Whittle's decision to follow Henchard doggedly serves as Hardy's bittersweet eulogy for an age that prized personal loyalty and the reciprocal if unequal obligations of master and servant above individual economic freedom and the promise of political equality.

III

For all of its archaic features, Casterbridge is only a modern equivalent of an ancient polis and therefore in several crucial respects differs from a community like republican Rome or ancient Thebes. Thus far I have highlighted only the archaic elements in Casterbridge and the premodern features of Henchard's character. I wish to emphasize however, that even before Henchard's fall from eminence, Casterbridge already contains within itself modern characteristics that do not become fully manifest until the close of Hardy's novel. Despite the archaic class structure of Casterbridge under the mayor's rule, the social stratification of this provincial city lacks the rigidity of that in the ancient polis or feudal Europe. Henchard begins life in Casterbridge as an itinerant haytrusser; like most of his fellow members on the Town Council who rose from humble stations, this preeminent civic leader has no hereditary or permanent claim to rule his fellow citizens. Though Henchard assumes the leading role in a political body, the Town Council or Corporation, whose rights and privileges were established by royal charter in the seventeenth century, the mayoralty remains an *elected* position subject to the changing whims of Casterbridge's leading citizens. Moreover, Henchard's economic power does not derive from any legally codified form of entail or aristocratic right. His wealth depends on his success as a financial middleman and economic speculator rather than on feudal privileges—rents, tithes, compulsory labor, and so forth—due the aristocratic lord of a landed estate.[21] In accordance with the dawning age of laissez-faire capitalism that Farfrae's leadership heralds, Henchard's financial fortunes become ever less secure; no individual concentration of wealth is protected from the vagaries of the competitive market. Finally, Henchard's political authority, even at the peak of his power, never extends to those activities that have traditionally been the preserve of a ruling nobility: warfare and foreign policy. Like his fellow burghers, Henchard is absorbed only in prosaic middle-class concerns, like commerce, agriculture, and domestic responsibilities. Even in the most archaic and historically undeveloped region of mid-century England, the effects and ethos of bourgeois modernity have already begun to manifest themselves.

Given the proto-modern character of even this most provincial backwater of early Victorian England, Hardy's greatest narrative challenge—and one which he only partially succeeded in meeting—was to locate and dramatize whatever archaic heroic elements persisted in the bourgeois existence of Casterbridge. The political activities of the traditional aristocratic hero—the foundation or preservation of a regime, and above all the exercise of martial virtue—are no longer available to Hardy's hero. Politics in its proto-modern form in Casterbridge has lost much of its mortal seriousness and epic glory. Hardy nevertheless endeavors to bring out a heroic substratum of bourgeois life still discernible in the final phase of Casterbridge's historical development. Hardy uncovers a human drive or impulse—what we have called the struggle for recognition—that effectively spans the historical gulf between the premodern and modern eras in Casterbridge. The proto-modern form in which Henchard expresses his Achillean temperament is "commercial combat" (p. 143).[22] Henchard pursues success in the marketplace with the same aggressive ferocity with which Achilles pursues glory on the battlefield. During a transitional period between the mercantilist and capitalist periods of English history, economic competition becomes Henchard's sublimated form of heroic endeavor in a manner that corresponds to the way social climbing and amatory conquest become Julien Sorel's forms of Napoleonic activity in a postrevolutionary age.

Henchard's economic form of heroism can be better understood in light of the English philosophic foundations of the modern liberal democratic regime. Hobbes and Locke championed commercial enterprise over traditional aristocratic pursuits as the chief activity for the modern citizen. They regarded commercial activity as a means of taming man's vainglorious pursuits and aggressive impulses. In their view, men would no longer fight over elevated matters such as religious salvation and political glory; the modern state would redirect the contentiousness of citizens into more prosaic and productive channels. Later economic theorists such as Adam Smith and David Ricardo understood commercial competition within a free market as a means by which the wealth of all could be increased.[23] The modern liberal tradition was founded upon the hope that the pursuit of happiness would consist of a peaceful striving for material gain and personal security and not a violent struggle for martial glory, aristocratic honor, and religious salvation.

Like Robinson Crusoe, Henchard is a fictional reflection of these philosophic and economic developments. Henchard's commercial career begins with a kind of public Homeric boast that subtly conflates the desire for material prosperity with that for social status and pure prestige:

> I haven't more than fifteen shillings in the world, and yet I am a good experienced hand in my line. I'd challenge England to beat me in the fodder business; and if I were a free man again I'd be worth a thousand pound before I'd done o't. (P.40)

Henchard begins, as does Defoe's shipwrecked hero, an impoverished and isolated individual, forced to rely on his own initiative to survive in a seemingly inhospitable world. When he leaves the furmity woman's tent near Weydon-Priors, Henchard enters into a solitary landscape in which he must make his fortune by means of physical strength, determination, ingenuity, rational calculation, and courage. Pitted against the indifferent (but ultimately fruitful) world of nature, initially lacking membership in any social group, Henchard, like Crusoe, finds that his material needs and desires are nevertheless heightened by a concern for prestige and public recognition. Like Defoe's character, Henchard ultimately makes himself the leader of an entire community largely by virtue of his economic prowess. At a transitional moment between preindustrial mercantilism and laissez-faire capitalism, Henchard's acquisitiveness can appear in a heroic light.[24] For Hardy's bourgeois hero, the struggles for recognition and for commercial success appear to be, at least initially, fully compatible.

Hardy further enhances the heroic stature of his protagonist by carefully omitting the eighteen years of Henchard's life during which, in a long and presumably arduous struggle, he rises from penury and obscurity to wealth and eminence. This narrative elision lends greater credibility and force to one of the governing myths of bourgeois culture: the glamorous tale of the self-made man.[25] Unlike Defoe, Hardy covers over the prosaic details: the drudgery of physical labor, the slow painstaking process of capital accumulation, the mundane commercial disappointments and successes—in short, the ordinary, unheroic, and occasionally demeaning tenor of economic enterprise that must have characterized two decades of Henchard's life. Hardy omits exactly the material which had been the typical subject matter of the modern bourgeois novel from Defoe to Dickens: the slow incremental rise of a character, first into the middle class and then into prominence within that class. Hardy's economic hero emerges suddenly, after two decades of business activity, fully formed, already wealthy, powerful, and successful, seemingly unsullied and unburdened by the prosaic demands of economic life, his social prestige in no way compromised by the manner in which it was acquired.

IV

Within modern society, the successful businessman might appear courageous and heroic, but he does not normally seem tragic. This is of course precisely what the philosophic founders of the modern commercial state had envisioned. By taming the heroic impulse, the commercial regime was supposed to replace the potential for tragic conflict in society with the potential for harmonious cooperation. The progressive historical transition from a mercantilist era to that of a more fully modern phase of capitalism thus requires of Hardy's hero an ever-more complete subordination of the struggle for recognition to economic ends. Hardy's hero ultimately deviates, however, from the course that modern liberal philosophy and economics prescribe for bourgeois man, refusing to limit his striving for pure prestige to the economic arena. Instead, with ever greater obstinacy and to his mounting financial and political detriment, Henchard clings to outmoded forms of personal honor that are extra-economic and that increasingly conflict with the changing demands of a more competitive and dynamic marketplace. Henchard's predicament thus embodies a Hegelian tragedy: living at a moment of historical transition, Hardy's hero fails to resolve the contrary ethical, political, and economic demands of two distinct phases of social life in Casterbridge. Insisting upon anachronistic patriarchal prerogatives, falling back on archaic, inefficient, and nonscientific business practices, and clinging to obsolete mercantilist assumptions, Henchard ultimately compromises his material well-being in a vainglorious attempt to prove that his outmoded way of life is superior to that of Farfrae, a newcomer much more attuned to the new economic realities of laissez-faire capitalism and the increasingly democratic spirit of modern Casterbridge. Moreover, Henchard's unwillingness or inability to adapt his conception of personal prestige to the changing demands of the emerging society gradually leads to a desublimation of the struggle for recognition that runs counter to political and commercial modernization. Rather than channeling his aggressive impulses into nonviolent and economically productive undertakings, Henchard tragically attempts to reconvert commercial competition back into a more immediate and archaic form of heroic violence and personal revenge that eventuates in his murderous physical assault on his former friend and business partner.

Hardy's description of Henchard's commercial war with Farfrae makes explicit the connection between the hero's financial competitiveness and his atavistic but still powerful desire for a more direct and violent form of personal combat:

> A time came when, avoid collision with his former friend as he might, Farfrae was compelled, in sheer self-defense, to close with Henchard in mortal commercial combat. He could no longer parry the fierce attacks of the latter by simple avoidance. As soon as their war of prices began everybody was interested, and some few guessed the end. It was, in some degree, Northern insight matched against Southron doggedness— the dirk against the cudgel—and Henchard's weapon was one which, if it did not deal ruin at the first or second stroke, left him afterwards well-nigh at his antagonist's mercy. (P. 143)

What distinguishes this type of commercial competition from that of the following laissez-faire era is the extra-economic aim that animates it. Henchard craves personal revenge and a vindication of his social superiority rather than material security or greater prosperity.[26] Farfrae rightly feels that Henchard's declaration of commercial war is, in strictly economic terms, quite unnecessary. Even in the relatively small local market of Casterbridge, both he and Henchard can profitably pursue the corn trade (pp. 142–43). But in the manner of a Homeric contest or classical agon, Henchard aims at destroying Farfrae's livelihood rather than enhancing his own; he thereby implicitly assumes that his own successful struggle for recognition is incompatible with that of other businessmen.[27] Henchard remains attached to the old mercantilist notions of protected and monopolistically controlled markets, not simply because he cannot seem to fathom that competition is potentially mutually profitable, but more profoundly because he will not accept what he perceives to be his loss of social esteem as a result of Farfrae's financial success. Unlike commercial shares in an expanding market, Henchard's archaic sense of public honor and personal prestige can only be diminished when divided among competitors.

And yet, despite his willingness to risk both prosperity and pure prestige in commercial combat, Henchard proves ultimately incapable of satisfying the bloodier demands entailed in the ethical code of the Hegelian master. When he actually engages Farfrae in physical combat and has the opportunity to take his enemy's life in the hayloft, Henchard recoils from the deed, conscience-stricken and completely unmanned (pp. 296–97). Though "in a modern sense" he may have "received the education of Achilles" (p. 106), Henchard never learns to kill. He draws back from an act of physical violence that would forever place him beyond the pale of middle-class morality and carry him back to an earlier era of aristocratic duels and blood feuds. Hardy's bourgeois hero lacks the pagan ferocity and aristocratic disdain for mere life that characterize the Hegelian master. Ultimately he rates the aristocratic sense of personal honor and prestige lower than the life of another human being. Henchard reluctantly accepts a modern, post-Christian, and bourgeois redefinition of personal honor that demands that he preserve the life of an "inferior" whom he considers to have slighted him. Far from consistently exhibiting an aristocratic pathos of distance, Hardy's hero inclines towards the modern belief in the universal recognition and equality of all human beings. Given an opportunity to deny the furmity woman's accusation in court and be taken at his word, Henchard confesses his transgression and publicly insists that he is "no better" than a poor vagabond from the lowest ranks of society (p. 227).

I have suggested that Henchard insists on clinging to an outmoded mercantilist conception of commercial competition that dovetails neatly with his archaic conception of the struggle for pure prestige. But Hardy's hero is also something of a commercial innovator who provides the catalyst for Farfrae's economic revolution. It is, after all, Henchard who makes economically feasible Farfrae's initial residence in Casterbridge. In need of a skilled manager to assist him in a business grown too large for one man to supervise personally, Henchard allows his entrepreneurial success and dynamic commercial proclivities to lead him to introduce a new division of labor for the sake of economic efficiency. Farfrae offers Henchard modern accounting and managerial skills, as well as a revolutionary scientific process by which bad grain can be restored, or at least by which its impurities may be effectively disguised.[28] Critics have long noted the Faustian aspects of the bargain Henchard strikes with Farfrae.[29] Because he challenges the restraints imposed by nature on the farmer and merchant (that grain, once gone bad, cannot be restored to its original state), and because he seeks to overcome the limits of a small, inefficient, and technically unsophisticated commercial enterprise, Henchard becomes a kind of proto-capitalist overreacher. His initial enthusiasm for new technological advances, specialized managerial skills, and a more efficient division of labor thus illustrates the Faustian dimension of capitalism itself. Economic progress entails a relentless dialectical process: man overcomes the material restraints imposed by nature and convention, but the very success of primitive methods of doing business eventually makes necessary more advanced technological and commercial practices that render prior modes of economic activity obsolete. For Henchard, this process means that his desire for ever-greater economic success paradoxically produces a competitor whose superior commercial and entrepreneurial talents allow him to supplant Henchard as the leading businessman in the community.

Were Henchard simply to accept and develop Farfrae's new commercial innovations, he might avert financial disaster, if not continue to prosper. But having initially welcomed economic modernization, Henchard comes to resent and resist the new technologies and managerial practices inaugurated by his associate.[30] Whereas Farfrae wishes to divide their managerial duties for the sake of greater efficiency and productivity, Henchard wants to perform their supervisory rounds together because he enjoys the company of his employee and friend (p. 120). Their additional disagreements over introducing a new seed drill and disciplining a tardy worker point to the difference between a primitive, patriarchal, intuitive, and inefficient form of doing business and its modern, bureaucratic, technological, and more profitable counterpart. By contrast with Farfrae, who never deviates from his temperate and fully rationalized system of "small profits frequently repeated" (p. 186), Henchard consistently allows personal, noneconomic considerations to dictate his business practices.[31] His insistence on regarding Farfrae as both his employee and his most intimate confidante contributes over time to their strained working relations (p. 129). When Farfrae supplants the mayor in the affections of laborers and townsfolk as the most admired man in Casterbridge, Henchard fires his highly talented and productive manager in a fit of pique and jealousy, even though his decision adversely affects his trade. Henchard's spiteful efforts to frustrate Farfrae's courtship of Elizabeth-Jane prevent a natural rapprochement between the two men that would have led to a mutually profitable merger (p. 142). And his preoccupation with an intense personal rivalry fueled by Farfrae's romantic interest in Lucetta culminates in the economically unnecessary and financially ruinous commercial combat with his former employee.

Farfrae wins the trade war with Henchard precisely because as an embodiment of Scottish economic enlightenment he never allows a desire for revenge or honor to interfere with his financial judgment. By contrast, having rejected the advanced business practices his manager pioneers, Henchard reverts to evermore archaic, crude, and irrational commercial tactics. Returning to a primitive practice of the classical and pagan era that still survives in this economically backward region, Henchard relies on the auguries of a local weather prophet when making rash financial speculations. When bad harvests ruin his chief debtor (on whom Henchard has depended to cover his own disastrous speculation) and place him in severe financial straits, Henchard resorts to dishonest business practices; in desperation he misrepresents the quality of his grain, failing to preserve a strict correspondence between bulk and sample (p. 242). The arc of Henchard's commercial career thus follows that of a provincial but forward-looking mercantilist, who initially welcomes and then repudiates economic modernization, only to fall back on ever-more outmoded methods of commercial enterprise, until he finally resorts to fraud and violence as the only possible means of exacting revenge on a commercial and personal rival. Having once stood for the most progressive economic and social movements in Casterbridge, Henchard tragically destroys himself by actively resisting those very forces he helped to unleash.

This same tragic vacillation characterizes Henchard's disastrous domestic life, in which he is torn by his contradictory attachments to

patriarchal rule and to a more modern and progressive ideal of familial and personal relationships. As a young man, Henchard is fired by
the idea of upward mobility for himself and his family, but finds that
his preexisting patriarchal obligations are a hindrance to his economic success. His sale of his wife and child at the Weydon-Priors
Fair offers to resolve this tension, freeing him from domestic responsibilities while rewarding him with a financial premium. But while
this sale helps to launch Henchard on his commercial career, it has no
legal standing (domestic slavery was abolished in England in 1772)
and Hardy must aver to Susan's provincial naiveté to make the incident credible to his readers. Though critics have sometimes interpreted Henchard's sale of wife and child as an instance of proto-
capitalist reification, in fact Henchard's drunken sale of his family
marks a return to a premodern and precapitalist custom that allows
wives and children to be disposed of as mere chattel.[32] Admittedly
Hardy based this incident on historical events that occurred around
Dorchester in the 1820s, but his fictional recovery of these exceedingly rare provincial practices embodies another ghostly return of the
ancient past that haunts the vanishing world of Wessex. The chattel
status of a patriarch's family is in fact more characteristic of certain
tribal societies or of the Roman Empire than it is of early modern
civilization in Western Europe.[33] In any case, twenty years after his
fateful bargain with Newson, during which time Henchard has come
to epitomize the new rising man of the mercantilist era, he attempts to
make amends for his past transgressions, tacitly buying his family out
of their former bondage.

Unfortunately for Henchard, he never manages the transition to a
more modern and liberal conception of family life that his reunion
with Susan and Elizabeth-Jane seems to promise.[34] While he encourages his daughter's desire to educate, refine, and improve herself,
Henchard presumes to decide her matrimonial future with a patriarchal command: she must not marry Farfrae. And though he develops a greater respect, love, and tenderness for his daughter, especially after the death of his wife, his discovery of her true parentage
leads him to display "a positive distaste for the presence of this girl
not his own" (p. 160). Having established the basis for domestic
union—he has legally adopted Elizabeth-Jane—Henchard subsequently rejects a parental relationship not based on a strictly biological connection, that of *blood*. The archaic prejudices of a kind of
tribal patriarch reassert themselves, and Henchard effectively drives
Elizabeth-Jane from his home through neglect and misuse. Even

when he later wishes to regain Elizabeth-Jane's affection, Henchard feels that it is necessary to resort to a subterfuge and leads her to believe that he is her real (biological) father. Henchard's gratuitous self-banishment from Casterbridge, after he is reconciled with his adopted daughter and subsequently supplanted in her affections by Newson and Farfrae, is merely the protracted working out of the hero's conflicted attempt to fix his role as husband and father at a moment of historical redefinition of these terms. Although he learns to repudiate the brutality and petty tyranny of the old patriarchy, he finds that he cannot respond deeply to the more egalitarian domestic relationship that follows from the loss of patriarchal power. For Henchard, the price of domestic liberation is the loss of personal attachment to those closest to him. By virtue of his acceptance of Elizabeth-Jane's individual autonomy and his willingness to recognize her as a fellow human being, Henchard must sacrifice a secure sense of attachment based on the idea that she is his own. He and his stepdaughter are equal but estranged in the modern and more liberal world of a transformed Casterbridge.[35]

V

Largely content with the status quo, the populace of Casterbridge at first does not question the insular and unsophisticated character of provincial life, the relatively stratified hierarchy that governs social relations, the primitive condition of agricultural methods, or the basically masculine and patriarchal ethos of the community during Henchard's mayoralty. But this seemingly static state does not last; Henchard persuades a series of outsiders who arrive in Casterbridge to remain, and collectively they gradually effect the economic and social modernization of the community in ways that subtly undermine Henchard's authority. For example, Elizabeth-Jane and Lucetta contribute to the increasing domestication, sophistication, and liberalization of Casterbridge's everyday life. Kojève notes that for Hegel, woman as the representative of domestic life is one of the crucial agents of historical progress; in particular, she is indirectly responsible for the dissolution of the strictly patriarchal order of the pagan state.[36] Henchard's Casterbridge undergoes an analogous process in the course of Hardy's novel. Elizabeth-Jane is remarkable for her interest in books, her efforts to educate herself, her cultivation of social forms, and her desire for a greater measure of feminine independence. Lucetta introduces more elegant fashions and expensive tastes, cultivates a greater appreciation of aesthetic distinctions, and promotes a refinement of social manners. As a single woman of independent means, she comes to epitomize for Elizabeth-Jane, as for Casterbridge as a whole, a new, more autonomous conception of a woman's role in society. Moreover, as a female with a "past," Lucetta anticipates later heroines in Hardy's fiction, such as Tess, whose transgressions of prevailing sexual codes challenge patriarchal norms and point towards a modern liberal conception of greater personal freedom for women. To be sure, Lucetta is punished by her society for her willingness to contravene its conservative mores governing gender roles. She becomes the victim of outmoded social prejudices appropriately embodied in an archaic social ritual in which the effigies of prominent citizens are mockingly paraded through the streets of Casterbridge: the skimmington ride. And although neither Elizabeth-Jane nor Lucetta conforms to today's notions of a liberated woman, both represent a clear advance beyond the restrictive gender roles that prevail in Casterbridge under Henchard's patriarchal rule. Insofar as Henchard plays a critical role in these women chosing to remain in Casterbridge, he can be said to help bring about, however unwittingly, the social changes their presence accelerates.

While Farfrae's modern commercial undertakings are obviously more efficient and profitable than Henchard's mercantilist enterprises, it is not at all obvious that they are compatible with, much less conducive to, the domestic revolution promoted by Hardy's female characters. Farfrae's coldly efficient and technocratic economic activity would appear to be at odds with the revolutionary changes encouraged by Elizabeth-Jane and Lucetta: the heightened importance of domestic life; the greater equality of the sexes; a refinement in taste and manners; an increase in female freedom and autonomy; an augmented sensitivity to the feelings of women, children, and the socially disenfranchised. But in fact, Farfrae's modern form of business provides a powerful economic engine for just these social transformations. It is no accident that both of Hardy's heroines gravitate toward Henchard's rival and eventually marry him. Collectively, these successive couplings suggest a coherent though largely unacknowledged program of social modernization and embody a powerful alliance for civic change. Farfrae's economic transformation of Casterbridge tends to provide the material basis for new developments in education, arts, technology, fashion, and social intercourse; moreover, it helps to subvert the comprehensive communal character of the city, thereby allowing for the cultivation of an autonomous domestic sphere and the increasing empowerment of women.[37]

Initially the communal character of Casterbridge as polis invites Henchard to make little or no distinction between commercial and familial affairs; the public world of the patriarch fails to recognize an autonomous realm of domestic affairs and family life. However, as both a successful laissez-faire capitalist and a modern domesticated husband, Farfrae illustrates a new and revolutionary relationship between the domestic and the commercial, the private and the public aspects of life in Casterbridge:

> The curious double strands in Farfrae's thread of life—the commercial and the romantic—were very distinct at times. Like the colours in a variegated cord those contrasts could be seen intertwisted, yet not mingling. (P. 187)

By insisting on a demarcation of the public world of commerce from the private world of family, Farfrae guarantees a kind of inviolability to the latter. Personal considerations no longer affect business decisions, and commercial concerns correspondingly no longer interfere, at least directly, with domestic affairs. To the degree that the two spheres influence one another, they simply serve to support, rather than to subvert or subordinate, the values of each other.

Farfrae's attention to matters of particular concern to the women of Casterbridge (song, dance, books, fashion, sentiment, love) enables him to become what we might term the first successful public relations man in the town. By appealing especially to their tastes, desires, and fantasies, Farfrae in effect creates or anticipates a new market hitherto ignored during the time of Henchard's civic and commercial preeminence. Whereas Henchard puts on outdoor municipal entertainments featuring traditionally masculine forms of agonistic competition, "boxing, wrestling, and drawing blood generally" (p. 133), Farfrae's public event offers singing and dancing in a safely enclosed pavillion (p. 135). Henchard provides his rough and ready contests as an act of civic pride and personal magnanimity—he pays for these celebrations himself and gives away all leftover food to the poor. The magnanimous patriarch attempts to dictate the pleasures of the populace according to his own rough Achillean temperament, though with a charitable intent. By contrast, Farfrae covers the expense of his fête by charging all comers a fee. A skillful entrepreneur, he successfully anticipates the more heterogeneous and domesticated desires of Casterbridge consumers, taking special account of the tastes of its female population, and thereby makes a profit.

Although apparently quite impersonal when doing business, Farfrae nevertheless wins the support and admiration of the community by playing to its sentimental longings, yearnings made all the stronger by the fact that Casterbridge is entering a phase of accelerated economic and social modernization. While he often publicly exhibits a passionate desire to return to the archaic life of the Highland clans, Farfrae has in fact eagerly left Scotland for the sake of entrepreneurial success and in the hope of participating in global commercial developments in America. By assuming the romantic posture of a Scottish Highlander filled with a deep lyric attachment to his geographically and historically distant homeland, Farfrae capitalizes on the burgeoning nostalgia of his market for a simpler premodern past. Like the presidents of major American corporations who enter our domestic lives through personal appearances in television advertisements, Farfrae, adorned in his quaint Scottish garb and singing the ballads of Burns, becomes a self-promoting public relations symbol for his own commercial enterprise.

Hardy's slyly satiric treatment of Farfrae's Scottish genius may have a double thrust: he embodies simultaneously the commercial success of a novelist like Walter Scott and the enlightened commercial principles of such Scottish intellectuals as David Hume, Adam Smith, and Adam Ferguson, who helped to provide the theoretical foundations for laissez-faire economic reform.[38] More particularly, Farfrae's successful commodification of his regional identity suggests the way in which economic modernization subsumes and transforms the archaic elements of premodern life. Once these traditional societies and their distinctive customs have ceased to exist as viable and living alternatives to modernity, they can be commercially preserved, packaged, and then marketed to consumers who enjoy the quaint features of a vanished life. Farfrae's audience, especially Elizabeth-Jane, indulges in a form of archaeological tourism, that becomes popular once premodern alternatives no longer pose a real threat to Casterbridge's increasingly modern way of life. Like Scott's novels, Farfrae's celebration of the Scottish Highlanders and their poetic tribal customs appeals to English consumers only long after the last meaningful political opposition to English rule north of the Tweed had been crushed at the battle of Culloden in 1746. Farfrae's theatrical representation of the life of the Scottish clans anticipates the postmodern leveling and commodification of premodern history and all forms of regionalism.[39] His holiday pavillion looks forward to the more elaborate forms of theatrical regionalism in our own time, such as Frontierland at Disney World and the conversion of Pennsylvania Dutch communities, Indian Reservations, and colonial Williamsburg into tourist attractions.[40] Finally, Farfrae's success paradoxically reflects the way in which Hardy himself marketed the name and cultural life of "Wessex" in a series of novels that proved financially profitable.[41]

Farfrae's innovative commercial enterprises prove more popular than Henchard's not only with the women of Casterbridge, but also with the common laborers and the poor. Abel Whittle sums up the sentiments of this group after Farfrae has taken over Henchard's business:

> 'Tis better for us than 'twas. . . . We work harder, but we bain't made afeard now. It was fear made my few poor hairs so thin! No busting out, no slamming of doors, no meddling with yer eternal soul and all that; and though 'tis a shilling a week less I'm the richer man; for what's all the world if yer mind is always in a larry? (P. 245)

It is ironic that Whittle, who eventually reverts to a kind of loyal bondsman of Henchard, should give voice to the newfound dignity and self-respect of the common laborer under Farfrae's management. Nevertheless, the passage makes clear that what the workers especially value is the recognition or esteem accorded them by Farfrae; economic gains are represented as less important to the working class than a greater sense of public recognition. Elsewhere in his nonfictional writings, Hardy makes clear the contrast between the rural laborer before mid-century and the same type after the liberal economic reforms of the Victorian era. Comparing the early nineteenth-century rural laborer with their feudal "thralls of Cedric who wore their collars of brass," Hardy argues that "enlightenment enabled him to rise above the condition of a serf who lived and died on a particular plot, like a tree."[42] Hardy goes on to describe the greater freedom, independence, and proud self-assertiveness of late Victorian workers, who no longer humbly submit to the sort of contempt and despotic excess formerly meted out by tyrannical farmers and managers.[43]

Admittedly, Abel Whittle's remarks suggest that from a strictly material perspective, the rural laborer actually sees a decline in his financial prospects as a result of economic modernization, and this has led a number of critics to assume that Hardy is here anticipating the depressed state of British agriculture that followed several decades latter in the 1870s.[44] However, a closer reading of the novel and of Hardy's nonfictional writings suggests his more optimistic appraisal of the material consequences of economic liberalization.[45] In his preface to the novel, Hardy notes that the repeal of the Corn Laws dramatically lowered the price of bread, thereby making it affordable and consistently available to the working poor, the group most threatened by harvest shortfalls and famine (p. 33). Hardy's comment reflects the fact that the historical event that finally convinced Peel and the Parliament to repeal these laws was the Irish famine of the 1840s, which led to the death of nearly a million Irish peasants.[46] Moreover, his conviction that economic liberalization would materially benefit the rural laborer was perfectly consistent with the views of many mid-Victorian radical defenders of the poor, such as Richard Cobden, founder of the Anti-Corn Law League. In his nonfictional essays and autobiograpical writings, Hardy expresses the opinion that the economic prosperity of the common agricultural laborer had increased substantially after mid-century:

> My opinion on the past of the agricultural laborers in this county: I think, indeed know, that down to 1850 or 1855 their condition was in general one of great hardship. . . . Things are of course widely different now [1902]. I am told that at the annual hiring-fair just past, the old positions were absolutely reversed, the farmers walking about and importuning the labourers to come and be hired, instead of, as formerly, the labourers anxiously entreating the stolid farmers to take them on at any pittance. Their present life is almost without exception one of comfort, if the most ordinary thrift be observed.[47]

Elsewhere, Hardy speaks of the "pecuniary condition" of rural laborers having been "bettered, and their freedom enlarged," in the second half of the nineteenth century.[48] I do not wish to make Hardy out as a simple advocate of laissez-faire economics; he did, for instance, have complimentary things to say about union organizers of agricultural labor, such as Joseph Arch, a quasi-socialist.[49] Nevertheless, it is clear that for Hardy, writing at the end of the Victorian age, the liberal political and economic reforms of the nineteenth century, adumbrated by Farfrae's economic modernization of Casterbridge, had generally contributed to the social and economic progress of the entire British population, including the working class in both rural areas and urban centers.

Under Farfrae the opinions and desires of all classes and both genders are at least implicitly consulted in civic and commercial matters. In every sense of the term, Farfrae's rule is more popular than Henchard's. The fall of the patriarchal hero is thus the harbinger of a more humane and egalitarian age in Casterbridge. By the close of Hardy's novel, the archaic character of Casterbridge has been compromised in every respect. Over the course of just five or six years, Casterbridge experiences the first effects of the revolution in modern technology, the rationalization of commercial activity, the incremental growth in the freedom of women, the introduction of new fashions and refinements in social manners, a democratization of political life, a general increase in material prosperity, and an erosion of local autonomy. The ceremonial visit of a member of the royal family (based on Prince Albert's journey to Dorchester in 1849) signals the increasing integration of this regional society into modern British life, and the emergence of a new national consciousness among the citizenry. As the new mayor of Casterbridge, Farfrae welcomes his royal guest as a patron and champion of economic and scientific progress in Victorian England (p. 285). Henchard's individual tragedy thus becomes an emblem of the passing away of an anachronistic communal existence, which ultimately succumbs to the forces of modernity.

VI

Although Hardy's dramatization of social and political change in Casterbridge loosely conforms to a Hegelian conception of tragic conflict, the belatedness of the historical moment he dramatizes tends to mute the tragic resonance of his narrative. Earlier novelists such as Scott or later ones such as Achebe and Vargas Llosa focus upon historical conflicts that arise from political and social differences that seem far more profound than those that separate Henchard and Farfrae. The historical distances between Scottish Highland clans and eighteenth-century Londoners, twentieth-century British colonial officers and Igbo tribesmen, the subjects of a virtually medieval theocratic society and the citizens of a modern democratic Brazilian republic, seem virtually unbridgeable by contrast to that which divides a proto-modern bourgeois mercantilist from a modern capitalist bourgeois. In comparison to the historical conflicts dramatized by Scott, Achebe, and Vargas Llosa, which typically culminate in widespread violence and the complete collapse of a traditional society, the historical clash of *The Mayor of Casterbridge* seems considerably less wrenching for most of those who live under the old order. In fact, in Hardy's novel, the triumph of the forces of liberal modernity on the whole appears to represent a general improvement in the lives of a majority of the inhabitants of Casterbridge.

The relatively short distance traveled between Henchard's Casterbridge and Farfrae's tends to deny to the fall of Hardy's hero the tragic resonance and revolutionary consequences that characterize the tragedies of figures such as Scott's Vich Ian Vohr, Achebe's Okonkwo, and Vargas Llosa's Counselor. Since Henchard anticipates and even initiates certain limited but progressive changes in Casterbridge, he cannot be said to embody an uncompromising resistance to modernity, much less a fully developed and politically grounded aristocratic way of life. In fact, as a civic leader and bourgeois merchant Henchard often seems to represent less a principled reaction to modernization than an incomplete realization of it.

Stendhal's heroes, however diminished and incapable of reliving the historical drama of an immediately preceding era, can at least look back to a revolutionary clash between political figures who represented fundamentally different ways of ordering social life: Louis XIV, Robespierre, and Napoleon. By contrast, the clash between Henchard and Farfrae reflects the more incremental and evolutionary course of English history punctuated by the succesive political leadership of such figures as Pitt, Canning, Grey, Peel, Disraeli, and Gladstone, whose political and philosophic differences could ultimately be settled through the mediating institutions of parliamentary debate and representative government. Looking back on the political history of modern England from a late Victorian perspective, Hardy reflects in his work the relatively nonviolent and ameliorative process by which Britain modernized itself. To be sure, there were moments of high tension—the Peterloo massacre of 1819, the widespread public agitation for the Reform Bill of 1832, the rise of Chartism in the late 1830s—that raised the prospect of open civil war. But in the event, the transition to full-fledged modernity was achieved in England through slow, largely peaceful, incremental change that contrasted sharply with the French experience of the regicide of Louis XVI, the violence of the Terror, and the civil war in the Vendée.

If Hardy's propensity for incremental and progressive liberal reform, the relatively peaceful and evolutionary nature of domestic British politics in the nineteenth century, and the historical belatedness of an author for whom modernity was a fait accompli all serve to diminish the violence of the clash of traditional and modern ways of life in *The Mayor of Casterbridge,* they also contribute to a peculiar sort of posthistorical literary anxiety that leads Hardy to try to amplify the tragic resonance of his fiction through the use of purely formal aesthetic contrivances. As Norman Friedman and Irving Howe have argued, the novel contains two superimposed but separable plot lines, one involving Henchard, Susan, Elizabeth-Jane, and Newson, the other involving Henchard, Farfrae, and Lucetta.[50] These two plot lines only appear to converge; in actuality they culminate in two distinct catastrophes: one domestic and personal, brought about in large part by the furmity woman's revelation of Henchard's past; the other economic and political, the result of Henchard's commercial war with Farfrae. As Howe puts it, "there is no necessary or sufficiently coercive reason why the consequences of a personal sin should coincide in time and impact with the climax of a socio-economic failure."[51] Were it not for his conflict with Farfrae ending in bankruptcy, Henchard might well have survived the scandal in the courtroom without undue loss of economic and political power.[52] By the same token, Henchard would have been financially ruined even without the fresh revelation of his past misconduct.

To be sure, the domestic and socioeconomic failures of Hardy's hero are thematically and even historically connected; they both proceed from the difficult transition from a proto-modern to a modern social and economic order. Nevertheless, this structural bifurcation in plot suggests a more general tendency on Hardy's part to multiply the number of calamities that coincidentally befall his characters without regard to any strict standard of narrative logic or plausibility. In addition to his loss of political authority, financial ruin, and repeated public humiliations, Henchard endures the death of his wife Susan, the discovery that Elizabeth-Jane is not his biological daughter (his real daughter already having died), the repeated loss of his step-daughter's affection, the collapse of his friendship with Farfrae, the disappointment of his matrimonial plans with Lucetta, the frustration of his efforts to preserve her name from public scandal, a new bout of alcoholism, and so on. Perhaps Hardy felt that by continually intensifying Henchard's suffering, he would ennoble his character, enhance his symbolic stature, and deepen the tragic dimension of his career. But the cumulative effect of Henchard's misfortunes (to say nothing of those suffered by the other principal characters) lends more support to Elizabeth-Jane's morose and ascetic-

Christian belief that life is "a general drama of pain" (p. 354) than it contributes to a convincing realization of traditional tragedy in the modern bourgeois era.[53]

As part of his effort to lend a tragic aura to his novel, Hardy made use of the traditional literary convention of suggesting that a divine order surreptitiously directs the events of his narrative. Critics have commonly understood the presence of the gods in Hardy's work to be part of his more general project of adapting the formal elements of classical Greek tragedy to a modern bourgeois novel.[54] And as our analysis of his archaeological narrative method suggests, Hardy's interest in recuperating the formal elements of Attic tragedy serves his larger aim of contrasting the archaic features of both hero and city with those of incipient modernity. But the patina of effects borrowed from Greek tragedy, especially the use of the gods, is nonetheless symptomatic of Hardy's more fundamental anxiety that the final transition from the proto-modern to the modern does not of itself produce the kind of tragic collision that distinguished earlier historical transitions or literary representations of them. Hardy's conscious leveling of all premodern epochs suggests that he must make extensive use of archaic "props" in order to give his narrative the appearance of a historically significant tragic collision.

If critics insist upon understanding *The Mayor of Casterbridge* on the model of Greek tragedy, it is the result of their having in effect been taken in by Hardy's artistic sleight of hand. For Hardy's self-conscious use of the formal elements of Greek tragedy serves to re-mystify the real process of modernization; economic inefficiency appears in the guise of personal fate and historical obsolescence as divine punishment. The shortcomings of grafting the forms of Greek tragedy onto a novel concerned with the economic fall of a middle-class politician become especially evident towards the end of the narrative. The central plot of the novel, concerned with the deeds of a political and economic hero, reaches its climax with Henchard's bankruptcy in Chapter 31. Henchard's violent confrontation with Farfrae in the hayloft, and his subsequent attempt to drown himself are two potentially tragic endings to a heroic existence. But Henchard draws back from these fatal steps, sparing first Farfrae and then himself. Much more the modern bourgeois than the traditional aristocratic tragic hero, Henchard opts to live with the consequences of his public humiliation, hoping to find in his relationship with Elizabeth-Jane a form of domestic happiness that will compensate for his total loss of wealth, power, and prestige.

The Henchard who makes this decision has already ceased to be a public figure or a historically significant actor. From the moment of his financial collapse, Henchard rapidly declines in political importance and heroic stature until he is no more than "a fangless lion," "an inoffensive old man" willing to submit to "snubbings and masterful tongue-scourgings," a broken-down and perpetually drunken haytrusser, economically and emotionally dependent upon his stepdaughter (p. 330).[55] Now that the main socioeconomic and political action of the novel has drawn to its close, Hardy must invoke the spectre of Oedipus and the motifs of classical tragedy to lend his story the aura of Greek drama. Henchard's self-imposed exile from Casterbridge is meant to function as a final reassertion of his heroic identity, creating as it does a parallel with the quintessential tragic hero of Thebes. Unlike Oedipus's self-banishment, however, Henchard's is politically ungrounded, stemming from a purely personal and psychological motive—Henchard's fear that he will lose Elizabeth-Jane's affection to Farfrae and Newson. Moreover, Henchard's histrionic gesture of self-banishment is, as Hardy himself seems to have realized, undercut by his subsequent return to Casterbridge in the penultimate chapter.[56] Henchard's brief visit makes necessary a second self-imposed sentence of exile, which inevitably cheapens the effect of the first and reveals both acts as empty theatrical gestures. The second act of self-banishment makes perfectly clear that Henchard's exile has always been revocable, and completely without the force of a legal sentence. Like Julien Sorel, Henchard resorts to a desperate act of self-dramatization, casting himself in the role of a banished tragic hero of Attic tragedy; however, unlike Stendhal's hero, Henchard does not manage to involve his community directly in his punishment or even to stage his self-castigation as a public performance.

Exile in *The Mayor of Casterbridge* lacks the political significance that lends tragic dignity to the banishment of Oedipus. I have suggested that Casterbridge possesses something of the autonomy and insularity of a polis. But by the close of the novel, this autonomy has been compromised, and in any case the city's political authority has never been absolute, nor has it extended to such matters as banishment. The mayor of Casterbridge, whoever he may be, has never possessed the authority to banish anyone.[57] Given the fact that many laborers in Victorian England regularly wandered from town to town seeking work, as Henchard himself does in the opening chapters, banishment from a given township, even if it were legally permissible, would not be the cruel and terrifying sentence it was in the ancient world.

Indeed there are no external reasons, no political or economic obstacles, that prevent Henchard from once more launching forth on a new commercial enterprise:

> And thus Henchard found himself again on the precise standing which he had occupied a quarter of a century before. Externally there was nothing to hinder his making another start on the upward slope. . . . But the ingenious machinery contrived by the Gods for reducing human possibilities of amelioration to a minimum—which arranges that wisdom to do shall come *pari passu* with the departure of zest for doing—stood in the way of all that. (P. 340)

Hardy's reference to the gods here is a particularly telling instance of his invoking the machinery of Greek drama at precisely that point at which his hero's tragedy has become politically ungrounded. What Hardy offers at this point is a purely psychological tragedy that is projected outward onto an indifferent universe in the form of Henchard's superstitious belief in a malevolent deity (p. 154). The futile gesture of self-banishment by a man only forty-six years old and in perfect health is only a psychological, not a political necessity.

Having ceased to be a civic figure long before he withdraws from Casterbridge, Henchard loses nothing by his self-banishment that he has not already forfeited. The very fact that only Elizabeth-Jane is present at Henchard's first departure from Casterbridge, and that no one at all is at his second, makes clear that banishment in the novel lacks a public context or any significant political consequences for the community. Whereas cities like Thebes and Rome are plunged into civil war by virtue of the banishment of heroes like Oedipus and Coriolanus, Casterbridge has achieved a new social equilibrium under Farfrae long before Henchard's "exile" and death. Henchard's last will and testament merely confirms what he already knows—he has become irrelevant to the community he once ruled. Because the political institutions of a modern bourgeois regime are designed to transfer power peacefully and smoothly from one elected official to the next, without civil strife, the fall of a bourgeois politician and businessman cannot have convulsive effects on his society. Accordingly, in modern democratic societies, businessmen regularly suffer bankruptcy and local politicians lose elections without their resorting to murder, suicide, or self-imposed exile, and without our feeling that their lives are the stuff of classical tragedy.

VII

While Casterbridge gradually conforms to the facts of modern economic and political life, Henchard lingers, just beyond the margins of the city, a living fossil cut off from the new community and modernity itself.[58] Though the conclusion of Hardy's novel lacks both the dramatic necessity and political significance of classical Greek tragedy, it seems thematically consistent with Hardy's representation of the equivocal merits of modernization. For even if Henchard's banishment is not demanded by his community, it nevertheless signals the hero's own final rejection of modern existence. Hardy's description of the barren landscape into which his hero disappears is highly evocative:

> [It was an] ancient country whose surface never had been stirred to a finger's depth, save by the scratchings of rabbits, since brushed by the feet of the earliest tribes. The tumuli these had left behind, dun and shagged with heather, jutted roundly into the sky from the uplands, as though they were the full breasts of Diana Multimammia supinely extended there. (P. 350)

By leaving Casterbridge, Henchard once more slips back into an archaic world associated with the Romans and the earliest Celtic tribes. If only on a symbolic level, Henchard's self-banishment functions as a return to a premodern era. But of course, such a desperate rejection of modernity means the extinction of the hero, who in death is reclaimed by a primitive and lifeless landscape containing only the half-submerged ruins of the distant pagan past. The rejection of modernity, however principled, inevitably means annihilation.

By the same token, in Hardy's fiction the acceptance of modernization does not necessarily spare one from suffering or even annihilation. Again and again in Hardy's novels, we find that every progressive movement in history must inevitably be paid for by a propitiatory sacrifice. In Hardy's symbolic economy of historical violence, almost every advance in social life elicits a "return of the repressed," an irruption of the archaic that momentarily reawakens in order to exact vengeance upon the agents of change. Henchard's efforts to leave his personal past behind, to create a new, more progressive existence for himself in Casterbridge, call forth the reappearance of the witchlike furmity woman who denounces him in court; his engagement of a progressive business manager is symbolically balanced by the brief appearance of an ancient weather prophet who "misleads" the hero, steering him towards his financial ruin. Nor is Henchard the only sacrificial victim: the modern marriage of Farfrae and Lucetta, which tacitly ignores the traditional moral taboo against the premarital sexual experience of the bride, disturbs from its historical rest an archaic practice—the skimmington ride—that scapegoats the violators of the old customs. This symbolic equilibrium is not a function of strict narrative logic; it is, rather, the result of Hardy's implicit assumption that at some deeper level, historical progress must be paid for in blood and that the requisite sacrificial victims are as likely to be selected from among those who strenuously resist the movement of history as from among those who strive to accelerate its progress. Moreover, as becomes evident in Hardy's late work, *The Dynasts,* the ancient gods who demand blood are insensibly merged with spirits or intelligences who articulate a neo-Hegelian understanding of a progressive universal history.

But if progressive and reactionary protagonists are just as likely to end up on the "slaughter-bench" of history, it is nevertheless true that Henchard is unusual among Hardy's protagonists insofar as he is more clearly attached to a world that is passing away than to one coming into being. More typically the lament of Hardy's characters is that of a progressive like Jude, who finds himself too far ahead of the curve of history: "our ideas were fifty years too soon to be any good to us."[59] In the better world toward which Hardy's novels obliquely point, Jude would be admitted to Christminster despite his social class, the divorce laws would be amended so that he and Sue might marry, improved economic conditions would not leave Tess at the mercy of Alec, and the antiquated social conventions and sexual mores that govern Angel's conduct would no longer pose insuperable barriers between him and Hardy's heroine. What ultimately distinguishes *The Mayor of Casterbridge* from Hardy's other best-known novels is the hero's dissatisfaction with historical progress; whereas Hardy's other characters desperately long for the end of history, Henchard recoils from this prospect.[60] Henchard is the last, rather than like Jude, the first of his kind.

Though I do not wish to disparage the considerable achievement of Hardy's other great novels, I believe that *The Mayor of Casterbridge* engages the problem of modernity in a more profound manner. For it is only in this work that Hardy manages to dramatize powerfully the equivocal bargain that makes possible historical progress. While his other major novels reflect a more conventional liberal sense that the progressive reform of a corrigible society does not always proceed quickly enough to satisfy everyone, in *The Mayor of Casterbridge* Hardy offers a more penetrating examination of the real costs and the enormous stakes of the Faustian compact with history. Only in this novel does Hardy represent both the grievous injustices and the powerful attractions of a hero and a community not yet fully modernized.

The course of Hardy's career suggests that the spirit of neo-Hegelian historicism, the sense that the end of history is both inevitable and knowable, gradually undermines the novelist's commitment to dramatizing the tragic dimension of historical movement. One conventional understanding of Hardy's career is that the increasing pessimism of his fiction met with growing hostility from his readers, eventually prompting him to abandon the novel as his preferred literary form. But I would suggest that at least up to World War I, the real trajectory of Hardy's imagination is toward an increasing acceptance and explicit endorsement of a neo-Hegelian view of the end of history, a view that measures the tragic collisions of historical change from an ever more remote and Olympian vantage point and thereby minimizes their tragic significance.

Throughout his early literary career Hardy was an avid reader of progressive thinkers such as Darwin, Huxley, Spencer, Hume, Mill, and Comte. During the period in which he was most productive as a novelist, Hardy was already under the influence of the mainstream of progressive liberal English thought, which converged at crucial points with the historicist elements of French positivism. Hardy's subsequent exposure to the philosophic works of Hegel, Eduard von Hartmann, and Schopenhauer merely provided him a fuller and more powerful articulation of the historicist premises already evident in his early fiction. By 1886, when *The Mayor* was first appearing in print, Hardy was already mulling over "the dictum of Hegel—that the real is rational and the rational the real—that real pain is compatible with a formal pleasure—that the idea is all."[61] By 1907, Hardy articulated a position convergent with Hegel's, though he was rather disingenuous in offering it as purely his own:

> That the Unconscious Will of the Universe is growing aware of Itself I believe I may claim as my own idea solely—at which I arrived by reflecting that what has already taken place in fractions of the Whole (i.e. so much of the world as has become conscious) is likely to take place in the Mass . . . that is, the Universe—the whole Will becomes conscious thereby, and ultimately, it is to be hoped, sympathetic.[62]

Hardy never mentions history in this passage, but it is quite clear from the context that his notion of the Unconscious Will is merely a variant of what Hegel termed the "ruse of reason." Hardy's history of civilization points toward a rational and humane objective, even though progress might not be the conscious intention of individual human actors. Moreover, this history is truly universal; what happens first in one "fraction of the whole" will eventually take place everywhere.

The Dynasts stands as the logical if aesthetically unsatisfying consequence of Hardy's commitment to "the modern expression of a modern outlook," in which the tragic movements of universal history are seen from the godlike position of the "Intelligences" located at the end of history.[63] Ostensibly an "Epic-Drama of the War with Napoleon," which treats a "vast international tragedy," a "Great Historical Calamity, or Clash of Peoples," *The Dynasts* offers an anemic and tedious staging of precisely those events that Hegel and Kojève understand to mark the beginning of the posthistorical era.[64] One might expect that Hardy's return to the subject of history on the grand scale would reinvigorate the dramatic possibilities of his narrative; here at last we seem to have a genuine and substantive political confrontation, with the fate of Europe hanging in the balance. But in fact, we find just the opposite. One senses instead the extreme artificiality of Hardy's "epic-drama," the obtrusive "postmodern" reliance on anachronistic dramatic conventions borrowed from Greek drama, the tired rehearsal of political clashes that now seem historically remote and whose outcome is perfectly well known, the hyper-self-consciousness of political actors who question their roles in the drama and constantly reflect upon how history will judge them. Hardy's great historical figures seem diminished, as if they had assumed the modest guise of his novelistic characters. In Hardy's hands, Napoleon becomes a marionette of the Universal Will, which works through his petty figure to accomplish the end of history. Cast as a vainglorious dictator intent upon crushing English liberties, Bonaparte unknowingly serves to strengthen the English nation, and thereby in the long run forwards the globalization of modern British political principles. Though the work of history is accomplished, there is little dramatic tension, as the fates of both Napoleon and Europe are foreordained, known to the "Intelligences of the Overworld," who preside over the action, if not to the mundane actors themselves.

Hardy remarks that "by surveying Europe from a celestial point of vision—as in *The Dynasts*—that continent becomes virtually a province—a Wessex, an Attica, even a mere garden—and hence is made to conform to the principle of the novels, however far it out-measures their region."[65] His comment reveals how the advanced historicism of his method threatens to reduce the tragic action of history even on a continental scale to inconsequence. From a universal perspective, the modernization of the European continent seems neither more important nor any less certain than that of some backward province of England. Seen from the end of history, the Napoleonic wars are just another chapter in the universal narrative of modernization that takes its place alongside the stories of incremental social change in Wessex. Hardy's "celestial" point of view marks a final disengagement with history, and therefore with tragedy, since this perspective forecloses the possibility of a radical alternative to the present, all historical movement having been already accounted for.

First published in 1903, *The Dynasts* marks the apogee of Hardy's (and Britain's) confidence in the unswerving and inevitable meliorstic advance of history towards its end. The major political events of the early twentieth century—two world wars, a global economic depression, and the rise of fascism and communism—were to shake profoundly European confidence in the inevitability and even desirability of the liberal democratic order. But before those cataclysms forced a reopening of the question of the end of history, Joseph Conrad explored the problem of modernity, not just in relation to Western European history, but in reference to the non-Western world as well. In a diary entry of 1890, Hardy suggested that the early Victorian Dorset laborer resembled a "remote Asiatic." Exhibiting "corresponding levels of culture," these oriental and occidental counterparts were living proof of the "persistence of the barbaric idea."[66] And yet, for all his seeming backwardness, Hardy's rural peasant made the transition to a modern European conception of civilized existence with comparative ease and within a single generation. By contrast, the Asiatic peoples who appear in Conrad's *Lord Jim* adhere to a way of life that remained, even at the turn of the century, more radically opposed to that of modern Europe, and their resistance to the forces of Western modernity consequently proved both more heroic and tragic than that of Hardy's country laborers. At the height of British imperialism, Conrad explores the possibility that a representative but disaffected member of modern European society might choose to flee its confines and seek out an alternative premodern mode of existence in what is now called the Third World. Anticipating the collision course on which the incursions of Europeans launched the non-Western world in the postcolonial era, Conrad also dramatized the tragedy that engulfs those peoples who attempt to reconcile the desire for modernization with the wish to preserve the traditional aspects of an indigenous society.

2

Conrad: The Flight
from Modernity

The shallow sea that foams and murmurs on the shores of the
thousand islands . . . which make up the Malay Archipelago
has been for centuries the scene of adventurous undertakings.
The vices and the virtues of four nations have been displayed in
the conquest of that region that even to this day has not been
robbed of all the mystery and romance of its past—and the
race of men who had fought against the Portuguese, the Span-
iards, the Dutch and the English, has not been changed by the
unavoidable defeat. They have kept to this day their love of
liberty, their fanatical devotion to their chiefs, their blind fidelity in friendship and hate—all their lawful and unlawful in-
stincts. Their country of land and water . . . has fallen a prey
to the western race—the reward of superior strength if not of
superior virtue. To-morrow the advancing civilization will
obliterate the marks of a long struggle in the accomplishment
of its inevitable victory.

Joseph Conrad, *The Rescue*

I

What for Hardy had been a provincial matter, the modernization of a
backward region of England, reappears in Conrad's fiction as a
global process, the imminent Westernization of the world. If in *The
Mayor of Casterbridge* we witness the march of history from within
the political boundaries of England, in Conrad's fiction we catch a
glimpse of the movement of world history as it appears to those who
live on the periphery of British (and Western European) imperial
influence. Like Hardy, Conrad believes that the "victory" of "advancing civilization" is "inevitable"; he is, however, much less confident that it will mean unqualified progress for the non-Western peo-

ples whose traditional ways of life are to be extinguished forever. Though in recent years Conrad has come in for much criticism as an apologist for Western imperialism, modern capitalism, and European racism, even as brief a passage as the above suggests that his attitude toward European modernity and the heterogeneous traditional societies of non-Western peoples was far more complex than is now customarily granted.[1] If the "superior strength" of the West assures its triumph over its non-Western "prey," this technological and military advantage does not necessarily correspond to any higher form of political and social "virtue." And if for Conrad the triumph of Western modernity is a historical certainty, it is no less the consequence of a tragic collision of cultures. For the race of men who fight in vain against the incursions of Western invaders do not relinquish their sovereignty gladly, and in defending their premodern ways of life these people exhibit personal and civic virtues—love of liberty, personal fidelity and responsibility, martial courage, and above all, a form of nobility—which in Conrad's eyes suggest their ethical equality with, if not their moral superiority to the typical bourgeois of modern Europe.[2]

Conrad's ambivalent attitude toward modernity and his qualified enthusiasm for traditional and non-Western societies are consistent with his personal history and family heritage. An expatriate Pole whose childhood was spent in internal exile in Vologda after his politically liberal parents were found guilty of activities aimed at subverting Russian imperial domination of Poland, Jósef Teodor Konrad Korzeniowski was no typical jingoist of late-nineteenth-century British imperial civilization. By virtue of his wanderings around the world and his sense of linguistic and cultural displacement that resulted from his nomadic career, Conrad actually more closely fits the mould of today's migratory postcolonial authors, such as Salman Rushdie. Orphaned at eleven when his parents died of the poverty and hardship inflicted by an authoritarian Czarist government, Conrad was readily capable of identifying with the colonial victims of imperialist oppression. Though he was eventually to claim British citizenship and make his name as an English writer, he remained something of an alien in his adopted country. Speaking English with a heavy Polish accent, criticized for his occasionally unidiomatic prose, visibly identifiable as a foreigner, Conrad was acutely sensitive to the fact that many of his fellow citizens continued to regard him as an exotic "oriental" Slav, not fully English or even Western. This felt distance from his Anglo-Saxon neighbors helps to explain why even when defending the socially progressive character of Western civilization, Conrad felt compelled to attack its "half-conscious prejudice of race-difference" and to champion the spiritual, intellectual, and material achievements of certain Asian nations such as Japan.[3]

Admittedly, Conrad's career in both the French and British Merchant Service made him a direct participant in the spread of European cultural and commercial influence around the globe, and he was not averse to celebrating in private letters and public pronouncements what he took to be the achievements of British imperialists in Sarawak and Malaya.[4] But by the same token Conrad remained throughout his life a vociferous critic of Dutch imperialism in the Malay Archipelago, Leopoldine (Belgian) imperialism in the Congo, and German and Russian imperialism in central Europe and Asia. In particular, Conrad strenuously objected to the eighteenth-century partition of Poland by Austria, Prussia, and Russia and agitated for the liberation of his native land and its reestablishment as a sovereign postcolonial nation.[5] As an outspoken critic of Russian imperialism and an ardent Polish nationalist, Conrad was in many respects closer to postcolonial writers such as Chinua Achebe or Ngugi wa Thiong'o than to turn-of-the-century British writers such as Kipling or Rider Haggard.

Conrad's having descended from the *szlachta,* the Polish landed gentry who historically exercised authority over Ukrainian serfs, has on occasion been taken as evidence that he identified with the reactionary elite within England who accepted and promoted the ideology of British imperial rule.[6] But Conrad's distant aristocratic heritage just as likely served to disenchant him with the commercial ethos of bourgeois modernity that characterized late Victorian England. The two decades he spent toiling in the Merchant Service did not prevent him in later years from offering a scathing critique of "industrious democratic States" ready to wage world war in the name of "peaceful . . . industrial and commercial competition."[7] In any case, to the degree that Conrad identified with his aristocratic forbears, he was embracing a premodern form of social organization that was at odds with the increasingly egalitarian and mercantile character of modern Britain. Accordingly, Conrad seems to show a special fondness in his fiction for anachronistic types who live by historically archaic codes of aristocratic behavior (Decoud and the Blancos in *Nostromo,* Dain Waris and the Bugis nobles in *Lord Jim*) and a distinct animus against arriviste merchants looking to exploit the commercial advantages of European imperial power (Hirsch in *Nostromo,* the Station Manager in *Heart of Darkness,* Cornelius in *Lord Jim*). In short, Conrad's aristocratic sympathies were just as likely to make him a critic as a supporter of European imperialist attempts to modernize the non-Western world, and perhaps help explain his romantic affinity for those "primitive" non-Western societies of the Malay Archipelago that still remained outside the orbit of middle-class European modernity.

Conrad's divided political sympathies, his simultaneous admiration for Western and non-Western cultures, for modern and traditional societies, his deeply ambivalent attitude toward what he regarded as the inevitable course of world history, are all powerfully dramatized in *Lord Jim.* Originally intended as the companion piece to *Heart of Darkness,* this tragic story of a bourgeois Englishman who flees the modern world in order to become a lord in premodern Patusan serves as a counterweight to the tale of Kurtz's similarly ambitious but ultimately more nihilistic venture in Africa. The juxtaposition of *Lord Jim* and *Heart of Darkness* reminds us that imperialism was not a uniform and homogeneous phenomenon, but took widely divergent forms, depending in part on the imperial nations involved and especially on the motives and aims of the imperialists. These two works portray contrasting visions of cultural hybridization, of efforts to bridge the divide between what have come to be called the First and the Third World. Kurtz's Faustian desire to combine the progressive ideals of an enlightened European despot with the martial courage and political dynamism of a semidivine warrior-chieftain eventuates in tyranny, violence, disease, and madness. Jim's autocratic efforts to modernize a traditional non-Western society while basically respecting its religious beliefs, cultural practices, and social forms meets with temporary success; however, the tremendous strains inherent in his endeavor lead to the death of the hero and the collapse of his short-lived regime. Kurtz dies a feverish lunatic, steeped in blood, his final recommendation to the Western world the genocide of the Africans he has enslaved and exploited: "Exterminate all the brutes!" By contrast, Jim dies a tragic hero, a willing sacrifice to the traditional customs and exacting ethical demands of a non-European community that he has endeavored to serve and that he embraces as his own.

I am aware that such a reading of *Lord Jim* runs counter to the prevailing view of Conrad's novel. Although Jim has always had his detractors, in the past twenty-five years critical opinion has shifted overwhelmingly against him.[8] Arnold Davidson's skeptical appraisal of Jim represents the current critical consensus: "We, as readers and critics, can hardly indulge our taste for heroes and find in Jim some redeeming greatness. . . . As a lord he was always a sham."[9] In keeping with this low opinion of Conrad's hero, many critics dismiss the second half of the novel, the chapters dealing with Jim's exploits in Patusan, as contrived, unconvincing, and ideologically suspect.[10] Fredric Jameson characterizes the second half of the novel as a "wish-fulfilling romance," "a degraded narrative," which claims to have "'resolved' the contradiction and generated the impossible hero, who, remaining problematical in the *Patna* section of the book as . . . the hero of a genuine novel must do, now solicits that lowering of our reality principle necessary to accredit this final burst of legend."[11] Patusan itself has come to be regarded as a fantasy projection of the Western imperialist mind, "a kind of enchanted island . . . where children like Lord Jim can pretend to be heroes."[12] Accordingly, critical interest has been disproportionately devoted to the first half of Conrad's novel. When Jim's career in Patusan is discussed in any detail, it is usually viewed in light of the *Patna* affair, that is, within the context of an emblematic failure on the part of a self-deceived middle-class protagonist in the service of Western European imperial interests.

The eagerness with which recent critics undercut Jim's claims to greatness and dismiss out of hand Conrad's exploration of his hero's political career in Patusan follows from an understandable hostility to the many abuses carried out in the name of European imperialism. Indeed Conrad's tale of Jim's rise to power in Patusan superficially resembles stories like Kipling's "The Man Who Would Be King" or H. Rider Haggard's *King Solomon's Mines*. It appears to be a variant of an imperialist myth often used to legitimate Britain's rule over its colonies: the fabulous tale of the invincible white man who becomes the semi-divine ruler of a grateful native people. While such readings have a certain plausibility, I would like to reconsider the novel in a quite different context, as an anticipation of later *postcolonial* novels, rather than as a simple reflection of Western imperialist ideology at the turn of the century. Conrad proved to be remarkably prophetic in many of his novels; *The Secret Agent* adumbrates the psychological portrait of the political terrorist in many later twentieth-century novels, and at times *Nostromo* reads as if it were a product of the Latin American Boom of the 1960s. My argument will be that *Lord Jim* similarly anticipates the concerns of many postcolonial novels that deal with the problem of modernization in traditional societies. With this shift in perspective, Jim's career assumes a strikingly different character, bearing a strong resemblance to those of subsequent Third World political leaders who have struggled to modernize their newly independent nations in the postcolonial period. If we take seriously Jim's opinion of himself—that he has permanently left the world of Western Europe behind; that he has become a member and leader of the native community rather than an agent of outside political powers; that he wishes to improve the social and material conditions of *his* people without regard to the political, cultural, and commercial interests of his British and European detractors; that he desires to preserve the freedom and autonomy of Patusan—then it becomes possible to view Jim's story as emblematic of the tragic course followed by the Europeanized elites of many newly independent postcolonial nations, political figures caught between the desire to modernize their countries and the equally strong wish to preserve the traditional basis of their indigenous cultures. In short, although it would be difficult to maintain that, strictly speaking, Conrad shared a postcolonial *perspective,* it is possible to entertain the idea that he anticipated many of the specific *concerns* about modernization characteristic of contemporary postcolonial authors.

Lest my interpretation seem too farfetched and detached from the immediate historical context in which *Lord Jim* was written, I point out that Jim's "postcolonial" career had nineteenth-century antecedents with which Conrad was intimately familiar: the remarkable lives of James and Charles Brooke, the rajahs of Sarawak, who reigned from 1841 to 1868 and from 1868 to 1916 respectively.[13] As the independent rulers of a native state in northeastern Borneo, the Brookes founded and then governed a sovereign nation composed of many different ethnic groups, a country which remained independent of European imperial control until it became a British protectorate in 1888, and even thereafter maintained its relative autonomy until the invasion of Japanese forces during World War II. I do not wish to ignore the obvious fact that the Brookes and Jim are of European descent, racially distinct from the people they rule, as opposed to the indigenous elites that emerged in the postcolonial period. In fact, even a great many indigenous rulers have been ethnically distinct from the mass of subjects they governed; among those who have come from a minority within a newly independent nation are Amin, Assad, Hussein, Moi, and Qaddafi. However, significant historical continuities can be found between the careers of these Western autocrats and their twentieth-century postcolonial counterparts—rulers such as Nkrumah, Kenyatta, Nasser, Ataturk, Nehru, and Sukarno—based on their common goals as would-be modernizers of non-Western nations occupying precarious and vulnerable positions on the periphery of European modernity, subject to international economic conditions and superpower rivalries beyond their control. The failures and successes of Conrad's protagonist, first in the immediate service of Western interests and later as an independent ruler of a native state, turn out to be strikingly similar to those that characterized the careers of many autocratic postcolonial leaders.

Thus I will argue that the non-Western setting of *Lord Jim* is the key to understanding the political achievements of its protagonist. By taking seriously what Conrad presents as the distinctive virtues of a non-Western community, we will be able to identity and appreciate Jim's unusual political talents, qualities that elevate him in the eyes of the inhabitants of Patusan, whose sense of what makes a heroic leader is often different from that of their modern Western counterparts. *Lord Jim* is designed to lead the protagonist out of the bourgeois world of postrevolutionary Europe and into a premodern world in which the virtues and vices of an autocrat once again become possible, and perhaps even necessary, given the political conditions that prevail. Conrad's hero leads a "fantastic" life in Patusan for the same reasons that the protagonists of Gabriel García Márquez's *The Autumn of the Patriarch* and Salman Rushdie's *Shame* do: theirs is not yet the tepid posthistorical world of Western liberal democratic modernity. Jim's ascension to political supremacy in Patusan seems incredible judged by the standard of the stable bourgeois world from which he comes. But it is perfectly in keeping with the turbulent political reality he finds in the Far East, the kind of community that has over the years in fact produced an extraordinary number of authoritarian figures who have risen from obscurity to rule an emerging nation. Only such circumstances can make a Lord out of a Jim. Our over-familiarity with Conrad's title has made it lose its force. We must strive to recapture the dissonance it originally embodied between the common ordinary name "Jim" and the exalted aristocratic title of "Lord."[14] Conrad's novel depends for its power on the full realization of all that is implied in this peculiar dissonance: the extraordinary prospect that two historical modes of life could somehow be fused together in a single political figure. For if Conrad's hero anticipates later postcolonial rulers, he does so in large measure because of his attempt to call upon the values and institutions of the past in order to make possible a transition to the future. Like the dictators of Chinua Achebe's *Anthills of the Savannah* and Henri Lopes's *The Laughing Cry,* who (at times disingenuously) look back to tribal custom in order to justify their authoritarianism, Jim sees in the traditional political and social institutions of premodern Patusan the means by which to provide himself with the authority and legitimacy necessary to carry out a modernizing enterprise. And like those representative postcolonial autocrats, Jim discovers that he cannot finally reconcile the conflicting demands of two historically antithetical systems of value. The effort to found a regime equally respectful of an ethos that is modern, Western, and democratic and one that is traditional, non-Western, and autocratic leads to a tragic political catastrophe for both Jim and his people.

By attending to the commonly neglected second half of Conrad's novel, I hope to redress an imbalance in the criticism of *Lord Jim,* but do not wish thereby to neglect the *Patna* episode entirely. Indeed, as I view it, both halves of the novel are essential to Conrad's scheme, which is precisely to juxtapose the situation of the would-be middle-class hero in the posthistorical world with his situation in a premodern world in which history has yet to be completed and in which fundamental political problems still demand heroic action and tragic choices. If the latter half of the novel stages the tragedy of modernization, the first half portrays the discontents of modernity itself, a world in which heroic activity in the service of a cohesive community has come to lack meaning and significance, in large measure because the very idea of political solidarity has become problematic. Whereas Patusan is the arena in which the tragic historical destiny of a developing community is dramatized, the *Patna* is the stage on which the endgame of the posthistorical individual is played out.

The formal bifurcation of *Lord Jim* into high-modernist novel and "degraded" romance, hitherto regarded as a structural flaw, thus becomes thematically central, mirroring the political, historical, and cultural divisions that are Conrad's chief concern. Only occasionally have critics noticed that the second half of the novel is itself divided into two parts, and no critic has yet made anything of this peculiar fact.[15] I suggest that the novel's tripartite structural division reflects a deliberate return to the subject matter of traditional political tragedy via a series of generic transformations: from modern(ist) bourgeois novel to epic (or heroic) romance and from epic romance to tragic narrative.[16] These generic modulations suggest Conrad's dissatisfaction with the postrevolutionary European novel insofar as it had come to reflect the unsatisfying realities of modernity, the tyranny of history itself. Nevertheless, Conrad's daring recovery of the epic and tragic narratives of an earlier age within the context of a modernist work means that the former are subsumed under the aegis of the latter. In formal terms, Conrad's work suggests a kind of posthistorical recapitulation of outmoded literary genres. The result is that *Lord Jim* simultaneously acknowledges and reacts against the inevitable historical process that has made its existence possible. As we shall see, one of the deep ironies of Conrad's work is that the "end of history" seems to provoke a renewed desire for the very political problems and crises that the movement of history was supposed to have overcome. A still deeper irony is that the flight from modernity seems to precipitate only a further acceleration of world history, as Conrad's hero inevitably recreates in a premodern world the very conditions he had hoped to escape.

II

Conrad's narrator Marlow detects in the failed first mate of the *Patna* a quality that distinguishes him from his feckless fellow officers and helps to explain Jim's subsequent actions in court and in Patusan: he suffers from a loss of recognition; he feels *shame*. It is precisely his deep and lingering sense of shame that impels him to seek out a new situation in which to distinguish himself in the eyes of other human beings, to become a lord and master in the Hegelian sense. Jim proves very different from Chief Officer Augustine Podmore Williams, the first mate of the crew that abandoned the *Jeddah* (historical model of the *Patna*) off the coast of Africa in 1880 with 953 Muslim pilgrims aboard. The scandal that his desertion created did not prevent Williams from continuing as an officer on other merchant vessels or from establishing a lucrative commercial career in Singapore, where he and his family lived for several more decades. In contrast to Jim, Williams did not allow his scandalous conduct to foreclose the possibility of his pursuing a comfortable bourgeois existence. Jim, on the other hand, relentlessly flees a modern world not because he cannot make a living, but because he values his reputation in the eyes of other men above the material prosperity that their society affords him.

But whatever the inner qualities that distinguish the failed hero from his self-satisfied contemporaries, had Conrad kept to his original intention of treating only the *Patna* incident in detail, Jim would remain for us merely another frustrated modern bourgeois at odds with the historical limits of his destiny, a maritime Julien Sorel vainly questing after the ever-elusive opportunity to prove his heroism in the posthistorical world. What therefore makes possible the astounding transformation of the humiliated bourgeois of the first half of the novel into the semidivine autocrat of the second half is the radically different historical and political environment that Jim encounters for the first time in Patusan:

> Had Stein arranged to send him into a star of the fifth magnitude the change could not have been greater. . . . There was a totally new set of conditions for his imaginative faculty to work upon. Entirely new, entirely remarkable. (P. 133)

Still outside the sphere of Western imperial control, Patusan is a remote backwater of world history, the habitat of "old mankind" (p. 152), a "land without a past" (p. 166), where even the memory of the earliest European traders and explorers from the age of James I has been lost. Jim's journey beyond the limits of European influence enacts an Odyssean return to a historical epoch reminiscent of the West's own premodern classical past: "a Homeric peal of laughter" can still be heard in Patusan (p. 163). Accordingly, in much the same way that Vargas Llosa later invokes the troubadour ballads and chivalric romances of the European Middle Ages when his characters enter the feudal world of the Bahian sertão in *The War of the End of the World,* Conrad abandons the conventions of the modernist novel for those of older and apparently outmoded literary forms, the epic and the romance, which suddenly regain their verisimilitude in Patusan:

> But do you notice how, three hundred miles beyond the end of telegraph cables and mail-boat lines, the haggard utilitarian lies of our civilisation wither and die, to be replaced by pure exercises of imagination, that have the futility, often the charm, and sometimes the deep hidden truthfulness, of works of art? Romance had singled Jim for its own. (P. 172)

Though Conrad exaggerates the primitive character and "utter isolation of this lost corner of the earth" (p. 151) to legitimate the romance of Jim's new life, he firmly grounds his story in the complex historical, political, and geographical realities of the Malay Archipelago in the middle of the nineteenth century.[17] Far from some mythic kingdom of the Western imperialist imagination, Patusan is based upon Conrad's personal recollections of the Berau settlement on the Berau

River in eastern Borneo, as well as on detailed (though conflated and imaginatively altered) nineteenth-century accounts of the customs and political histories of other regions and peoples inhabiting Borneo and the Malay Archipelago.[18] The political institutions, the religious quarrels, the ethnic divisions, the social hierarchies, the dynastic struggles, the economic realities, and the cultural practices of Jim's adopted country all are rooted in historical fact. A succession of Indo-Malay kingdoms based in Java and Sumatra held sway over the native inhabitants (Dyaks) of the northeastern Bornean coast for several centuries before the arrival of Arab traders and "evangelists," who converted the region to Islam in the thirteenth century.[19] Arab dominance also eclipsed the imperial influence of the Chinese and Mongols, who had established trading colonies and settlements. Although the Portuguese, Spanish, Dutch, and English arrived in the Malay Archipelago in the sixteenth and seventeenth centuries, many independent, native-ruled states remained at the turn of the nineteenth century. In the 1820s and 1830s, before the arrival of James Brooke, the British maintained interests in Singapore and the Malay peninsula, and the Dutch in Java, Sumatra, and southern Borneo, but neither imperial power had extended its formal political influence to the northeastern region of the island, the areas known as Sarawak and Brunei.

When Jim arrives he finds Patusan roughly divided among three hostile factions struggling for political ascendancy. Rajah Allang, uncle and dependent of a remote sultan and a descendant of the Indo-Malay rulers of earlier centuries, claims formal suzerainty over Patusan. In fact he exerts real authority only over the Malays, as well as a certain village of fishing folk near the cost, presumably indigenous Dyaks, whom he treats as his personal slaves.[20] Doramin leads the Bugis, relatively recent immigrant traders from the island of Celebes, who are involved in a murderous commercial war with the rajah's Malays. Sherif Ali, remotely descended from thirteenth-century Muslim invaders, is a wandering "Arab" and Islamic militant who has enslaved tribesmen from the interior regions of Patusan, very likely members of at least two more ethnically distinct clans of Dyaks who have been at war with one another. While many of the Dyaks have converted to Islam, others remain animists. Religious differences between animists and Muslims, and between different Islamic sects, fuel Sherif Ali's *jihad* against Doramin, Tunku Allang, and all other "infidels" (p. 179).

Conrad unobtrusively records the impact of generations of European interlopers and traders. Jewel's grandfather was a highly placed official in the Dutch East India company, who married her Malay grandmother. Her father Cornelius is a Portuguese merchant working for Stein, who in turn holds a special permit from the Dutch government to trade in the region. A German political exile who fled Europe after the abortive revolution of 1848, Stein has inherited his business from an earlier Scottish trader named Alexander M'Neil. While the Dutch have made proprietary claims to the region, they have been content to control European commerce by licensing it to independent traders (such as Stein), reserving their resources for the formal administration of colonies remote from Patusan. Despite nearly four centuries of European presence in the Malay Archipelago, no Western power plays a role or has any immediate or compelling incentive to interfere actively in the internal affairs of Patusan (pp. 133, 142). The historical traces of European influence in Patusan, while hinting at the looming threat of Western imperialism, principally evidence the chaotic, multiethnic, and politically fractious situation that Jim stumbles upon when he first arrives, a condition that has almost as many affinities with a postcolonial as a precolonial state of affairs.

Thus Patusan is not an "enchanted island" of the Western imperialist mind, but a roughly accurate historical representation of a region characterized by what modern political scientists would term "uneven development." While some regions of Patusan—the interior reaches up river—remain in a relatively "primitive" condition, the coastal sections are in contact with the outside world, exhibiting more highly developed technologies, trading arrangements, and political structures. Whereas the Dyaks of the interior still appear attached to tribal chieftains and to clan rituals, the Malays along the coast have long lived under a more centralized dynastic administrative system. The mixture of heterogeneous languages, peoples, religions, political institutions, and social structures reflects hundreds of years of sedimented history, including long periods of Asiatic imperial control and European commercial influence, a situation in many ways characteristic of those postcolonial societies that lack any "natural" or "organic" unity—that is, societies that have yet to be fashioned into modern nation-states.

Unlike Julien Sorel, who finds himself condemned to the safe, secure, and placid world of postrevolutionary France, Jim stumbles into the unpredictable and chaotic political conditions of a premodern world, in which fundamental political change is still possible.

Jim meets with a Napoleonic opportunity that Stendhal's parvenu hero would envy: the chance to found a new regime. As a kind of modernizing autocrat, "the virtual ruler of the land" (p. 166), who centralizes administrative control of Patusan, Jim attains a "greatness as genuine as any man ever achieved" (p. 149). Conrad duly notes that the imposition of a stable new government requires the employment of force and violence in a land where "utter insecurity for life and property was the normal condition" (p. 139). While Jim does not exactly display a Napoleonic genius for warfare, he demonstrates a basic tactical skill and exploits technological advantages in weaponry whenever possible. In an episode borrowed directly from James Brooke's military exploits in Sarawak, Jim executes his plan of dragging cannons to the heights above Sherif Ali's fortification, where he and his men initiate a successful surprise attack on the enemy. Moreover, in a country in which the development of weaponry is at a rudimentary stage, Jim's personal valor can still determine the outcome of this battle fought hand to hand. As in the world of the *Iliad,* in Patusan political dangers assume concrete, human form, to which Conrad's hero responds with poise and resolution. So long as he faces an identifiable human enemy—Sherif Ali's assassins and spearmen, Tunku Allang's armed retainers, Gentleman Brown's desperadoes— Jim acts with a degree of physical courage that wins him widespread respect in a land that still glorifies the military prowess of its aristocratic leaders. Although in contemporary Western societies we have increasingly come to think of the battlefield triumphs or physical courage of our civic leaders as only incidental qualifications for election to public office, our relatively modest estimation of the importance of military skill in our leaders is in fact historically atypical. Throughout most of history, and in many postcolonial nations today, martial bravery and military success have established the popular basis for many a leader's claim to govern his people. Before we dismiss Jim's martial exploits as evidence of his childish, brutal, or reactionary character, we should recall that the military feats of such revolutionary figures as Bolívar, Mao, or for that matter George Washington were instrumental in their becoming the respected leaders of independent postcolonial nations.

Like James Brooke, who deftly maneuvered himself into power through a series of commercial deals and palace intrigues with the leaders of Sarawak and Brunei, Jim displays a certain Machiavellian grasp of political conditions in Patusan. He accurately sizes up the constellation of forces and successfully manipulates them to his advantage. Though like Brooke he has no official or even unoffical support from a European government, Jim is able to exploit Tunku Allang's misimpression that he is an agent of the Dutch. By not disabusing the rajah of this idea, Jim buys himself valuable time; his captors fear to execute him because that might provoke the intervention of a formidable Western imperial power. By the same token, Jim's revelation of his English background to Doramin helps to smooth the way to an alliance; the Bugis are much less apprehensive about the more remote and less powerful English colonial presence in the Malay Archipelago. Moreover, by solidifying his pact with the most recent immigrants to the island, the Bugis, Jim provides himself with an additional measure of political protection in his early days in Patusan. In the name of peace and justice, but no doubt in order to forestall further assassination attempts on him by Sherif Ali as well, Jim succeeds in uniting the Bugis against the leader of the local *jihad*. His crucial role in the military victory of the Bugis further enhances his stature among them and has the added advantage of intimidating Tunku Allang. In imitation of Brooke's actions in Sarawak, Jim's subsequent liberation of Sherif Ali's slaves forms the basis of his own "people," those native Dyaks particularly and unqualifiedly devoted to his personal cause. This body of former slaves and grateful followers ultimately provides Jim with the kind of real political power that makes possible his seemingly "fantastic" ascent to absolute supremacy in Patusan.

Were Jim's success limited to his seizing control of Patusan, he might appear little more than a kind of petty dictator, not much different from Kurtz, who gains power by virtue of violence, fraud, and exploitation of the superstitious beliefs and internecine divisions of the local population. However, Conrad goes to considerable lengths to present Jim as a liberal reformer, a leader who desires to unify and modernize Patusan without turning the society into a pale imitation or subordinate colonial possession of a modern Western state.[21] Jim's political revolution is not carried out for the sake of European commercial or political interests; under his government Patusan remains a small but independent community struggling to maintain its sovereignty in the midst of geopolitical competition among Europe's great powers.[22] Nonetheless, like James and Charles Brooke of Sarawak, Jim modifies or eradicates many longstanding customs in Patusan that he finds incompatible with a European tradition of modern liberalism.[23] Jim eliminates slavery and many of the exploitative economic privileges and monopolies of the Malay nobility; introduces a form of judicial rule based upon equality before the law that is less subject to the class prejudices and ethnic hostilities that have plagued relations among the Dyaks, Malays, and Bugis; establishes a precedent for magisterial clemency (by pardoning Tunku Allang), thereby moderating the violent excesses of a tribal ethic that approves of revenge; works to improve the economic and social prospects of the merchant and peasant classes; and tolerates a variety of faiths, while suppressing those forms of religious fanaticism that promote civil strife.

Jim's personal and governmental actions regarding racial relations in Patusan are particularly revealing, especially when seen against the background of British imperial policies of the time. After the Sepoy Mutiny of 1857, British colonial rule became acutely caste conscious, severe in its official insistence that all English officers avoid social, matrimonial, and sexual ties with the native population, particularly in equatorial zones. Jim's public acknowledgment of Jewel, a "half-caste" Malay woman, as his legitimate spouse constitutes a major breach of the nineteenth-century British imperial ethos. Moreover, Jim is united to the Bugis couple, Doramin and his wife, by a form of filial piety, and to their son Dain Waris by the equivalent of blood brotherhood, while relying upon the emigré Malay, Tamb' Itam, as his most trusted political agent and military aide. In short, Jim refuses to be bound by British racial prejudices and conventions, but instead willingly crosses racial barriers, redefining at will ethnic identity: he tells Marlow that in Patusan he lives among his *"own* people" (p. 220, emphasis added). Marlow substantiates Jim's view of himself, insisting that the white Tuan belongs completely to the people of Patusan: "it was they that possessed him and made him their own to the innermost thought, to the slightest stir of blood, to his last breath" (p. 152). To Marlow's European listeners, especially to the "privileged man," an old hand in the British imperial service (and the "you" of the following passage), Jim's conduct constitutes a complete betrayal of his British and European identity:

> You had said you knew so well 'that kind of thing,' its illusory satisfaction, its unavoidable deception. You said also—I call to mind—that 'giving your life up to them' (*them* meaning all of mankind with skins brown, yellow, or black in colour) 'was like selling your soul to a brute.' You contended that 'that kind of thing' was only endurable and enduring when based on a firm conviction in the truth of ideas racially our own, in whose name are established the order, the morality of an ethical progress. (P. 206)

Marlow's defense (and Conrad's implicit endorsement) of Jim's policies and actions thus tacitly repudiate the invidious racial prejudices that characterized British imperial rule. Jim hopes to move beyond both the violent ethnic conflicts that beset Patusan in the past and the practice of racial apartheid that characterized British colonial rule at its worst; he aims at in effect creating a new multiracial and multiethnic state.[24]

Jim's regime also marks an attempt to modernize Patusan along the lines of classical liberal economic thought, in particular to introduce free trade. When Jim first arrives as a would-be commercial agent for Stein's trading venture, he discovers that continuous and ruinous warfare exists between the Malays and Bugis because Rajah Allang violently enforces trade monopolies and feudal economic privileges inconsistent with a market economy. The existence of slavery drastically limits economic development based on wage labor, while the *jihad* waged by Sherif Ali against both the Malays and Bugis further curtails commerce in Patusan. Having once centralized political authority in his own hands, Jim embarks upon economic reforms consistent with the principles of free trade, eliminating slave labor, guaranteeing the free movement of goods along the river and coast, eliminating the rajah's monopolies, and securing the rights of private property for all citizens, regardless of class or ethnic identity.

Jim fancies himself something of an entrepreneur; before his death he is planning a coffee plantation in Patusan. This unrealized scheme has occasionally given rise to the charge that Jim would have become simply another exploiter of the native population. However, Conrad clearly intends that Jim's rule in Patusan be seen in sharp contrast to the blatantly abusive practices of Chester and Robinson, who propose that Jim join them in forcing Chinese coolies to extract guano from a deserted island. There is no evidence to suggest that Jim benefits financially at the expense of his people; he and Jewel continue to live in relative simplicity during his reign. In fact, Jim seems to adhere to the economic policy of native self-development and free trade that James Brooke attempted (though admittedly with only limited success) to introduce in Sarawak.[25] In an 1838 prospectus for his first commercial venture to Borneo, Brooke stated:

> Any government instituted . . . must be directed to the advancement
> of the native interests and the development of native resources, rather
> than by a flood of European colonization to aim at possession only,
> without reference to the indefeasible rights of the Aborigines.[26]

Unlike Dutch imperialists in Java, who introduced the much-hated *corvée* system of forced labor in the Malay Archipelago, Jim does not merely substitute a set of European feudal economic practices for an older native equivalent. As ruler of an independent society, Jim ceases to have any official ties either with Stein's company, or with any other European power. Patusan is therefore not subject to direct government interference in the market on behalf of outside commercial interests. While the local economy remains relatively undeveloped at the time of Jim's death, at least the groundwork for economic progress had been laid by the autocratic hero. In this respect, Jim's career in Patusan anticipates that of certain authoritarian Asian political leaders, such as Lee Kuan Yew of Singapore or Deng Xiaoping of China, who have embarked upon economic liberalization and modernization by means of a paternalistic and nondemocratic method of government.[27]

If Jim assumes the role of liberal reformer in Patusan, he nevertheless remains bound by the realities of traditional political life, in which authoritarian premodern and theocratic methods of government have been the historical norm. Despite his commitment to modernizing Patusan, Jim remains fundamentally a despotic figure, one whose power seems absolute, a leader shrouded in a sacred aura, a semidivine ruler (pp. 140, 162, 167). Conrad gives no hint that Jim intends to introduce anything like representative government or democratic rule; at most he delegates limited authority to the headmen of the villages, whom he appoints directly. Jim's rule remains fully charismatic in the Weberian sense, never routinized or institutionalized.

Moreover, while striving to modernize Patusan, Jim does not completely abandon the old ways or embark upon a thoroughgoing and total modernization of this native state. In contrast to the more idealistic Kurtz, whose radically modern attempt to impose enlightened rule by force leads to a form of imperialist tyranny far worse than any native antecedent, Jim leaves unchanged many of the social customs and political conventions to which the inhabitants of Patusan are strongly attached and which serve the purpose of giving this new community a sense of stability and "organic" rootedness in the past. While Jim abolishes slavery, he does not eliminate all class distinctions, since to do so would invite renewed social conflict and likely undermine the precarious peace that centralized rule has made possible. In a similar vein, Jim makes virtually no attempt to liberalize the social norms that govern relations between the sexes in Patusan. And in order to maintain his legitimacy, Jim must observe the feudal and tribal formalities that effectively regulate his conduct and make the rule of a single individual acceptable to the people of Patusan. He must visit the rajah regularly, running the risk that his coffee will be poisoned; in the most important matters of state, such as the initiation of hostilities against an enemy, he must confer with a council of nobles and elders to obtain their approval before he can act.

In short, Jim consciously preserves traditional customs that he understands to be based on little more than the habits and faith of the peoples of Patusan. Although he knows "the legend" that has "gifted him with supernatural powers" (p. 162) is no more than an irrational mystification, Jim understands that to introduce progressive changes he must preserve his people's nearly religious "belief" in him (p. 203). To embark upon a program of full-fledged enlightenment and secularization runs the risk of subverting his own legitimacy, and therewith the limited modernizing reforms that it has made possible. Jim tacitly assents to a form of political propaganda that will later characterize the postcolonial regimes of such figures as Haile Selassie, the Shah of Iran, Mohamed V of Morocco, and Mao Ze dong, each of whom indulged to varying degrees in self-deification as head of state. To be sure, Jim is only a petty idol or household god beside these others, but he shares with them the intention of employing a personal myth—a cult of personality—as a means for *imagining* or *inventing* a new national identity.[28]

Jim's political project in Patusan is in effect to create a nation where none had existed. Examined closely, the organic character of Jim's community begins to look artificial and contrived. In this regard, Marlow functions simultaneously as the subtle critic of the regime, who recognizes the fragility of the imagined community, and as the purveyor of Jim's myth of national unity. On the one hand Marlow's descriptions of Patusan enable us to see the polyglot, multiethnic, and syncretistic character of this fractious "nation," whose unification requires the skillful political use of force, guile, and mystification. On the other hand, Marlow becomes the poet laureate of the new regime and the trustee of the "amazing Jim-myth" (p. 171) that constitutes the ideological basis for a cohesive Patusan. If Jim's political enterprise succeeds, at least temporarily, it is in part because the attempt to craft an organic community out of the warring factions and disparate religious and ethnic groups of Patusan is made easier by the isolation and the small size of this society: "Thirty miles of forest shut it off from the sight of an indifferent world" (p. 138). The diminutive character of an historical backwater cut off from the rest of the world invites comparison not only with Hardy's Casterbridge, but more generally with the classical form of the regime—the polis.[29] By contrast to much more populous and geographically far-flung postcolonial nations such as Indonesia or Malaysia, Patusan bears a strong resemblance to a premodern classical polity. It is at least possible that its people actually know each other personally and meet one another on a regular basis. Moreover, for all its internal divisions along class, race, and religious lines, a substantial portion of Patusan's citizens are related to each other through blood or marriage. The artificial cohesiveness of Jim's imagined community draws for support on preexisting familial, clan, and tribal structures that create a genuinely "organic" (biological) network of social relationships.

Jim thus constructs something new out of the sedimented political history of the past. To be sure, the result is a political invention, based on a myth, that is subject to the shortcomings that beset all regimes founded on personal myths. But if Jim's respect for many premodern institutions and traditional customs answers to the historical limitations and political realities of Patusan as he finds them on his arrival, his preservation of them also reflects his (and possibly Conrad's) discontent with the modern world from which he has retreated.[30] Like Stendhal's Fabrizio del Dongo, Jim has sought to escape from a humiliation that seems entirely a personal failing, but which on closer scrutiny proves to be intimately connected to the new realities of the posthistorical world. Jim seeks out Patusan for much the same reason that Fabrizio leaves the battlefield of Waterloo for Parma. He hopes to return to the heroic possibilities of a bygone era, to find once again an arena in which personal courage and political action become historically meaningful. Before analyzing the ultimately tragic outcome of Jim's political career in Patusan, we must therefore consider how the decisions he makes and actions he takes as the leader of a new nation are premised upon a deep and abiding discontent with posthistorical modernity. To that end, I propose to read the *Patna* episode as illustrating the dangers and disappointments that shadow the end of history.

III

Jim goes to sea hoping to escape the limitations of a Western posthistorical existence in which the necessity, even the possibility, for politically meaningful heroic action seems no longer to exist. The England of Jim's youth contains "placid, colourless forms of men and women peopling that quiet corner of the world as free of danger or strife as a tomb, and breathing equably the air of undisturbed rectitude" (p. 208). As in *Heart of Darkness*, Conrad evokes the European homeland as a "whited sepulchre," a great tomb containing the tepid spirits of the dead, whose insubstantial forms remain untouched by political conflict or historical movement, exaltation or catastrophe, heroism or tragedy. For Marlow, precisely because England represents an historical achievement and a completed political enterprise, the reigning sentiment of its people becomes moral self-satisfaction mixed with profound boredom. In Conrad's view, neither the social distinctions among citizens in England nor the political issues that divide them are fundamental or historically meaningful; they are merely formal and superficial. Though England still possesses an aristocracy in name, Conrad is aware of how empty its claims to rule have become. In Conrad's England, a modern aristocrat such as Sir Ethelred, "the great Personage" of *The Secret Agent*, whose bloated physique and meaty handshake betoken "a glorified farmer," is reduced to pushing through Parliament a bill for the nationalization of the fisheries, while vaingloriously claiming to lead a "social revolution."[31] To a political expatriate like Conrad, who had experienced first hand the ongoing violent struggles in central and eastern Europe between autocratic and liberal forces, the politically temperate existence of a complacent democratic people bent on the steady pursuit of material self-interest might well bear a striking resemblance to what Nietzsche calls the era of the "last man."[32]

Rejecting the stultifying atmosphere of his father's parsonage, the young Jim believes a career in the Merchant Service will open up new historical vistas and prospects for heroic activity. The high-flown public rhetoric of the Victorian age typically represented officers of the merchant marine as daring adventurers upholding the honor and glory of the British Empire. Writing in 1877, at approximately the time Jim would have been finishing his apprenticeship on the training ship *H.M.S. Conway*, Thomas Brassey, a member of Parliament concerned with the legislative reform of the British Merchant Service, offered this appraisal of the responsibilities of its officers:

> On board a ship bound on a distant voyage the captain becomes responsible for something more than the mere performance of the duties strictly belonging to his profession. There is no position more full of responsibility, none in which there are greater opportunities of doing

good or harm, than that of a commander of a merchantman. In distant seas, far removed from the control of public opinion, a sea captain has unlimited powers of raising or lowering the character of his crew, and of alleviating or aggravating the inevitable hardships of their lot. The honour of the country is often in his charge. Our sailors are the pioneers of civilisation. It is from their character and conduct that semi-barbarous peoples form their first impressions of our nation.[33]

Brassey's imperialist ethos was underwritten by the queen of England, who annually awarded a gold medal to the outstanding apprentice on the *Conway*:

> to encourage the boys to acquire and maintain the qualities which will make the finest sailor. These consist of cheerful submission to superiors, self-respect and independence of character, kindness and protection to the weak, readiness to forgive offence, desire to conciliate the differences of others, and, above all, fearless devotion to duty, and unflinching truthfulness.[34]

The queen's declaration was incorporated into the rules for the management of the *Conway* as framed by the Mercantile Marine Service Association of Liverpool, a private business association of shipbuilders and owners that helped to defray the cost of training the officers of the Merchant Marine.

Despite the rhetorical exuberance of M.P.s like Brassey and the moral exhortations of the queen, Jim soon discovers that his career in the Merchant Service is "strangely barren of adventure," with its "prosaic severity of the daily task that gives bread" (p. 7). The British Merchant Marine turns out to be merely an extension of the deadening bourgeois existence from which Jim believed he was escaping.[35] The crews with whom he sails, especially those who have forsaken the more demanding routines of the home service for duty aboard foreign-owned vessels, are indistinguishable from bigoted, idle, and supercilious vacationers on a Thomas Cook tour:

> The majority were men . . . attuned to the eternal peace of Eastern sky and sea. They loved short passages, good deck-chairs, large native crews, and the distinction of being white. They shuddered at the thought of hard work, and led precariously easy lives. (P. 9)

It comes as no surprise that such irresolute self-indulgent individuals desert the *Patna* and its Asian passengers during a crisis. Faced with danger, they care only about saving themselves, with no concern for their reputation or for the safety of the pilgrims aboard ship. Their willingness to dispense with personal honor for the sake of self-preservation suggests that the bourgeois synthesis of master and slave morality Hegel predicted has failed to materialize at the end of history;[36] these officers preserve only the ethical virtues of the Hegelian slave, who values mere life above public esteem.

Brassey's comment that "something more than the mere performance of the duties strictly belonging to [the] profession" be required of officers in the Merchant Service hints that the maritime code that governs their behavior is insufficient to inspire heroism or altruism. What one finds in this code is hardly a statement of the chivalric or quasi-aristocratic ethos that most critics of Conrad's works have tacitly assumed the maritime code to contain, but, instead, hundreds of pages of Byzantine governmental statutes that minutely regulate merchant shipping but that make virtually no generalized ethical claims.[37] More nearly resembling the U.S. Uniform Commercial Code, the maritime code consists of several lengthy parliamentary statutes, including the Mercantile Marine Act of 1850, the Merchant Shipping Act of 1854, and subsequent amendments passed in 1862, 1875, and 1894.[38] These statutes establish a large semigovernmental agency, known as The Board of Trade, which effectively oversees mercantile shipping (it is this body that tries Jim in court), and set forth the regulations covering such uninspiring matters as proper load lines, the establishment of lights and fog signals, the methods for engaging and discharging sailors, the registration of vessels, the official form of a master's log book, the methods for calculating tonnage, the cubic dimensions of living space alloted to each sailor, and the penalties for overcharges by lodging houses that rent to seamen. Although some few parts of the statutes govern the specific responsibilities of captain, officers, and crew, even these lack any overarching statement of the moral objectives or endorsement of the heroic responsibilities of the Merchant Service. There is no mention of honor, glory, patriotism, courage, selflessness, altruism, or the "civilising mission" of the Merchant Marine—merely an elaboration of fines and penalties to be meted out for failure to observe regulations.[39]

Of course these statutes do not completely fail to articulate a set of moral valuations. The mercantile code was clearly intended to form the character and regulate the conduct of the officers in the Merchant Service. However, the particular form and content of these statutes says a great deal about the kind of character they seek to shape: a modern bureaucratic functionary scrupulously observant of commercial regulations, personal safety, and the protection of property; a modern "soul" whose conduct is incompatible with the traditional autonomy of an aristocratic hero. The comprehensive, intrusive, and detailed nature of these state regulations illustrates the general tendency of Western modernity to *rationalize* (in the Weberian sense) and *discipline* (in the Foucauldian sense) the conduct of all citizens, resulting in the homogenization of their "characters."

Jim discovers that the heroic possibilities of life in the Merchant Service are further limited by the specifically commercial ends for which his profession exists. Meeting the professional obligations of an officer requires neither patriotic sacrifice nor the pursuit of martial glory, only "inglorious toil" (p. 31) and a punctiliousness in honoring commercial contracts with the businessmen who own and charter the vessels he sails (p. 9). Even Brassey, who seems anxious to represent the Merchant Service in a heroic light, was especially concerned to improve the commercial efficiency of its officers. He strongly recommended that the curriculum for training apprentices be modified so as to include "the elements of a commercial education," which would "prove invaluable to the captain of a mercantile ship, as the representative of the interests of his owner abroad."[40] Accordingly, moral responsibilities aboard ship are often conceived principally in commercial terms. Brierly's chauvinistic comment, "I don't care a snap for all the pilgrims that ever came out of Asia, but a decent man would not have behaved like this to a full cargo of old rags in bales" (p. 42), is especially revealing in its suggestion that the Asian passengers aboard the *Patna* are valued only moderately higher than inanimate cargo. The reification of the pilgrims, their reduction in Brierly's thinking to mere merchandise, suggests one reason why Jim demonstrates so little attachment to their welfare. The conduct of trade with other nations requires neither respect for alien religious beliefs nor altruism on behalf of other human beings; it depends only upon the rational pursuit of material self-interest. Jim is not inclined to take seriously the opinion of those whom his fellow officers regard as "human cargo" (p. 11) shipped for profit; hence their regard for him is no spur to heroism.

Nevertheless, one cannot ignore the genuine shock and moral indignation felt by many of Jim's fellow officers in the Merchant Service upon learning of his cowardice and desertion. As Captain Brierly puts it: "This is a disgrace. We've got all kinds amongst us—some annointed scoundrels in the lot; but, hang it, we must preserve professional decency or we become no better than so many tinkers going

about loose. We are trusted. Do you understand?—trusted!" (p. 42).
Given that Brierly is so overwhelmed by the implications of this
disgrace for his own personal and professional self-image that he
eventually commits suicide, one wonders why Jim's membership in
the professional caste of merchant marine officers fails to provide him
with a sufficient degree of heroic resolution in the face of danger. The
modern rationalized commercial organization of the Merchant Service once again provides a partial explanation, for it decisively medi-
ates Jim's professional relationships with his "fellow" officers.
Though this "obscure body of men" believes itself bound together by
"a community of inglorious toil and by fidelity to a certain standard
of conduct" (p. 31), in actual fact they never assemble en masse; their
contractual obligations constantly disperse them around the globe.
Masters and mates are engaged and released, organized and shifted
according to the demands of economic efficiency and commercial
profitability; no cohesive esprit de corps need exist between Jim and
his crewmates, nor any lasting personal ties. Since each ship bears at
most a few and sometimes only a single member of this caste, this
"body of men" possesses only an attenuated or abstract unity. This
fluid, highly dispersed, bureaucratic, and impersonal organization
provides Jim with little incentive to worry about what view his fellow
officers aboard the *Patna* might take of his conduct. This situation
contrasts sharply with Jim's position in Patusan, where men like Dain
Waris and Doramin are bound by direct ties of kinship, and moreover live and act together as a group (as in the tribal council Jim
regularly consults). In these circumstances Jim can draw courage
from his comrades, but in the modern world of the *Patna* he can find
no such support. Jim's lack of courage on the *Patna* and his decision
to save his own skin thus indirectly reflect the modern utilitarian
principles of organization upon which his profession is founded,
principles ultimately derived from a modern philosophic doctrine
expounded by Hobbes and Locke that holds the preservation of one's
own life to be the paramount human obligation.[41]

The heroic tone of both Brassey's paean to the Merchant Service
and the queen's moral appeals to its cadets thus reflects a genuine if
unacknowledged anxiety about the potentially alienating effects and
disenchantments that shadow the global mission of Western modernity. The servants of the Merchant Service must not conceive of
themselves merely as bureaucratic functionaries, but as courageous
"pioneers of civilisation" unflinchingly defending "the honour of the
country." Flagbearers of England, champions of the British Empire,

the avant-garde of Western modernity itself—these men must be made to feel that they carry out a political task of genuine historic importance. But an unsettling paradox follows from this universalizing imperial ambition, one which Conrad returns to repeatedly in his fiction. In the very act of advancing this global project, the representatives of European modernity find that they become increasingly detached from the particular political community and culture that gave birth to their aspirations. For all their jingoist and imperialist rhetoric, Brassey's remarks pinpoint the principal obstacle facing those who serve the cause of modern Western civilization: the officers and crew of these merchantmen find themselves "far removed from the control of public opinion," in effect politically ungrounded when most in need of the conventional support of their countrymen.

The attenuation of a sharply defined and demanding public morality that accompanies the globalization of modernity provides a new perspective from which to interpret Jim's inglorious leap from the *Patna*. His cowardly act does not demonstrate, as some critics have claimed, the metaphysical groundlessness of all heroic or political action, but rather of only a certain kind of action in certain circumstances. Jim's failure shows that in Conrad's view the viability of heroism depends on the palpable presence of a political community to which the hero belongs and in whose eyes he can see himself.[42] Jim fails to act courageously on the *Patna* in large measure because he senses that the recognition of his community is denied to him. Marlow brings home this point by way of comparing Jim to the courageous French lieutenant who tows the derelict *Patna* to harbor. An ardent defender of the value of honor, the French lieutenant has served his country with considerable distinction on board a military vessel in times of war and national crisis. Always surrounded by his fellow countrymen, he has never had to make a distinction between his personal honor and that of his country. When Marlow asks whether a man might not act the part of a coward undetected, in private, and yet retain a public reputation for courage, the French lieutenant finds himself at a loss: "This, monsieur, is too fine for me— much above me—I don't think about it" (p. 91). The chief distinction between the French lieutenant and Jim turns on their capacity to feel themselves members of a political community that is palpably present and cohesive and that thus helps to guide their conduct.

Jim's failure aboard the *Patna* thus suggests an acute crisis both in the imperial ideology of Great Britain and more generally in that of modernity itself. For what Jim glimpses aboard this vessel thousands of miles from England is the deracinated character of an imperial identity and the profoundly disorienting effects of posthistorical existence. If the archetypal Western image of the ship one finds in Shakespeare's *The Tempest* and Melville's *Moby-Dick* is that of the political microcosm or regime in miniature, one discovers in Conrad's fiction its negation: the utterly fragmented or absent community. For the world that exists on board the *Patna,* the one in which Jim must play the roles of citizen and leader, is utterly denationalized and cosmopolitan: "She was owned by a Chinaman, chartered by an Arab, and commanded by a sort of renegade New South Wales German, very anxious to curse publicly his native country" (p. 9). The crew consists of five European officers of differing ethnic backgrounds hailing from remote parts of the Empire and two Malay pilots. The eight hundred passengers, "collected . . . from north and south and from the outskirts of the East" (p. 10), are a similarly cosmopolitan mix of Asians.[43] This multicultural assembly of peoples reflects the heterogeneous character of Britain's worldwide imperium. The individuals aboard the *Patna* share no common faith or language, no ethnic identity or social customs, no political traditions or historical experiences. They belong to the same community only in the most abstract and attenuated sense.[44] If the engines that drive the *Patna* are the products of Western capitalism and European imperialism, the cosmopolitan world that lives in her hold and above deck is the predictable consequence of the globalizing tendency of modernity.

The denationalized character of life aboard the Patna has a profoundly alienating effect on Jim. He lives amidship, "isolated from the human cargo" (p. 11), and insists that there is "nothing in common between him" and the rest of the crew (p. 64). When the *Patna* lies dead in the water and appears on the verge of sinking, Jim ignores his crewmates and fails to respond to the concerns of the pilgrims, whose language he does not speak and whose religious convictions he does not share.[45] Though he finds himself among the heterogeneous representatives of a far-flung global empire, Jim feels completely isolated at the height of the crisis and therefore immobilized: "He remembered he could do nothing; he could do nothing, now he was alone" (p. 61). He literally closes his eyes to everything and everyone around him, effectively severing the last connection between him and the impalpable "community" of human beings aboard ship and eclipsing any lingering chance that he might find recognition in the eyes of others for his actions.

Once again we can highlight what is distinctive about Jim's situation on the *Patna* by contrasting it with his circumstances in Patusan. There Jim is the willing "captive" of a political community, personally tied in a variety of ways to the people he governs. Much like Shakespeare's Prince Hal, he learns to speak to the humblest citizen in his native tongue, and more generally comes to share in the destiny and dreams of his people. His bond to Patusan is strong and lasting, because in his own eyes, as well as those of his followers, he has become the mythic embodiment of the land and its people, and as he sees it, he can never return to the world beyond its horizons. In short, Jim's commitment to Patusan is profound in a way that his commitment to the *Patna* is not. The roots Jim puts down in Patusan help explain why he is able to sustain his heroic conduct there. His lack of roots aboard the ocean-going *Patna* in turn helps to explain his failure to act heroically in these particular circumstances. The contrast Conrad develops between Patusan and the *Patna* suggests a disturbing disjunction between the conditions of modernity and the conditions of heroism. If, in Kojève's terms, the end of history brings about the "universal homogeneous state," in Conrad's nightmare version of modernity, this homogenization means the effacement of all meaningful differences among human beings, who, like the pilgrims on the *Patna*, are now lumped together indiscriminately in a vast cosmopolitan empire. Since among the distinctions effaced in this situation is that between the hero and the coward, Jim loses all support for heroic action aboard the *Patna*.

Thus, although it is quite possible to read Jim's failure aboard the *Patna* as illustrating a metaphysical crisis, the specific details of his predicament suggest that this crisis is in fact a product or symptom of a particular political and historical process. What is most peculiar about Jim's situation is not what is present, but rather what is absent—a political context within which human activity still has historical meaning. As Jim says: "I was so lost, you know. It was the sort of thing one does not expect to happen to one. It was not like a fight, for instance" (p. 79). In short, Jim's crisis on the *Patna* is nothing like the Hegelian struggle for recognition: there is "nobody to pass an opinion" (p. 74). Jim desperately searches for an identifiable human enemy, but he encounters only the perfect calm of the ocean and "that awful stillness preceding a catastrophe" (p. 55). His most visible "antagonist" is a lifeless object: the bulkhead. His effort to anthropomorphize it demonstrates a persistent desire to deal with a living foe rather than the inanimate product of modern technology: "The thing stirred and jumped off like something alive while I was looking at it" (p. 52). Jim's frustration with an inhuman opponent that will neither fight nor recognize him leads to a displacement of his aggression. He strikes out at a pilgrim who begs for water and at his fellow crewmen, who become the focus of his animosity.

Jim's conflict with the inhuman force of the sea might be understood as a transhistorical confrontation, an elemental struggle between man and the natural world, in which case his situation would be little different from that of traditional heroes like Achilles, who struggles with the river gods Skamandros and Simoeis in Book XXI of the *Iliad,* or Cuchulain, who in his madness battles the sea. But on closer examination, we can see that Jim's predicament is paradigmatic of a *posthistorical* crisis: human antagonists have receded or vanished because the work of history appears to be at or close to its end. The political power of modern Western man has become so extensive and so irresistible that the only antagonist left for him is nature itself. But having arrived at the limits of his historical success, he discovers that the entire edifice of the modern scientific project that has provided his political power forms only a weak defense against nature; it appears as an insecure bulkhead that cannot be relied upon to hold back the elements. If the modern project announced by thinkers such as Bacon was aimed at the conquest of nature, then Jim, taken as a distant heir of that enterprise, discovers that this goal remains infinitely far off. The existential dread Jim feels, his abstract but highly personal experience of his mortality, thus becomes ever more acute and overpowering in the absence of any meaningful historical activity. Jim is finally overcome not by the raw physical power of the elements—the *Patna* stays afloat—but rather merely by "the idea" of his impending death (p. 53). The denationalized character of life aboard the *Patna* has its existential equivalent in the increasingly depoliticized and abstract character of death itself, which has come to lack historical significance.

This paradigmatic crisis assumes a particular descriptive form in Conrad's fiction:

> A silence of the sea, of the sky, merged into one indefinite immensity still as death. . . . You couldn't distinguish the sea from the sky, there was nothing to see and nothing to hear. Not a glimmer. (P. 70)

> We were like men walled up quick in a roomy grave. No concern with anything on earth. Nobody to pass an opinion. Nothing mattered. . . . No fear, no law, no sounds, no eyes—not even our own. (P. 74)

This nihilistic epiphany, which reapppears prominently in many of Conrad's works—for example, *Heart of Darkness, Nostromo, The Secret Agent, Under Western Eyes,* and *The Shadow Line*—always discloses the absence of all conventional markers that denote a viable political community of which the hero is a member.[46] Kurtz in the African interior, the Roman legion on the Thames of primitive Britain, Decoud stranded on one of the Isabels, Razumov in Geneva, or Jim on the *Patna* have passed beyond the outermost bounds of a cohesive political community that can legitimate their actions, recognize their humanity, and lend historical significance to their lives. The specific political sources of these moments of radical alienation may differ: for Kurtz, Jim, and the Roman legionnaires, it is the propulsive expansion of imperialism that leads them beyond a meaningful political context; for Decoud and Razumov, it is the disintegrative effects of political revolution and terrorism that unnerve them. In Conrad's novels an absence of communal attachments thus characterizes both the prepolitical and the posthistorical world. In *The Secret Agent* the modern cosmopolis of London, with its inhuman scale, its denationalized ethnic restaurants, and its millions of disassociated inhabitants, marks not an escape from but an instance of the heart of darkness:

> Then the vision of an enormous town presented itself, of a monstrous town more populous than some continents and in its man-made might as if indifferent to heaven's frowns and smiles; a cruel devourer of the world's light. There was room enough there to place any story, depth enough there for any passion, variety enough there for any setting, darkness enough to bury five millions of lives. (P. 11)

At the center of the global empire, London in its cosmopolitan immensity exhibits the same impersonal and alienating qualities that Jim encounters at the periphery of its political sphere.[47]

The first half of *Lord Jim* is as famous for its radical high modernist techniques as for its representation of Jim's crisis aboard the *Patna*. Adorno's characterization of the formal features of high modernism as the appropriate vehicles for the representation of the alienated state of the modern subject requires only minor modification in order to link our thematic analysis of *Lord Jim* with a consideration of Conrad's narrative innovations. Conrad's two most striking formal devices—his use of a constantly shifting and radically subjective point of view and his constant disruption of conventional chronology—are themselves symptoms of what I have called posthistorical existence. Conrad's perspectivism is perfectly consistent with the alienated subject that no longer can see his world as "whole"; the geographic dimensions of the empire transcend the capacity of the imperial subject to see himself as part of a cohesive political community.[48] The achronicity of the narrative suits a posthistorical consciousness that can no longer conceive of any further linear movement in history. Prior historical moments can be formally reshuffled virtually at random since no one moment is privileged over any other: their order no longer matters at the end of history. And yet despite Conrad's stunning employment of these formal devices, he abandons them in the latter half of his work. Conrad's response to the impasse of modernity, at least in *Lord Jim,* is to return to a world in which history is not yet completed, a land where fundamental political issues are not settled and in which premodernist narrative forms—romance, epic, tragedy—still possess versimilitude: Patusan.

IV

In *The Theory of the Novel,* Lukács argues that the epic hero and the epic world form a unified whole. By contrast, the novelistic hero seeks to regain a sense of unity with his world and his society that he vaguely senses existed in the epic past. Every novel, Lukács argues, is an artistic projection of a wholeness lost through the dialectical processes of history. No novel can ever completely and actually regain this lost unity between man and his world because the novel remains merely an artistic product that can represent but not alter the factual conditions of modernity. In *Lord Jim,* the Patusan episodes that precede the arrival of Gentleman Brown momentarily embody the organic wholeness belonging to the epic world. But a return to the epic world is not the same as never having left it. As our previous description of Patusan has made clear, Jim is himself a secret agent of modernity, a novelistic hero carrying even to this remote region the germ of historical change. His attempted synthesis of modern and premodern, Western and non-Western societies proves unstable and his contradictory efforts to modernize Patusan and to shield it from the alienating effects of modernity lead to a political tragedy that once more enacts the loss of the epic unity of the hero and his world.

Over time, the tensions between Jim's liberalism and his continued reliance on autocratic rule prove troublesome. Jim's economic reforms antagonize characters such as Tunku Allang, his court retainer

Kassim, and the Portugese trader Cornelius—men who have long enjoyed the benefits of feudal privileges and mercantilist monopolies inconsistent with the new principles of free trade. Unfortunately, the very liberal sympathies that lead Jim to abolish the economic privileges of the old order inhibit him from using his authority to crush the remnants of this feudal elite. Protected by Jim's liberal toleration of political opponents, this group waits for an opportunity to undo his reforms. Moreover, by opening up Patusan to free trade, both domestic and foreign, Jim makes easier the interference of interlopers such as Gentleman Brown, who pose as merchants while engaging in piracy and fomenting political strife. The Malay feudal elite quickly seizes upon the arrival of Brown to conspire against Jim and indirectly brings about the political catastrophe that puts an end to his new order.

By the same token, Jim would not be any more successful were he simply to adhere to a more purely autocratic form of rule. For his charismatic powers and semidivine status prove as much a hindrance as an aid in resolving political problems in Patusan. Although he retains the power to settle "the deadliest quarrel in the country by crooking his little finger" (p. 164), Jim must make himself physically present throughout the whole of Patusan in order to enforce his laws. His absence while he settles disputes in the interior bush makes it impossible for his people to respond in a concerted fashion to Gentleman Brown's surprise raid. Moreover, even the slightest mistake on his part threatens to compromise Jim's reputation for invulnerability and infallibility. The precariousness of his divine rule ultimately contributes to his political tragedy; his single miscalculation in dealing with Brown destroys the basis of his legitimacy in Patusan. Jim's form of charismatic rule thus suffers from the inherent defects that characterize all "sacred" rulers, such as the Counselor of Canudos in *The War of the End of the World* or the Inca Atahualpa, Emperor of the Tawantinsuyu, whose political vulnerability to the intrigues of a few Western adventurers is analyzed by Vargas Llosa in his essay on the Spanish conquest of the Americas.[49] Founded upon an essentially irrational faith in the divine authority and superhuman power of a single individual, Jim's regime, like those of the prophet of Canudos and the sacred Inca, ultimately proves incapable of defending itself against the novel threat of an external enemy who proves more ruthless, flexible, and rational in his Machiavellian willingness to employ whatever means are demanded to guarantee victory. Moreover, the charismatic regime, lacking institutional supports that could outlive

Jim, necessarily collapses with the desacralization and demise of the divine leader; after the death of the white Tuan nothing remains of his political accomplishments.

The strictly internal tensions that emerge in Jim's regime—between the desire to liberalize economic and social relations and the continued reliance on autocratic political measures, between the rationalizing objectives of reform and the dependence on political mystification—prove barely manageable as long as Patusan remains largely insulated from the outside world. Patusan's isolation temporarily enables Jim to control the rate of growth, to allow only domestic considerations to dictate the pace of political reform and economic development. But like many postcolonial leaders tempted by the incompatible ideals of complete freedom from all outside influence and integration into an increasingly complex web of global economic and political relations, Jim must come to terms with historical developments and political forces that lie outside his control. Rejecting the historically limiting course of hermetically sealing Patusan's borders to all foreigners, in the manner of the Tokugawa shogunate of Japan, Jim runs the risk that the stability and cohesiveness of his newly fashioned community will begin to dissolve once outsiders, particularly denationalized representatives of the modern world, intervene in its internal affairs. It is no accident that Jim's eventual destruction is worked by Cornelius, who is half-Portuguese, and by Gentleman Brown and his polyglot renegades, those "emissaries" from "the world [Jim] had renounced" (p. 234). Even Marlow's friendly presence momentarily creates a disequilibrium in the regime, for it threatens to strip Jim of his semidivine aura. Because of Marlow, Jewel—Jim's first comrade in Patusan and his most passionate supporter—comes to suspect some secret weakness in Jim. Although Marlow attempts to lie to Jewel, in effect trying to remystify her consciousness, he comes close to revealing Jim's ordinary, indeed demeaning origins in the modern Western world. In each case, the intrusion of an alien representative of posthistorical modernity—individuals like Marlow, Brown, and Cornelius, who maintain only a nominal attachment to any nation-state or community that they can call their own—threatens to destroy the founding myth of Jim's new nation and to tear apart the synthetic achievement of the Tuan's political imagination. For as opposed to the myth of the organic and cohesive people of Patusan led by their own Tuan, Brown represents the incursion of the world Jim previously encountered aboard the *Patna*: a cosmopolitan crew of Americans, Chinese, Scandinavians,

Solomon Islanders, Englishmen, "mulattos," and other South Sea Islanders bound together by nothing more than a common desire for profit and personal survival (pp. 216–17).

Brown's arrival in Patusan brings into the open and considerably aggravates the political and ethical conflicts inherent in Jim's effort to create a new nation constructed according to both modern Western and traditional indigenous ways of life. Reflecting the liberal political values, secularized Christian morality, and democratic sympathies of his modern European upbringing, Jim's decision to give Brown a clear road out of Patusan represents his sharpest departure from the ethical judgments and political practices of a native elite on which he has relied for support and advice. To be sure, their Islamic faith places considerable importance upon mercy and tolerance; nevertheless Jim's most trusted friends and allies—Dain Waris, Doramin, and Tamb' Itam—much more accurately gauge the real political threat that Brown and his crew pose to the new regime and unanimously recommend the quick and violent extermination of their enemy, the "evil-minded strangers" (p. 221). Their adherence to a more exacting ethos of revenge, which places strict limits upon the extent of political tolerance and human solidarity, strongly resonates among a populace attached to its tribal and feudal traditions, and has the virtue of crudely but prudently discriminating between friends and enemies of the beleaguered regime.

Alone among his people and against their advice and wishes, Jim takes a more cosmopolitan and less narrowly chauvinistic view of this outside threat. Accordingly, he offers the following apology for his decision to set Brown and his crew free:

> They were erring men whom suffering had made blind to right and wrong. . . . They were evil-doers, but their destiny had been evil, too. . . . Men act badly sometimes without being much worse than others. (Pp. 238–40)

The Christian duty to forgive an enemy; the liberal belief that evil deeds are the result of suffering, misfortune, and ignorance; a democratic conviction in the moral equality of human beings—all these principles help to explain and justify Jim's fateful political decision.

But if Jim makes his decision on a principled basis, his reasoning nevertheless reflects Brown's efforts to alienate Jim from the nation and people he has come to regard as his own:

> He asked Jim whether he had nothing fishy in his life to remember that he was so damnedly hard upon a man trying to get out of a deadly hole

by the first means that came to hand. . . . And there ran through the
rough talk a vein of subtle reference to their common blood, an assumption of common experience; a sickening suggestion of common guilt, of
secret knowledge that was like a bond of their minds and of their hearts.
(P. 235)

Brown aims at rhetorically subverting Jim's heroic self-image, reminding him of his humble democratic origins and thereby shaking
his confidence in his political authority as a lord and semidivine
leader of a "primitive" non-Western people. Brown subtly undermines Jim's certainty in the political and ethical standards upon
which he has founded his regime. By (unknowingly) reminding Jim of
his earlier failure aboard the *Patna*, Brown appeals to his previous
experience of alienated individuality. As the representative of a denationalized modernity devoted to the narrow pursuit of self-
preservation and self-interest, Brown skillfully advocates a form of
moral relativism that would excuse Jim's earlier desertion as well as
the savage attacks of the pirates on Patusan, and subtly underwrites
Jim's decision to ignore the ethical claims of the people in Patusan
who demand revenge upon their political enemies.

Brown's "subtle reference" to the "common blood" he shares with
Jim further strains the imaginative bond the political hero has la-
boriously formed with a foreign people and their land:

You have been white once, for all your tall talk of this being your own
people and you being one with them. Are you? And what the devil do
you get for it; what is it you've found here that is so d———d precious?
(P. 232)

Brown attempts to reground Jim's identity by evoking a thinly veiled
doctrine of racial essentialism. Brown's racism indirectly threatens
the multiethnic and nonracial basis of the new Patusan that Jim has
carefully if incompletely cultivated and promises to divide the white
lord from his people. Brown also speaks as a culturally superior
representative of Western modernity, who can dismiss Jim's political
ambition as that of a historical laggard, a "mimic man" forever
chasing the more progressive European world from which he came.
In effect, he suggests that Jim's local superiority in Patusan is based
primarily upon his modernity, which is after all only the common
inheritance of anyone who hails from Western Europe. In Brown's
eyes, Jim as political leader will never amount to anything more than
a small-time parody of his much more successful and powerful counterparts in the modern West.

The protagonists of Gabriel García Márquez's *The Autumn of the Patriarch,* Augusto Roa Bastos' *I the Supreme,* Alejo Carpentier's *Reasons of State,* Henri Lopes's *The Laughing Cry,* Chinua Achebe's *Anthills of the Savannah,* and Salman Rushdie's *Shame* all reflect the much more critical and satiric view of the modernizing autocrat taken by Conrad's postcolonial literary successors, who have experienced firsthand the atrocities and absurdities committed by the historical counterparts of these dictatorial figures. The "heroes" of these novels are treated with far less dignity (they are much funnier) and with less sympathy (they are much more tyrannical) than Conrad's Jim, who in the end is allowed a tragic death.[50] I suspect that the reason for Conrad's more sympathetic treatment of the modernizing autocrat is, paradoxically, his deeper suspicions about the worth of modernity itself. For Jim redeems himself not by a last-ditch heroic attempt to overcome the conservative resistance to his political reforms, but by a willingness to be judged by a regime that finally condemns his fateful decision to protect the intruders from the modern world.

Jim's momentary identification with the dangerous emissary of modernity provides a necessary but not sufficient basis for the tragic resolution of the novel. Jim makes two decisions, equally integral to his tragedy: first, to let Brown go, and second, to remain in Patusan after Brown ambushes Dain Waris and his men. If Jim's decision to give Brown a clear road out of Patusan originates in his temporary alienation from the regime he founded, the assurances he provides his people honor his ultimate allegiance to a community that remains, despite the changes it has undergone under Jim's leadership, politically and culturally distinct from the modern West. Speaking in a local dialect, Jim deliberately and carefully frames his decision to set Brown free within the ethical and political horizons of Patusan:

> [Jim] declared to his hearers, the assembled heads of the people, that their welfare was his welfare, their losses his losses, their mourning his mourning. He . . . told them to remember that they had fought and worked side by side. They knew his courage. . . . And that he had never deceived them. For many years they had dwelt together. He loved the land and the people living in it with a very great love. He was ready to answer with his life for any harm that should come to them if the white men with beards were allowed to retire. (P. 238–39)

Faced with an apparent rupture between himself and his community, Jim reasserts the inviolability of his union with the regime by pledging his own life as a guarantee of his loyalty.[51] Jim may make a concession to the ethical and political values of the modern West, but he refuses to disavow the moral and civic obligations peculiar to a traditional community such as Patusan. In a final and futile attempt to negotiate the historical distance separating two ethical systems, Jim justifies his decision, not by converting his people to a modern sensibility, but rather by relying on the authority of his sacred word, by invoking his public reputation for infallible wisdom and dauntless courage, and by claiming the privileges that belong to the traditional lord who assumes full responsibility for the welfare of his people.

After his decision has led indirectly to Brown's treacherous ambush and the death of Dain Waris, Jim firmly rejects all proposals for flight or battle. Either would give the lie to his pledge before the assembled elders and demonstrate his ultimate indifference to the people and community he calls his own. Instead, Jim accepts his regime's punishment for a catastrophe he did not intend and could not have foreseen. By condemning himself, by honoring his sacred word to his people, Jim lives up to the strict traditional responsibilities of a premodern lord. By modern Western legal standards, Doramin's ritual execution of Jim seems vengeful, cruel, and unjust, while Jim's willing participation in his own destruction appears pathological, suicidal, and irrational.[52] But as Hegel argued, the traditional tragic hero does not follow modern legal, ethical, and psychological standards of guilt but rather affirms a more demanding conception of personal and political responsibility:

> When we [moderns] . . . act or estimate a particular action, we assume that only full responsibility can attach where the individual under consideration is in complete possession of the true nature of his action and its attendant circumstances. . . . The heroic character . . . adheres simply to all the consequences and makes good his personal responsibility for the whole.[53]

As he approaches Doramin, Jim acknowledges his assumption of heroic and tragic responsibility. To the cries: "He has worked all the evil. . . . He hath taken it upon his own head," Jim replies: "Yes. Upon my head" (p. 252). By affirming the ethical standards of his premodern community and accepting its right to judge his conduct, Jim legitimates both his civic ties to and elevated political status among its citizens. Marlow, who as a modern Western outsider has remained skeptical of "the fabulous value of the bargain" Jim has made with the people of Patusan (p. 152), reserves his most lavish praise for Jim's final act of tragic self-affirmation:

Not in the wildest days of his boyish visions could he have seen the alluring shape of such an extraordinary success! For it may very well be that in the short moment of his last proud and unflinching glance, he had beheld the face of that opportunity which, like an Eastern bride, had come veiled to his side. (P. 253)

In contrast to the existential dread that overcomes Jim when, as an alienated subject of modernity, he faces the abstract possibility of his meaningless annihilation at sea, in his final moments in Patusan Jim bravely meets a death made bearable if not glorious by its immediate political context. The hero's death—which significantly appears in the premodern and non-Western guise of a traditional Eastern bride—provides a definitive demonstration of Jim's political devotion to Patusan and momentarily heals the historical rift between the leader and his people.

Although he sacrifices himself for a traditional community, in some respects Jim remains a peculiarly modern figure. Like Julien Sorel, he affirms his identity as a tragic hero in a highly self-conscious, indeed literary manner. In the face of the obstacles modernity has placed in his way, Jim, like Julien, looks to the literature of prior ages for a model of heroic conduct. Whereas Julien carries around his copy of Napoleon's *Mémorial de Sainte Hélène* for inspiration, Jim sets off for Patusan with his half-crown edition of Shakespeare. But because he finds a premodern community where the seemingly antiquated notion of adventure becomes an everyday reality, Jim is able to live out his literary fantasy and proves that he is no mere Don Quixote, succeeding as a hero in ways that Julien Sorel does not. Though Jim may at times appear to be playing a role, there is nothing contrived or merely histrionic about his tragedy.[54] The two crucial decisions that lead to his destruction—the first to free Brown and the second to remain in Patusan and face Doramin's wrath—result, as we have seen, from Jim's sincere desire to affirm what is most admirable in two mutually exclusive systems of value. One cannot say that either decision was simply foolish or wrong-headed. To exterminate an almost powerless group of one's former European fellows, to desert one's adopted community, or to massacre one's friends, allies, and subjects must strike us as ignoble choices. Were Jim to opt for the values of the archaic or the modern worlds exclusively, he might spare himself a tragic fate, but he would thereby repudiate the extraordinary ambition and ethical breadth that constitute his greatness and in the end make him a tragic hero.

But if Jim's tragic death finally releases the individual hero from the bonds of the modern world and provides Conrad with a compelling romantic resolution to his novel, it offers little hope that the historical spread of Western modernity will be halted or reversed. Jim's tragic fall foreshadows the destruction of the very regime for which he gives his life. His tragedy strips Patusan of its noblest and most courageous individuals, those most worthy to succeed Jim in ruling the community, especially Dain Waris, Jewel, and Tamb' Itam. At the close of the story, the country once more verges on a state of anarchy, racial and tribal strife, and thus is all the more vulnerable to the encroachment of Western imperial powers. For Jim promises to be only the first in a relentless series of political interlopers who will revolutionize this "lost corner of the globe" and inevitably pull it into the orbit of the emerging world system. It is, after all, Jim's presence and apparent political success in Patusan that suggests to a subsequent intruder, Gentleman Brown, the plan of seizing the entire country for himself (p. 223). The second chance afforded Jim in Patusan thus amounts only to the opportunity to reenact the tragic drama of Western history in a non-Western setting; the romantic flight from the limits of modernity paradoxically reinitiates a tragic historical progress that points, however obliquely, to the inevitable obliteration of the premodern world.

For all of Conrad's sincere interest in and deep sympathy for traditional and non-Western societies, he tends to present the inevitable victory of modernity from a Western perspective. Although Conrad portrays many of the Asian characters of Patusan in a favorable, even heroic light, they remain in the background, secondary figures in Jim's drama. In *Lord Jim* the story of a modern European hero dominates the political tragedy of a non-Western society. By turning to the novels of postcolonial writers such as Achebe and Vargas Llosa, we can begin to understand the tragic movement of history from the perspective of non-European peoples. In *Things Fall Apart* and *No Longer at Ease,* Achebe embodies the tragic confrontation between Western modernity and a traditional African society in the stories of two representative African heroes: Okonkwo, the greatest warrior of the traditional Igbo community of Umuofia; and his grandson, Obi Okonkwo, a rising member of the new African elite that is to rule the postcolonial nation of Nigeria. Achebe's representation of their African tragedies in one sense confirms and in a deeper sense challenges Conrad's prophetic narrative representation of global modernization.

II

THE WIDENING
GYRE

3

Achebe: Beasts of
No Nation

I

As Nigeria's most prominent novelist, Chinua Achebe would seem an unlikely advocate of the Hegelian view of history, especially given that Hegel's attitude toward Africa seems to represent European racism at its worst. In Hegel's infamous formulation, Africa is:

> the land of childhood, which lying beyond the day of self-conscious history, is enveloped in the dark mantle of Night. . . . For it is no historical part of the World; it has no movement or development to exhibit . . . What we properly understand by Africa, is the Unhistorical, Undeveloped Spirit, still involved in the conditions of mere nature, and which had to be presented here only as on the threshold of the World's History.[1]

While Hegel's characterization of Africa is commonly viewed as an example of Eurocentric criticism at its most pernicious, it nonetheless remains a challenge to the artist, critic, or historian who wishes to explain the distance between precolonial African communities and postcolonial African nations.[2] For the fact that Hegel's dismissive view of Africa and the African is both demeaning and untrue does not in itself invalidate the more basic Hegelian thesis that different societies are to be understood in terms of a world-historical process of cultural development. Even for African writers sensitive to the false claims to universality often made by Western critics, the temptation to understand the sudden and comprehensive changes of African society in terms of modernization is powerful and persistent.[3] In his recent essay, "What Has Literature Got to Do With It?" Achebe states unequivocally that "the comprehensive goal of a developing nation like Nigeria is, of course, development, or its somewhat better variant, modernization."[4] Although Achebe has explicitly repudiated the Eurocentric bias of Western accounts of Africa, the historicist legacy of Hegel's thinking remains imbedded in the political and philosophic language he uses to describe the sweeping changes that have occurred in Africa since the nineteenth century.

There are, of course, great differences between the articulate, dignified, and heroic Igbo people of Achebe's *Things Fall Apart* or *Arrow of God* and the uncultured and barbarous Africans of Hegel's "land of childhood." Yet throughout his novels, short stories, and critical essays, Achebe remains in accord with a Hegelian conception of history insofar as he traces a historical development of the Igbo people that points towards some conception of modernity. The very terms "developing nation" and "modernization" that Achebe employs in his essays imply a linear and progressive conception of history, which, though punctuated by tragic conflict and political turmoil, precludes the possibility of a return to traditional or premodern forms of political life. Amplifying his statement that the comprehensive goal of a developing nation is modernization, Achebe states emphatically: "I don't see much room for argument about that. What can be, and is, vigorously debated is the quickest and safest route for the journey into modernization and what items should make up the traveller's rather limited baggage allowance."[5]

For Achebe, as for many African writers, the moment in which the destination of a people is determined is the colonial one in which African and European civilization confront each other in a decisive struggle. The greatness of *Things Fall Apart* lies in Achebe's ability to reveal both what was truly at stake in that tragic conflict and why it was that the confrontation was decided in favor of modernization. Strictly speaking, Achebe dramatizes only a local struggle around the turn of the century in the Igbo heartland of West Africa between Protestant missionaries backed by British imperial power and the inhabitants of several Igbo villages. Clearly, the many confrontations between Europeans and Africans on the African continent over several centuries varied considerably according to particular political, geographic, and social circumstances. Nevertheless, Achebe focuses on an underlying ethical conflict between two civilizations that eventuated in the destruction of the traditional Igbo way of life. For

Achebe, that tragic struggle does not simply come to an end with the death of Okonkwo, the representative or "typical" hero of the Igbo people (in Lukács's sense of the term), but rather continues to affect the character and direction of the future development of Nigerian society. In *No Longer at Ease,* set in the Nigeria of the mid-1950s, Achebe offers a reprise of the tragic confrontation of *Things Fall Apart,* but in a mediated and modernized form. And that same tragic conflict of modern European and traditional African ways of life also proves to be the historical source of the political chaos that engulfs Kangan—a thinly fictionalized version of postcolonial Nigeria—in Achebe's most recent novel, *Anthills of the Savannah.*

Originally planned as the first and third parts of a trilogy that was to trace the lives of the Igbo people through three generations from the precolonial era to Nigerian independence, *Things Fall Apart* and *No Longer at Ease* embody radically different conceptions of tragedy that reflect the fundamental changes that have occurred in Africa in the wake of its encounter with European civilization. These two novels trace a literary historical movement outlined in Hegel's theory of tragedy: the "classical" or objective tragedy of *Things Fall Apart* gives way to the modern and subjective tragedy of *No Longer at Ease.* In Achebe's words, the "clear and momentous confrontations" of the former novel are superseded by a "succession of messy, debilitating ambushes" in the latter.[6] Reversing the generic movement of the two parts of *Lord Jim,* Achebe's two novels trace a formal modulation that mirrors the historical development from the epic world of a traditional tribal society to the increasingly modern and bureaucratic world of a postcolonial nation-state. While Okonkwo's tragedy bears a strong resemblance to that of Jim in Patusan, Obi's misfortunes in the Nigeria of the 1950s compare with those of Jim aboard the *Patna.* And just as the conclusion of *Lord Jim* obliquely points towards the continuing dangers that confront the partly modernized community of Patusan after the death of its political leader, Achebe's two early novels prophetically look forward to the political crises and social calamities that continue to plague the emergent nation long after its initial confrontation with the modern West. In *Anthills of the Savannah* Achebe addresses the postcolonial problems of tyranny and political corruption, the monstrous hybrid products of the meeting between traditional African and modern European cultures.

II

For Hegel, the African is without a universal conception of Law or God, and therefore without a conception of justice or morality that transcends immediate individual sensuous need. Within Hegel's philosophy of history, the African stands in for Hobbes's theoretical characterization of man in the "state of nature"; that is, he remains in a condition that precedes the development of "culture."[7] It is this kind of dehumanizing portrait of the African that Achebe has been at pains to address throughout his career, and which has, for example, prompted his now famous and scathing criticism of Conrad's *Heart of Darkness* as an inaccurate and unjust representation of an Africa "trapped in primordial barbarity."[8] In his clearest formulation of the fundamental issue that has preoccupied him as a writer, Achebe states: "This theme—put quite simply—is that African people did not hear of culture for the first time from Europeans; that their societies were not mindless but frequently had a philosophy of great depth and value and beauty, that they had poetry and, above all, they had dignity."[9] *Things Fall Apart* serves Achebe's aim in a manner that remains exemplary among African fiction of the last thirty years. But it has become difficult to acknowledge the scale of Achebe's achievement without also acceding to the claim that it embodies *uniquely African* values. The only alternative would appear to require a "totalizing" or "universalist" approach that reimposes a set of Western cultural norms upon an African novel, thereby reappropriating the work for a European literary tradition. What this Manichean dualism fails to recognize is the possibility of exploring comparisons between Achebe's novel and Western works of literature that would, in turn, suggest that the Western tradition is by no means uniform or entirely alien to a traditional African sensibility.[10]

A remarkable example of such an unexpected resonance is the strikingly Homeric quality of *Things Fall Apart,* evident in certain ethical and political norms that link the Igbo community of *Things Fall Apart* with the Mycenaean civilization depicted in the *Iliad.* These two societies share a common ideal of human excellence, an ideal bodied forth in the kind of individual they most highly esteem: Okonkwo and Achilles. Achebe describes his first novel as centered upon "the man who's larger than life, who exemplifies virtues that are admired by the community."[11] Like Achilles, Okonkwo is "a man of action, a man of war" (p. 7). His "fame" among the Igbo rests "on solid personal achievements" (p. 3), foremost of which are his exploits as the greatest wrestler and most accomplished warrior of the nine villages. He is a man renowned and respected for having brought home from battle five human heads; and on feast days and important public occasions, he drinks his palm wine from the skull of the first warrior he killed. (p. 8). While the Igbo people, like Homer's Greeks, admire their great warriors, they do not pursue war for its own sake; Umuofia fights only if "its case was clear and just and was accepted as such by its Oracle—the Oracle of the Hills and Caves" (p. 9). (One is reminded of the many oracles in Greek myth, such as the one Agamemnon must obey before the Greeks sail to Troy.) Okonkwo's reputation therefore depends on the fact that his physical and military prowess serve the higher political aims of defending Umuofia against its enemies and preserving justice among the rival clans. However, his personal achievements are not limited to the exploits of the athlete and warrior. Through patience, industry, and skill, he has become a successful and prosperous farmer. Like many of the Greek heroes of the *Iliad* and the *Odyssey,* he has become a powerful and respected patriarch, capable of providing for an extensive household, and an honored leader in the conduct of the community's affairs. As one of the leading men of the community, he has also become a member of its most secret and important cult, the *egwugwu.* (Donning the masks of the ancestral spirits, who in turn are believed to incarnate themselves in the cult members, the *egwugwu* ritually settle disputes within the clan and help administer justice in the village.) In this patriarchal society, the possession of property, women, children, titles, and political power is a necessary component of the noble life. *Things Fall Apart* thus celebrates an epic standard of achievement that, to paraphrase Achebe, speaks for the depth, poetry, and dignity of traditional Igbo culture in much the same way that the *Iliad, Beowulf,* the *Eddas,* or the *Nibelungenlied* do for the civilizations that produced them.

Unlike Achilles' many would-be imitators in European bourgeois literature, including Julien Sorel and Michael Henchard, Okonkwo is no romantic dreamer or frustrated entrepreneur. His heroic status is grounded in the often harsh political and social realities of turn-of-the-century Igbo life. Achebe's representation of Umuofia and Mbanta draws heavily on his broad knowledge of historical and anthropological works devoted to West Africa as well as to the oral tradition that has kept the Igbo past alive down to the present day.[12] The affinities between traditional Igbo and Mycenaean ideals are thus rooted in far more than a merely literary similarity; broad parallels suggest themselves precisely because the two cultures, though neither was internally homogeneous, and though the two were separated from each other by geographical and historical distance, were organized around roughly similar social structures and an ethos that celebrated a comparable notion of human virtue. Responding to the question of whether Aristotle's conception of the tragic hero informs *Things Fall Apart,* Achebe has stated that the similarities between his novel and Aristotle's *Poetics* owe a great deal to the historical continuities between traditional African and ancient Greek civilization:

> If we are to believe what we are hearing these days the Greeks did not drop from the sky. They evolved in a certain place which was very close to Africa. Very close to Egypt which in itself was also very close to the Sudan and Nubia which was very close to West Africa. So it may well turn out, believe it or not, that some of the things Aristotle was saying about tragedy were not really unheard of in other cultures. . . . I think a lot of what Aristotle says makes sense. Putting it in a neat, schematic way may be peculiar to the Greek way of thinking about the hero. But that idea is not necessarily foreign to other people: the man who's larger than life, who exemplifies virtues that are admired by the community, but also a man who for all that is still human. He can have flaws, you see; all that seems to me to be very elegantly underlined in Aristotle's work. I think they are there in human nature itself, and would be found in other traditions even if they were not spelled out in the same exact way.[13]

Setting aside the vexed question raised by Martin Bernal's *Black Athena* and Cheikh Anta Diop's *The African Origin of Civilization* of whether the roots of Greek culture were Afroasiatic, we can still say that Achebe's statement draws attention to certain similarities between particular Greek and African civilizations in a way that breaks down the Manichean dualism of the West and its Other. In fact, the differences between the ethos of Homer's Mycenaean heroes and that of their Igbo counterparts in Achebe's novel are far less striking than those between either of them and the moral standards and political norms that prevail among most contemporary European, American, and African intellectuals.

It is naturally tempting for contemporary critics to argue that the justice or morality of patriarchal Igbo society is suspect, that Okonkwo's "heroism" is merely an ideological apology for despotism, violence, cruelty, and oppression. But this position comes dangerously close to that of Hegel, who, as we have noted, insisted that the African possesses no conception of law, justice, or morality. No doubt many of Achebe's readers would be far more comfortable were he to present his ancestors as less alien, and more in sympathy with the ethical norms and social sensibilities of the modern world. But Achebe has steadfastly eschewed the kind of romanticized "technicolour idyll" that he criticizes in Camara Laye's *The Dark Child,* a work that in his view refashions history to suit contemporary African moral sensibilities and political objectives. Achebe insists upon presenting traditional Igbo society in a comprehensive and realistic manner, without "glossing over inconvenient facts."[14] Achebe draws attention precisely to those aspects of the society most troublesome for the majority of his contemporary readers, aspects quite incompatible with modern standards of justice and morality.[15]

For example, Achebe portrays the strict and inflexible gender roles that inform Okonkwo's conception of virtue: "No matter how prosperous a man was, if he was unable to rule his women and his children (and especially his women) he was not really a man" (p. 37). Okonkwo is quite ready to enforce his authority by violent means; he beats his wives and children, and nearly kills his second wife Ekwefi for implying that he is an incompetent hunter (p. 28).[16] Although Okonkwo loves and admires his daughter Ezinma for her "spirit," for that very reason he would be happier had she "been a boy" (p. 46). Clearly, in a society in which polygamy, the ritual payment of a bride price, and physical violence of husbands against wives is deemed appropriate, the role of women is subordinate and distinctly circumscribed,[17] a matter which Achebe's feminist contemporary, the Igbo writer Buchi Emecheta, has powerfully addressed in such novels as *The Bride Price.*

Nor does Achebe conceal many other aspects of Igbo life that are profoundly undemocratic. Although he does not dwell on the custom in any detail, he mentions the practice of slavery in the nine villages (p. 33). And he gives ample consideration to the caste known as *osu,* individuals dedicated to a god, and therefore taboo. They and all who descend from them are confined to a special area of the village, prohibited from marrying the freeborn and from attending any assembly of free citizens, forbidden all titles of the clan, and destined to be buried in the Evil Forest, a place of ritual contamination and religious dread. Occupying the lowest rank in the Igbo social hierarchy, below even that of slaves, the *osu* are the untouchables of the Igbo community.

Perhaps the features of Igbo culture most alien and problematic for contemporary Western sensibilities are certain of its religious rituals and conventions. The corpses of *ogbanje*—"evil" children who are believed repeatedly to die and return to their mothers' womb to be reborn without ever reaching adulthood—are ritually mutilated and disposed of in the Evil Forest. Twins, illegitimate children, and those striken with certain diseases are also left to die in the Evil Forest. Most disturbing is the practice of religiously sanctioned human sacrifice. The Oracle of the Hills and the Caves calls for the ritual execution of Ikemefuna, Okonkwo's adopted son, just as the Oracle of Abame requires the sacrifice of a white stranger who appears among the clan riding a bicycle.[18]

All of these conventions and practices pose grave difficulties for Achebe's readers, and especially for contemporary American and European critics who look to Third World fiction to supply a corrective to what they understand to be the evils of Western civilization. To be sure, the fact that certain of these practices, such as the ritual human sacrifice and dismemberment of the *pharmakos* (scapegoat), were common in ancient Greece suggests that the origins of Western civilization were as "barbaric" as those of modern Africa.[19] But such a comparison does nothing to establish the moral legitimacy of those practices within a postcolonial African context, nor does it serve to diminish the distance between the ethical universe of Achebe's contemporary reader (whether African or Western) and that of his characters. Achebe anticipates these difficulties; his interest in functional anthropology reflects his intention of demonstrating that traditional Igbo society, with all its limitations, shortcomings, and injustices, was nevertheless grounded upon an ethical foundation that is at least comprehensible, if still antipathetic to a contemporary reader. For example, Achebe suggests that the Igbo practice of ritual human sacrifice was ultimately linked to the communal objective of preserving peace. The ritual murder of Ikemefuna strikes his stepbrother Nwoye as a great calamity that the traditions of the clan cannot satisfactorily explain or justify, and which ultimately drives him to join the Christian church in defiance of his father Okonkwo. However, Achebe reminds his reader that Ikemefuna comes to Umuofia as part of the settlement of a quarrel with a neighboring village. The original occasion for the dispute is the killing of a daughter of Umuofia during her visit to the market held at Mbaino. When revealed to the assembled citizens of Umuofia, her murder initially provokes in them a "thirst for blood" (p. 8). At this critical juncture custom intervenes to avert an outbreak of mass inter-clan violence. The elders of Umuofia ask Mbaino to choose between two alternatives: war or "the offer of a young man and a virgin as compensation" (p. 8). While the Oracle's demand for Ikemefuna's sacrifice appears to have no rational basis, it does embody an inner logic that seeks to limit bloodshed: a wife for a wife and a life for a life. The killing of Ikemefuna is cruel and violates modern liberal norms of justice—the boy is not personally involved in the killing of Ogbuefi Udo's wife in Mbaino and therefore in our eyes is innocent. But his sacrifice does serve to prevent a war between the two clans and therefore helps to ensure the long-term security of both villages.

Okonkwo's endorsement of the ritual sacrifice of Ikemefuna thus suggests not the absence of exacting ethical standards among the Igbo people, but the existence of a strict premodern morality that values the welfare of the clan and tribe above that of the individual. The archaic ethos of Umuofia thus makes greater demands on the leading members of the community—such as Okonkwo—than does the gentler and more forgiving morality of a modern liberal society. Just as Jim proves his heroism in Patusan by assuming the collective guilt of his community, expiating it through his ritual self-sacrifice, Okonkwo demonstrates his heroic assumption of communal responsibility by countenancing the ritual execution of the adopted son he has grown to love. Though the village elders and leading men of Umuofia regard his *active participation* in Ikemefuna's sacrifice as unnecessary and even inadvisable, Okonkwo's hubristic insistence on augmenting his communal obligations is nevertheless perfectly consistent with Hegel's conception of the archaic heroic character who willfully assumes *personal* responsibility for the whole of his society.

In order to understand fully the integral role of human sacrifice in traditional Igbo society, we may turn to the work of René Girard, whose *Violence and the Sacred* examines the political and social function of ritual violence within premodern communities. Girard argues that ritual sacrifice circumvents a cycle of bloody revenge that otherwise threatens to destroy these societies. He suggests that what seems particularly offensive within our contemporary judicial framework, the innocence of the ritual victim, who is apparently chosen at random, is essential to the effectiveness of the sacrifice. The very fact that the ritual victim is *not* directly related to the antagonists in the dispute means that he is located outside their network of familial and clan relations and hence that his death does not requite a reciprocal act of revenge. As Girard sees it: "to make a victim out of the guilty

party is to play vengeance's role, to submit to the demands of violence. By killing, not the murderer himself, but someone close to him,
an act of perfect reciprocity is avoided and the necessity for revenge
by-passed."[20] In ritual terms, the innocence of the victim is understood as a sign of his *purity,* indicating that he is free of the contamination of violence and that his sacrifice will provoke no further
acts of retribution. The symbolic identity of the ritual victim as both
inside and outside the community, as being close, but not too close to
the participants in the dispute helps to explain why Ikemefuna is
temporarily adopted by Umuofia. His brief life in the village establishes his marginal status as belonging neither completely to Mbaino
nor Umuofia. His sad sojourn in Okonkwo's household thus transforms him into the "pure" ritual victim needed for an effective sacrifice that staves off a blood feud. Girard concludes that "primitive
religion is no 'cult of violence' in the contemporary sense of the
phrase. Violence is venerated insofar as it offers men what little peace
they can ever expect."[21]

Functional anthropology offers to explain a wide variety of customs and practices that might otherwise seem pernicious.[22] For instance, Achebe points out that the taking of titles among the Igbo
people, a practice that may strike an egalitarian critic as aristocratic
and elitist, worked to redistribute wealth within the community. The
ceremony of entitlement involved a lavish festival thrown for the
entire clan at the expense of the honored individual. Accordingly,
the system of titles helped to prevent any one man from amassing so
much wealth as to dominate the affairs of his village completely.[23]
This custom thus satisfied the craving for individual honor while
preserving a limited equilibrium of wealth within the clan. Similarly,
the practice of bride price, whereby the groom and his family purchased the bride from her father, appears to reduce women to the
status of property. But here again, the practice also served another
purpose: if the wife was mistreated and left her husband, the bride
price was retained by her father's family. If on the other hand, she left
her husband without just cause, the bride price was returned to the
groom. The custom thus served as a means to solidify the marriage
and to help ensure that a wife (and her blood relations) possessed
some measure of financial influence over her husband. A husband
could not treat his wife with utter impunity. A practice that appears
on the surface to reflect the utterly helpless condition of Igbo women
in fact served to provide them with some small measure of security
and power.

III

Achebe does not necessarily approve of all traditional Igbo practices, nor does he feel that it would be politically advisable for a contemporary African writer to celebrate them uncritically. Although they may offer to make alien practices comprehensible, functional anthropological accounts do not necessarily make these customs compatible with or preferable to those of contemporary Western society anymore than these same explanations demonstrate the appropriateness of these conventions for postcolonial Nigerian society. Achebe insists that it is the task of the contemporary African writer to question the justice and morality of precolonial tribal life: African writers "cannot pretend that our past was one long, technicolour idyll. We have to admit that like other people's pasts ours had its good as well as its bad sides."[24] To emphasize his point, Achebe presents several Igbo characters in *Things Fall Apart* who comment on the problematic character of their traditions. Ogbuefi Ezeudu, the oldest man of Umuofia and one of its priests, suggests that the customs of the clan are neither beyond criticism nor reform. Referring to the way the clan punishes those who violate the sanctions of the Week of Peace, he says, "It has not always been so. . . . My father told me that he had been told that in the past a man who broke the peace was dragged on the ground through the village until he died. But after a while this custom was stopped because it spoilt the peace which it was meant to preserve" (pp. 22–23). The priest is also conscious of differences between the customs of Umuofia and those of other clans. He notes, for example, that in the village of Obodoani, if a man dies during the Week of Peace his body is cast into the Evil Forest: "It is a bad custom which these people observe because they lack understanding. They throw away large numbers of men and women without burial. And what is the result? Their clan is full of the evil spirits of these unburied dead, hungry to do harm to the living" (p. 23).

Although he recognizes that disrespect for ancestral ways threatens to lead to social disintegration and chaos, Ogbuefi Ezeudu feels that customs must nevertheless accord with "understanding." For the old priest, "understanding" requires a comparative knowledge of the different customs of other clans and of the different customs that in past times existed in his own clan. By allowing his character to make this distinction, Achebe calls into question the racist stereotype of the African as hopelessly mired in superstition and irretrievably bound to tribal customs that invariably escape his critical examination.

Although the specific customs under discussion may be of only local concern, the sort of conversation Ogbuefi Ezeudu carries on with younger members of the clan would not be out of place in Plato's *Laws*. Achebe's dialogue fulfills many (though not all) of the essential functions of philosophic activity as defined by contemporary African thinkers such as Kwasi Wiredu and Kwame Anthony Appiah. Ancestral beliefs are not transmitted uncritically from one generation to another, but instead become the subject of transcultural comparison, rational argumentation, and discursive clarification.[25] Ogbuefi Ezeudu is not merely concerned with the preservation of his community, for which the faithful observance and communication of ancestral ways would suffice, but with the critical consideration of what kind of community Umuofia should be. Moreover, Ezeudu's critical reflections on the appropriateness and wisdom of the ancestral ways of his clan possess a significance that transcends this historical moment; they have an important bearing on the political opportunities and choices facing Nigeria on the eve of its independence in 1958. His probing comments implicitly caution Achebe's reader against an uncritical acceptance of "authentic" precolonial traditions and a too narrow identification with tribal identity in an imminent postcolonial situation that will demand the overcoming of divisions among different ethnic groups, such as the Igbo, Yoruba, and Hausa-Fulani.

The transcultural significance of this dialogue suggests that Achebe is not completely persuaded by the conventionalist or historicist thesis that human thinking remains completely bound by the intellectual horizons of a given community or historical period. Achebe's respected elder priest insists that an intellectual distinction can and should be made between a good custom and a bad one, between a tradition that is preserved because it accomplishes an end deeemed desirable by the community (in fact by all communities), such as keeping the peace, and one that is properly abandoned because it fails to attain that end. The presence of this dialogue in Achebe's novel gestures toward the notion that the standards by which a particular community ought to be properly judged are not entirely relative to or circumscribed by the traditional beliefs and practices of that community.

Achebe might have tried to resolve the tension between traditional Igbo practices and those demanded by a modernizing postcolonial African nation by appealing to some contemporary form of cultural and moral relativism; that is, he might have espoused the commonly held opinion that political justice and morality are *purely* matters of convention and that it is impossible for any member of a community to step outside of his historically given situation in order to evaluate the justice of his society objectively. According to this view, the moral differences between traditional Igbo society and contemporary post-colonial African or modern Western societies are merely relative, to be accounted for by shifting historical or cultural paradigms, but posing no fundamental or insuperable political and ethical problems for Achebe or his readers. Achebe hesitates, however, to adopt such a position, qualifying his relativistic assessment of political morality with a demand for at least adhering to a common standard of justice within each and every community:

> For a society to function smoothly and effectively its members must share certain basic tenets of belief and norms of behaviour. There must be a reasonable degree of consensus on what is meant by virtue and vice; there must be some agreement on the attributes of a hero, on what constitutes the heroic act. Different societies will not hold identical ideas on these questions in every part of the world or at every time in history. And yet, in spite of local and historical variations, we do not know of any society which has survived and flourished on totally arbitrary notions of good and evil, or of the heroic and the cowardly. Our very humanity seems to be committed to a distinction between these pairs however fuzzy the line may sometimes appear.[26]

Insofar as Achebe recognizes that each society depends upon a locally shared set of moral distinctions, he is still in agreement with those who argue that ethical "value" is merely a contingent or conventional matter, though not a completely arbitrary one.[27] Nevertheless the conclusion of the passage charts a course away from the position staked out by a number of more radical antifoundationalist theorists. Achebe appears to accede to the Aristotelian precept that a universal human capacity—reason—is called upon to determine which particular conventions are best suited to a given local condition. While the same laws are not always and everywhere equally suited to all communities and peoples—many modern Western standards of behavior are inappropriate for traditional Igbo society—a universal principle of judgment guides the wise individual in choosing the most appropriate laws for a given society. Elsewhere Achebe goes on to insist that "the frontier between good and evil must not be blurred; . . . that somewhere, no matter how fuzzy it may be to us, there is still a distinction between what is permissible and what is not permissible."[28]

No doubt for many, Achebe's position is indefensible, resting as it does on a hypothetical frontier between good and evil that exists "somewhere" that he cannot precisely name. But Achebe's reluctance to embrace radical relativism stems in part from his recognition that it cannot provide a complete account of the political and cultural confrontation between the forces of evangelical British imperialism and traditional Igbo civilization. For what serves to destroy Umuofia and its culture is precisely the introduction of a new morality that threatens to relativize and hence obscure traditional moral distinctions. Antifoundationalism obviously acknowledges—indeed is premised upon—the existence of different moral systems, but it is undisturbed by their diversity insofar as they represent only relative rather than fundamental distinctions. That is to say, antifoundationalism implies a theoretical neutrality toward the kind of ethical and political conflict that Achebe dramatizes. If we were to employ the terminology of one prominent antifoundationalist critic, Stanley Fish, what happens to the Igbo people is not a catastrophe or a fundamental revolution in their society but simply an instance of "change," a shift in the conventional paradigms of their community. It is certainly possible to read the events of Achebe's novel within a relativist framework, but to do so is to risk minimizing and seriously misrepresenting what happens. For given that Fish's model of "change" is derived from his experience in a contemporary American professional academic community, his antifoundationalist thesis tends to reduce political revolution and social collapse to mere changes in intellectual fashion. The differences among regimes, among precolonial, colonial, and postcolonial African life, become in short, merely "academic."

A more serious problem is raised by the underlying premise of the antifoundationalist thesis: that there are "no consequences" to theory, except for those who happen to be in "the business" of theorizing, that is to say academicians. (And such consequences are limited to their professional success or failure, the rise and fall of their reputations among the professoriate). Achebe's novel suggests something quite different, namely that the very existence of certain societies depends upon their adherence to certain foundational premises. For the Igbo villagers, the introduction of Christianity leads to a subversion of their most fundamental—that is religious, political, ethical, and cultural—assumptions, and this subversion in turn leads directly to their inability to resist the incursions of British imperialism and preserve their traditional way of life. This suggests that although its proponents such as Fish and Rorty may trace the conventionalist thesis back to the pre-Socratics, contemporary antifoundationalism proves to be the rhetorical articulation of an ethos particularly suited to modern liberal democracies and especially to the professionalized academy. The antifoundationalist thesis is a luxury afforded by and consistent with a liberal democratic ethos that values tolerance as a means of minimizing conflict in a secular society. In this respect, antifoundationalism can be traced back to Locke's *A Letter Concerning Toleration* and Hume's critique of religion, but with the important difference that what was formerly offered as a political solution to the incessant religious strife of Western Europe in the seventeenth century is taken by its contemporary advocates to be a theoretical given on which all forms of political and social life necessarily rest. Contemporary American antifoundationalism takes for granted the existence of secular modern liberal governments in a way that was impossible for earlier thinkers, who originally sought to provide the philosophic foundations for the separation of church and state. This is not an oversight that Achebe, as a Third World writer still engaged in the struggle for the development of a modern African nation, is likely to make. Acutely aware of the dangers and benefits of a society that does not distinguish between civil and religious rule, he dramatizes life in a community in which the unquestioned superiority of secular government has yet to be demonstrated or widely accepted. Were the Igbo villagers of *Things Fall Apart* already persuaded of the antifoundationalist thesis, or even open to it as a theoretical proposition, they might have met the challenge of the Christian missionaries by assimilating or effectively neutralizing (relativizing) an alien set of religious and cultural beliefs. But this is simply to put forward the truism that if Igbo conventions and beliefs had already been influenced by contemporary liberal thought in some form, the Igbo would not have found the presence of Christian emissaries to be a fundamental threat to their society; they would have been post- rather than pre-Christian, postmodern rather than pagan.

When Uchendo, an elder of Mbanta, hears for the first time of the destruction of Abame by the white men, he understands this calamity to have arisen out of a profound difference between two cultures: "The world has no end, and what is good among one people is an abomination with others" (p. 99). On the surface, Uchendo's pronouncement seems consistent with a relativistic understanding of cultural values; however, the force of his statement emphasizes the incompatibility of different ethical systems and acknowledges the profound danger that the intrusion of the white man represents for the Igbo community. Uchendo concludes his speech with a comment that magnifies rather than minimizes the difference between the Igbos and the whites: "We have albinos among us. Do you not think that they came to our clan by mistake, that they have strayed from their ways to a land where everybody is like them?" (p. 99). Although Uchendo openly acknowledges the contingent basis of social norms, the lesson he draws from this observation is the narrowly ethnocentric and conservative one that different races ought to be kept separate. If one of the justifiable charges against the hegemonic pretensions of Western society is its potential for suppressing difference in the name of some pseudo-universal truth, then it is also true that the spirited defense of the local, the conventional, and the indigenous can lead just as easily to mutual ignorance and suspicion among different peoples.[29] Moreover, as Wiredu suggests, the historical retreat into the local and conventional left many precolonial African societies politically vulnerable to the incursions of external modernizing forces for which they could not adequately account.[30] Within the restrictive cultural context of traditional Igbo life, Uchendo's "conventionalism" cannot in practice be distinguished from the worship of the ancestral, and therefore cannot provide the villagers of Umuofia with the "understanding" they require to respond decisively and effectively to the challenge of the Christian missionaries.

IV

By rendering revolution or catastrophe as "change," it is possible to elide the fundamental incompatibility of different regimes and ethical systems. *Things Fall Apart* becomes *Things Change (But Not Really)*. But rather than assimilating Achebe's novel to a relativistic model of paradigm shifts, we can read *Things Fall Apart* as dramatizing the Hegelian tragic conflict between two ways of life that are fundamentally at odds with one another.[31] For Achebe, this conflict is *inescapable*. It was impossible for the political and ethical differences between the British and the Igbo to have been mediated in a peaceful fashion. Whatever accommodation is ultimately possible between premodern Umuofia and modern Nigeria, between Igbo and European traditions in the postcolonial epoch, can occur only through the violent and comprehensive reordering of the communal life of Okonkwo's people.

In a strange and brilliant fashion, Achebe's account of the destruction of Umuofia recreates Nietzsche's narrative of the master-slave dialectic in *On the Genealogy of Morals.* Achebe dramatizes the collapse of a noble and heroic pagan culture when it is corrupted by a slave revolt in morals. One of the underlying ironies of Achebe's novel is its stunning racial reversal of the roles of master and slave: In *Things Fall Apart* it is the African black (chiefly Okonkwo) who speaks for aristocratic paganism and the European white (principally Reverend James Smith) who takes the part of slavish Christianity. As in Nietzsche's work, the movement in Achebe's novel from paganism to Christianity, from a noble to an egalitarian culture, represents a form of social decline, a loss of cultural vitality in the traditional Igbo way of life.

Christianity appeals initially to the downtrodden and socially disaffected members of Igbo society. The first converts to Christianity are *efulefu,* "worthless, empty men," those without titles (p. 101). They are commonly represented in the language of the clan as those who sell their matchets and come to battle armed only with their empty sheaths (p. 101). Women, twins rescued from the Evil Forest, and *osu* swell the ranks of the newly converted.[32] Although each of these groups has a different reason for its discontent, all are united in their enthusiasm for a religious community that grants them a form of social equality and personal dignity. An especially seductive feature of this new religion is its open rejection of the hierarchies of the clan. The Igbo missionary, Mr. Kiaga, quickly enlarges his new church in Mbanta by subverting the traditional order of rank: "Before God, there is no slave or free. We are all children of God and we must receive these [*osu* as] our brothers" (p. 111).

Initially, the leaders of Mbanta are largely unconcerned by the defections to this new religion, since in their opinion they have lost only "the excrement of the clan" (p. 101). However, they underestimate the powerful effects of Christian *ressentiment.* Eventually, the new religion attracts even those who are or might have become leading men in the clan, but who for a variety of reasons become disaffected individuals like Ogbuefi Ugonna, Nwoye, and Enoch. Achebe's description of the latter character reveals a typical victim of Christian *ressentiment,* whose vehemence brings the church into direct conflict with the clan:

> Enoch was short and slight of build, and always seemed in great haste. . . . On Sundays he always imagined that the sermon was preached for the benefit of his enemies. And if he happened to sit near

one of them he would occasionally turn to give him a meaningful look, as if to say, 'I told you so.' It was Enoch who touched off the great conflict between church and clan in Umuofia. (P. 131)

Enoch is the son of the snake priest, and hence, like Nwoye, a renegade master who helps to lead the slave revolt in morals. For Enoch, the values of Christianity—mercy, pity, charity, equality—are attractive precisely because they provide him with a moral weapon with which to attack the paternal authority of his clan.

Although Achebe sympathizes with the plight of women, slaves, *osu*, and other marginalized and subordinate groups within the clan, and acknowledges the moral and social attraction of Christianity for them, he insists upon representing their religion in its militant and subversive form. The gentle, tolerant, and forgiving missionary, Mr. Brown, and his successor, the zealous, militant, and inflexible Reverend Smith are not so much opposites as two different but necessary faces of the same revolution in morals. No doubt many, perhaps even most, of the converts merely seek communal acceptance and relief of their wretched state rather than empowerment or revenge. But in practice the two desires cannot be kept separate; Nwoye embodies the desire for a more humane treatment of twins intermingled with a violent hatred of his father. Revolutionary conflict between the new and old religions cannot be averted by appeal to the pacifistic spirit of Christianity.

We have become so habituated in the United States to the association of Christian evangelism with what are often called "traditional family values" that we may fail to recognize the shocking implication of Mr. Kiaga's scriptural recitation: "Blessed is he who forsakes his father and his mother for my sake. Those that hear my words are my father and my mother" (p. 108). These words of greeting to Nwoye promise to reorder the hierarchy of the Igbo family fundamentally. Okonkwo and the elders of the village are no longer the true fathers; their place has been usurped by a god who refuses to acknowledge the lineal distinctions that structure the life of the village. The religion of the clan is based upon ancestor worship; consequently spiritual and biological fatherhood are synonymous (p. 108). By contrast, evangelical Christianity threatens to dissolve the biological basis of the communal order. As one wise elder of Mbanta puts it:

I fear for you young people because you do not understand how strong is the bond of kinship. . . . An abominable religion has settled among you. A man can now leave his father and his brothers. He can curse the gods of his fathers and his ancestors. . . . I fear for you; I fear for the clan. (P. 118)

The new religion strikes directly at the foundation of Igbo society: the inviolability, sanctity, and authority of the clan.

Hegel lays considerable importance on the universalistic (and hence modernizing) dimension of Christianity, which he understands as mirroring the cosmopolitan character of citizenship in the late Roman Empire.[33] One of the distinct advantages of Pauline Christianity, later consciously adopted by Islam, was its transnational conception of community. The church of believers was not in principle bound by nationality, race, ethnicity, gender, or language. The truly revolutionary effect of this dynamic conception of human solidarity becomes evident in *Things Fall Apart*. For the newly converted Christian, the status of father and mother, parent and child, is not fixed by kinship ties, by blood, but instead by the "word of God," which founds a new order, an alternative community no longer based on membership in the clan.

Enoch's physical unmasking of an *egwugwu* in public during an annual religious ceremony is a sacrilege clearly intended to challenge the authority of the clan. But what is not immediately apparent is the unerring logic of his particular action. Enoch's affront is a literal and symbolic repudiation of the importance of kinship: it proclaims that the ancestors have no claims on the living and that ties of blood are not binding on members of the community. The inability of the clan to respond decisively to the challenge of the new church is due, at least in part, to the ethical restraints and conceptual limitations that follow from ancestor worship and the sanctity of kinship ties. "As for [the] converts, no one could kill them without having to flee from the clan, for in spite of their worthlessness they still belonged to the clan" (p. 110). Okonkwo's bellicose heroism is helpless in the face of an enemy within the clan; he cannot fight against his own kinsmen without destroying the very principle he intends to defend.

Okika, a friend of Okonkwo and a great man in Umuofia, gives an impassioned speech at the dramatic climax of the novel that raises the possibility that the clan will radically depart from custom, and by attacking its own kin, do what its ancestors would never have done (p. 144). However, Okonkwo's murder of one of the *kotma*, the official messenger of the court of the British District Commissioner, circumvents the customary proceedings by which the clan could reach a consensus on this matter and act as a body.[34] Achebe thus does not dramatize an actual change in the clan's conception of its identity, though he does raise it as an unfulfilled historical possibility. In any case, the refusal of the clan to fight, their horrified reaction to Okonkwo's action, and their subsequent flight suggest that such a change was not likely, much less imminent. Moreover, it is clear that this revolutionary change in the clan's identity would have itself destroyed its traditional way of life. At best, a united Umuofia would paradoxically be immediately at war with itself. It follows that civil strife would intensify rather than diminish the crisis of clan identity. For to distinguish between those inside and outside the clan would now depend upon a conceptual distinction—which gods one worships—rather than on an organic fact—one's inheritable membership in a biologically homogeneous community. Which is to say that Umuofia would save itself only by undermining the absolute authority of that very principle—kinship—that has hitherto sustained its identity and cohesion. In the process it would, in effect, have tacitly accepted the very transvaluation of morals and social affiliation that Christianity threatened to impose in the first place.

The only other practical alternative left to the clan is the expulsion of the converts, but this in turn encourages the gradual extinction of the community through the attrition of its members. Okonkwo meditates upon the twilight of the clan:

> Suppose when he died all his male children decided to follow Nwoye's steps and abandon their ancestors? Okonkwo felt a cold shudder run through him at the terrible prospect, like the prospect of annihilation. He saw himself and his father crowding round their ancestral shrine waiting in vain for worship and sacrifice and finding nothing but ashes of bygone days, and his children the while praying to the white man's god. (P. 108)

The collapse of an aristocratic warrior ethic, the destruction of patriarchal authority, the demise of the gods, the slow depopulation of the village, the disappearance of the clan, and the annihilation of the representative Igbo hero are all adumbrated in this elegiac passage. Achebe powerfully presents the triumph of the slave revolt in morals as seen from the perspective of one of the last heroic spokesmen for the old noble order.

The clan resorts to half-measures against the new converts; after the unmasking of the *egwugwu,* it burns down the church. However, Ajofia, the leading *egwugwu* of Umuofia, allows Reverend Smith to remain among the Igbo people: "You can stay with us if you like our ways. You can worship your own god. It is good that a man should worship the gods and the spirits of his fathers" (p. 134). In many respects, Ajofia's speech exemplifies a tolerance and magnanimity that belie the prejudiced European belief in the barbarism of the African. On the other hand, this same speech reveals that Ajofia cannot or will not contemplate the possibility of a religion that is *not* based on the worship of the gods and the spirits of one's ancestors. Ajofia's toleration of a diversity of beliefs depends upon his conviction that every race or tribe properly worships *its own* lineal progenitors. What his statement omits is the possibility of an evangelical religion—like Christianity or Islam—in which a god does not belong to a particular people, but instead lays claim to the allegiance of all peoples. Ajofia's principle of toleration ultimately rests upon an unqualified attachment to his own people and their traditions, rather than upon a universalistic conception of a common human inheritance.

Achebe tacitly acknowledges the often murderous rivalries that existed among different clans and tribes prior to the arrival of the white missionaries. The tribal wars evoked at the beginning of the novel suggest a remote but important source of the ill-treatment meted out to Okonkwo and the other leaders of Umuofia by the "foreign" *kotma* who serve the British imperial government (p. 138). Achebe is understandably reluctant to dwell on a phenomenon that was often invoked by the British to justify colonial rule in Nigeria. Nevertheless, Uchendo's nostalgic recollection of a golden age in the remote past when "a man had friends in distant clans" (p. 96) obliquely acknowledges the increasingly violent relationships among the clans that had come to define Igbo life by the turn of the century, a state of affairs that resulted in part from the oppressive power wielded by the Aro. This clan had forged an alliance with the Abam, who brutally enforced a trade monopoly for the Aro, a trade heavily dependent upon the abduction of slaves from other Igbo clans. From the seventeenth century onwards, the Aro exercised power over surrounding clans through their mercenaries, the Abam, with a consequent intensification of tribal conflict over succeeding generations. Only with the projection of British imperial power into the interior of Igboland, the destruction of the Aro oracle at Arochukwa, and the brutal twenty-year campaign of "pacification" against the Igbo peoples in the first two decades of the twentieth century (the background of the raid on Abame) were tribal hostilities finally suppressed.[35]

Contemporary anti-imperialist criticism often supposes that British success in Africa was the result of a merely technological and military superiority. But Achebe, an arch anti-imperialist himself, suggests otherwise. He notes that Mr. Kiaga, many of his fellow missionaries, and the court messengers who supplied the manpower for the British imperial forces were themselves from the indigenous African population. This suggests for Achebe not some essential lack of integrity in Africans, but rather a structural limitation in the precolonial social organization of the Igbo people. So long as the basic unit of social organization remained the clan, a rough balance of power among different ethnic groups could be preserved. Even during the period of Aro hegemony in Igboland, the clans maintained their social cohesiveness and political autonomy. But the fractious relations among the clans proved fatal to them when they were confronted by a much larger and more cohesive social organization—the Christian church backed by British imperial power—which was capable of exploiting and manipulating inter-clan and intertribal rivalries.[36]

The pretensions of Christianity to universality help to explain why it was such a powerful political adversary of traditional Igbo ways. *Things Fall Apart* dramatizes Christian missionaries uniting individuals from different clans, tribes, and races. The group of missionaries that comes to Mbanta consists of a white man, four Igbos from "foreign" clans, and one black from another tribe, possibly the Yoruba (p. 102). Achebe thus draws on the colonial history of the region, which involved the inexorable spread of the Church Missionary Society up the Niger River from the mid-nineteenth century onwards. The pioneering efforts of the C.M.S. were led by the freed slave and eventual Bishop of the Niger, Samuel Ajayi Crowther (who was not an Igbo) and the Reverend J. C. Taylor, another ex-slave (who was an Igbo). Together they established a C.M.S. station and school at Onitsha (the historical model of Achebe's Umuru) run entirely by Africans, though later missions were generally supervised by whites.[37]

The British imperial policy of "divide and conquer" reveals the sinister side of Christian universalism. The sometimes strained relationship between Christian missionaries and British imperial officials endured and even flourished, in part because Christianity not only provided a wedge into many traditional African communities by exploiting already existing divisions within and among the clans, but also supplied a glue that helped to hold the heterogeneous subjects of the empire together, however briefly and haphazardly. The sorts of connections that Gibbon, Hegel, and Nietzsche identified between Christianity and late Roman imperialism are thus pertinent to the colonial history of Achebe's Igbo communities. Christianity helped to provide a new basis for common membership in a far-flung empire that encompassed many different peoples and widely divergent cultures. It served the Empress Victoria just as it did the Emperor Constantine.

V

In one of the rare amusing scenes in *Things Fall Apart,* Achebe rehearses a theological debate between Mr. Brown (modeled on G. T. Basden, missionary to Ogidi and friend of Achebe's father) and Akunna, an elder of Umuofia (p. 126). The humor of this dialogue derives in part from the white man's presumption that an appeal to rational argument will help persuade his Igbo interlocutor of the superiority of Christianity. The rhetorical and analytical savvy with which Akunna defends the animistic beliefs and polytheistic customs of the clan underscores Achebe's point that the European missionaries, for all their confidence in the higher truth of Christianity, were not capable of logically demonstrating it. This leads Mr. Brown to proselytize through more indirect, but ultimately more effective means: the establishment of schools, the encouragement of trade, and the construction of a small hospital. Given the centrality of the ideological struggle between traditional Igbo and Christian beliefs to the tragic action of the novel, it is easy to overlook these seemingly incidental developments.[38] But Achebe's detailed portrait of evangelical Christianity reveals it to be closely allied, if not coextensive with the forces of European modernization.

As we shall see in our consideration of Vargas Llosa's *The War of the End of the World,* the alliance between Christianity and modernity is at best fragile and can easily collapse into open hostilities. But in the case of Achebe's novel, the evangelical Christianity of the Church Missionary Society had already made its peace with the forces of Western modernization. Mr. Brown's Protestantism is particularly amenable to the dynamism of a market economy, modern science, and educational enlightenment. The willingness of protestant Christianity to join forces with the secular process of modernization facilitates the conversion of the Igbo people:

> The white man had indeed brought a lunatic religion, but he had also built a trading store and for the first time palm-oil and kernel became

things of great price, and much money flowed into Umuofia. . . . Mr. Brown's school produced quick results. A few months in it were enough to make one a court messenger or even a court clerk. Those who stayed longer became teachers. . . . From the very beginning religion and education went hand in hand. (Pp. 126–28)

Achebe is aware of the fact that the C.M.S. often cooperated not only with the official representatives of the British imperial government, but also with Liverpool trading companies that did business along the Niger river and later in the West African interior.[39] But unlike many of his Marxist contemporaries, such as Ngugi wa Thiong'o and Sembène Ousmane, Achebe does not view the introduction of a market economy into Africa as an unmitigated calamity, particularly since trade in palm oil and kernel helped to supplant the slave trade carried on by the Aro and Abam. Though an eloquent critic of unrestrained self-interest, Achebe nevertheless insists that materialism among the Igbo was both traditional and respectable long before the arrival of non-Africans.[40] Accordingly, he tends to favor a program of modernization in postcolonial Africa that would begin with "concrete aspirations like economic growth, health for all, education."[41] As a writer himself, Achebe is no doubt sensitive to the advantages of literacy which Mr. Brown's school offers to the Igbo people for the first time.

We should nevertheless keep in mind that all the modern innovations that the C.M.S introduces to Igbo society serve in some direct or indirect way the interests of British imperialism and help to erode the solidarity and viability of the traditional life of the clan. Religious education and the spread of literacy help to create the bureaucratic infrastructure necessary for the administration of colonial rule in Nigeria.[42] Health care, which would seem to be ethically neutral, nonetheless surreptitiously undermines the traditional authority of the *dibia*, medicine men such as Ogakbue Uyanwa. Indirectly, at least, modern medical care supplants another pillar of the community's socioreligious structure, since its "magic" is greater than that of the clan. And as our investigation of *No Longer at Ease* will suggest, a market economy, even if materially beneficial to the mass of Nigerians, undermines the communal loyalties and familial attachments that undergird traditional tribal life.

The ambivalence Achebe feels towards evangelical Christianity in league with modern Western education, science, and a market economy resembles the doubts Stendhal, Hardy, and Conrad share about modernity. From the perspective of the clan elders and their representative hero, Okonkwo, the intrusion of the modern West into Umuofia leads to the tragic collapse of a flawed but fundamentally noble society. From the more distant historical perspective of post-colonial Nigeria, the destruction of traditional Igbo life appears as a necessary phase in the historical development of a modern and inde-pendent African nation. The tragedy of Okonkwo is subsumed and transformed by a larger historical movement that leads to the assimi-lation of all forms of human life to a single global model: the modern secular state.[43]

Seen from the "end of history," the introduction of a Western religion—evangelical Protestantism—into Igboland appears as another Hegelian "ruse of reason." While the Christian missionaries Reverend Brown and Mr. Kiaga are in a fundamental respect just as misguided in their religious beliefs as are the oracles, *dibia,* elders, and priests of the Igbo, these Protestant evangelicals nevertheless unwittingly serve to advance the rationalization and modernization of life in Umuofia and Mbanta. Which is to say that the most impor-tant changes they help to bring about in Igbo society are often only indirectly related to their profession of the Christian faith. To be sure, capitalism (to say nothing of literacy and medical technology) need not be indissolubly linked with the prior introduction of Protestant-ism or even Christianity into an economically undeveloped part of the world. (The examples of modern Japan, South Korea, Singapore, Hong Kong, and Taiwan call into question the validity of Max Weber's thesis concerning the Protestant origins of modern capital-ism).[44] Nevertheless, Achebe's novel does suggest that Protestant Christianity can serve as *a* vehicle, and sometimes the decisive vehi-cle, by which certain important features of modernity are introduced into a traditional society. In the Igbo villages of *Things Fall Apart,* the Christian missionaries not only help to encourage trade, they also inculcate in their converts certain beliefs—such as the idea that all are equal in the eyes of God the Father—that can provide the ideological basis for the future development of modern forms of egalitarianism and democratic individualism.

But lest we lose sight of the particular context of this fundamen-tal change, we should recall Hegel's observation that history is a slaughter-bench. For Achebe's Okonkwo, there is no future, literally or even imaginatively. His premonition of a time when his own off-spring have abandoned the ancestral shrine, leaving the hero discon-solate among the ashes, proves fatefully prophetic. Okonkwo's tragic death illumines with one final incandescent flicker the destruction of a heroic culture. Occurring "off-stage" with great suddenness, his suicide is never seen from his perspective; it consequently requires some effort to recover the psychological dimension of his self-destruction. The District Commissioner's view of Okonkwo's death is commonly understood to be Achebe's ironic comment upon the Eurocentricism of writers like Conrad and Cary.[45] What is perhaps less well appreciated is that even the final spokesman for the clan, Obierika, does not completely grasp the implications or motivations of his friend's death: "That man was one of the greatest in Umuofia. You drove him to kill himself; and now he will be buried like a dog" (p. 147). As a young man, Okonkwo felt shame over the memory of his father, an untitled individual who was buried in the Evil Forest; why is it then that Okonkwo, who has always feared and avoided bringing shame or dishonor upon himself, chooses to end his life in such an ignoble manner?

Obierika's assessment of Okonkwo's end is only partially correct, for it is not only the British, but also the Igbos who drive him to suicide. Okonkwo offers to lead the Igbo villagers in a noble, violent, though probably futile struggle against the Christian and British threat. Unfortunately for him, the clan fails to follow his lead. The result is not merely that Okonkwo is left physically and politically vulnerable—the inevitable subject of punishment under the colonial judicial system—he is also bereft of his faith in the ethical norms that provided the basis of his heroic self-image.[46] His commitment to heroism and nobility has meaning only in relation to the cultural, political, and religious practices of the clan. The refusal of his clansmen to act against the new government in effect leaves him without a viable community and consequently without a sense of personal identity. For Okonkwo, the distinction between a "great man" and a "dog" has been effectively eroded and therewith the meaningful differences between the noble and the base, the admirable and the abominable.

Still living amidst the ruins of a declining noble culture, Obierika speaks for a noble and increasingly anachronistic perspective that sees in the hero's death a tragic catastrophe. As the progressive representative of historical change, the District Commissioner understands Okonkwo's suicide as nothing more than a minor, if interesting episode in the lengthy transformation of Igboland into a modern British colony. The book that the District Commissioner intends to write, *The Pacification of the Primitive Tribes of the Lower Niger,* is itself to be only one chapter in the comprehensive narrative of Hegelian world history. While Achebe's irony invites us to dismiss the District Commissioner as the unfeeling and pompous representative of a racist and imperialist perspective, the novel ultimately *subsumes* rather than rejects the official British view. *Things Fall Apart* explicitly ironizes the Western "historical" view of colonialism by placing it within a tragic context; but it also implicitly accepts the irreversibility of colonial history, and tacitly incorporates a Hegelian narrative as the subtext of its action.

VI

During a job interview, Obi Okonkwo, the protagonist of *No Longer at Ease* (1960), offers a theory of tragedy that many commentators feel aptly characterizes Achebe's second novel:

"You say you're a great admirer of Graham Greene. What do you think of *The Heart of the Matter?*"

"The only sensible novel any European has written on West Africa and one of the best novels I have read." Obi paused, and then added almost as an afterthought: "Only it was nearly ruined by the happy ending."

The Chairman sat up in his chair.

"Happy ending? Are you sure it's *The Heart of the Matter* you're thinking about? The European police officer commits suicide."

"Perhaps happy ending is too strong, but there is no other way I can put it. The police officer is torn between his love of a woman and his love of God, and he commits suicide. It's much too simple. Tragedy isn't like that at all. I remember an old man in my village, a Christian convert, who suffered one calamity after another. He said life was like a bowl of wormwood which one sips a little at a time world without end. He understood the nature of tragedy."

"You think that suicide ruins a tragedy," said the Chairman.

"Yes. Real tragedy is never resolved. It goes on hopelessly forever. Conventional tragedy is too easy. The hero dies and we feel a purging of the emotions. A real tragedy takes place in a corner, in an untidy spot, to quote W. H. Auden. The rest of the world is unaware of it." (Pp. 43–44)[47]

Given an opportunity to define his notion of "real tragedy," Obi surprisingly ignores the example of his own grandfather, Okonkwo, who embodies the kind of tragic hero that his grandson dismisses as merely literary and conventional.[48] Rather than looking to his own family history, Obi draws for critical inspiration on two sources—an old Igbo man from his village and W. H. Auden. Superficially, Obi's theory seems rooted in an indigenous African understanding of tragedy, as represented by the traditional wisdom of the village elder. But in fact, the "native" element of his theory is itself a product of the imposition of evangelical British imperialism upon earlier precolonial Igbo life. The reflections of the elder are the musings of a *Christian convert*. Obi further transforms the "indigenous" conception of tragedy by applying the critical standards he has acquired through a colonial education. (He is sent to a British university in the United Kingdom, where he studies English literature before returning to a civil service job in Nigeria). Obi's understanding of tragedy has been decisively influenced by a European bourgeois literary and critical tradition. Indeed, his "new" theory approximates that of George Eliot: it represents tragedy as an essentially private and antiheroic matter concerning an ordinary individual whose suffering goes unnoticed by the rest of the world.[49]

As I suggested above, *No Longer at Ease* functions as a modern and subjective tragedy that historically supersedes the earlier "classical" and objective tragedy embodied in *Things Fall Apart*. This generic modulation reflects the rapid and sweeping sociopolitical changes that transformed West Africa between the late nineteenth century (when Okonkwo's story begins) and the mid-1950s (when Obi's takes place). Achebe carefully omits all mention of "Nigeria" in *Things Fall Apart;* the word does not appear until the second chapter of *No Longer at Ease,* where the reader learns "It was in England that Nigeria first became more than just a name to [Obi]" (p. 19). In his second novel, Achebe moves his characters from the traditional Igbo village into the modern cosmopolitan world created in the wake of European imperialism. Whereas the action of *Things Fall Apart* is largely confined to the small closely knit tribal communities of Umuofia and Mbanta, the drama of *No Longer at Ease* moves from Lagos to London, from Liverpool and the Madeiras to Freetown and Iguedo. The varied international settings of the second novel clearly mark an advanced stage of globalization that has transformed the lives of the provincial Igbo people of the earlier novel. Like Hardy, Achebe records the gradual extinction of local and regional cultural identities. Umuofia—which in Igbo means "people of the bush"—meets a fate similar to that of Casterbridge; it slowly loses its distinctive regional and autonomous character as it is subsumed by a new larger political entity, the emergent nation of Nigeria. The first mention of "Nigeria" in Achebe's novels thus signals the introduction of

one of the central themes of his later work, the not altogether successful attempt to found a new regime, specifically a modern African
nation-state, that will take its rightful place in the international community of the postcolonial era.

Achebe's depiction of Lagos emphasizes the alien and cosmopolitan character of the new Nigeria. The city is not primarily Igbo in
character. Much of the everyday dialogue on the street—for example,
the taxi driver's shout of "*Ori oda*"—is carried on in the rival language of Yoruba.[50] Though Lagos remains rooted in its past as a
center of Yoruba culture, by the late 1950s the city has become home
to many different tribes, races, and linguistic groups. Its citizens generally communicate via English or the more commonly spoken
pidgin, rather than an indigenous tribal tongue. The city is filled by
masses of people who are unknown to each other and who have little
in common. The villagers of Umuofia are shocked to discover that the
inhabitants of Lagos cannot attend their "neighbor's" wedding unless they receive "one of these papers on which they wrote R.S.V.P.—
Rice and Stew Very Plenty" (p. 17).

This vast new metropolis sometimes produces in Obi a peculiarly
modern form of discomfort and psychic disequilibrium that is unknown to members of the clan in *Things Fall Apart*—anomie.
Though he champions the cause of the new Nigerian nation and
thinks of himself as an exemplary representative of a sophisticated
rising generation in Nigeria, a member of the new African elite, Obi
sometimes feels lost, alienated, and alone amidst the multiethnic
crowds of modern Lagos, much the way Jim does aboard the *Patna*.
Though there are many reasons for his eventually accepting the bribe
that brings his career in the civil service to an end, his succumbing to
political corruption is made easier by his moral and physical isolation
in Lagos, where he is increasingly cut off from his family and clan.
His acceptance of the fateful bribe occurs in the privacy of his apart-
ment, where his fellow clan members can no longer watch him and
therefore no longer reproach him for his misconduct. Much like Conrad's hero aboard the *Patna,* Obi finds that his social isolation in a
cosmopolitan setting helps to subvert his heroic resolution and to
undermine his faith in an exacting and high-minded ethical code.

For many of Achebe's Igbo characters, "Nigeria" itself remains
something foreign and unwelcome: "In Nigeria the government was
'they.' It had nothing to do with you or me. It was an alien institution
and people's business was to get as much from it as they could
without getting into trouble" (p. 38).

Though he fails in his attempt, Obi's heroic aspirations aim at the construction of a new government that would no longer be an "alien" institution and of a new nation in which the welfare of "you or me" would be consonant with that of all citizens. Obi thus represents, at least initially, the hopes and ambitions of the new Nigerian *nation* as opposed to his grandfather, who spoke for the *clan* of Umuofia. Whereas Okonkwo becomes a traditional tragic hero because of his resistance to modernization, Obi becomes a modern tragic figure in part because of his unsuccessful effort to accelerate the same process.

At the close of *Things Fall Apart* one expects that the vestiges of tribal life will be swept away by the incoming flood of evangelical Christianity. As several critics have noted, however, in *No Longer at Ease*, Christianity has not completely triumphed and traditional village life has not entirely vanished. C. L. Innes points out that in Obi's home village of Iguedo, traditional Igbo religion and Christianity have blended into a kind of syncretistic hybrid.[51] Viewed from the perspective of Okonkwo at the turn of the century, Christianity represented the leading edge of European modernization; seen from the perspective of the new Nigerian elite of the 1950s, Christianity seems nearly as vestigial and anachronistic as do many of the precolonial tribal traditions. The conflict between traditional and modern forces in *No Longer at Ease* consequently does not manifest itself in the struggle between tribal religion and Christianity—as was the case in *Things Fall Apart*. Achebe understands that modernization is a dynamic process left incomplete by the introduction of Christianity into West Africa. His second novel accordingly concerns a much later post-Christian, postreligious phase of historical development, the chief engine of which is a market economy. The business of modern Lagos is not religion, but business.

By themselves neither European Christianity nor imperial British rule are sufficient to create modern Lagos. The growth of the city depends upon increased commerce. Achebe is clear about the reasons that Igbo villagers leave Iguedo to come to the capital. At a meeting of the Umuofia Progressive Union (U.P.U), the president of the organization naively suggests that it is "work" that brings so many of his clan from the countryside to Lagos; he is corrected by one of the group's members: "It is money, not work. . . . We left plenty of work at home" (p. 79). The widespread desire of the villagers for the greater prosperity available in the modern city draws them from their ancestral homes. *No Longer at Ease* provides a critique of a market economy, but it is a cultural rather than an economic one. In Achebe's view, economic liberalization transforms Nigeria precisely because it answers the material needs of its inhabitants, not because it materially exploits them. Achebe finds fault with a market economy not because it does not work well enough, but because it often works too well.

Critics are quite right to see that many elements of clan life survive in the world of *No Longer at Ease;* these elements have, however, undergone a great transformation under the influence of economic liberalization. The U.P.U. is ostensibly a cultural organization created in order for the clan to reconstitute itself in areas outside its ancestral homeland. In fact, the clan has become a small-scale bureaucratic organization largely devoted to forwarding the financial interests of an ethnic minority within the new Nigeria; as such it in many respects resembles any business or trade organization that aims to advance the fortunes of a special interest at the expense of the economy as a whole. On many occasions, its leaders speak out in favor of the high-minded goals of national progress and economic liberalization—the "march towards political irredentism, social equality, and economic emancipation" (p. 37). But in fact, the U.P.U. seeks forms of political favoritism from the central government that benefit its interests at the expense of other tribes, clans, and villages: "Our people have a saying 'Ours is ours, but mine is mine.' Every town and village struggles at this momentous epoch in our political evolution to possess that of which it can say: 'This is mine.'" (p. 37).

Achebe illustrates the ways in which the ethical aims of traditional Igbo society have been redirected towards material ends without the people necessarily having embraced the ethical and political principles that make a market economy viable. When Obi returns to his village he hears a group of women singing "The Song of the Heart," the lyrics of which reflect the traditional ethos of the clan:

> He that has a brother must hold him to his heart,
> For a kinsman cannot be bought in the market,
> Neither is a brother bought with money. (P. 123)

By contrast, the secretary of the U.P.U. refers to his kinsman Obi as the "possession" of the clan; he states explictly that the scholarship provided by the U.P.U. to Obi is an "investment which must yield heavy dividends" (p. 37). Though we shall see that kinship ties still possess considerable importance for the U.P.U., it is clear that kinship itself has taken on an increasingly commercial character that it lacked in the world of *Things Fall Apart.*

In general, *No Longer at Ease* illustrates the ways in which the ethical standards of the clan have been transformed into increasingly modern bourgeois commercial values. The traditional Igbo conception of greatness has given way to a new modern European criterion. Back in Iguedo, the old man of the village, Odogwu, compares Obi to the heroes of the past, such as Okonkwo, Ezeudu, and Obierika:

> These men were great in their day. Today greatness has changed its tune. Titles are no longer great, neither are barns or large numbers of wives and children. Greatness is now in the things of the white man. And so we too have changed our tune. (P. 57)

We hear a note of nostalgia and loss in Odogwu's words in praise of Obi and Iguedo. But his view nevertheless agrees with that of the U.P.U. Whereas the glory of the clan once resided in its great military prowess and in the martial accomplishments of its warriors, in the mid-twentieth century the prestige of the clan depends upon the economic success and political influence of its favorite sons. Tribal warfare now takes the form of competition among clans and villages for the largest share of governmental favor, which in turn, translates into greater wealth for those receiving special consideration from the central government. Christianity has turned out to be merely an intermediate ethical phase that makes possible the transition from a noble to a mercantile and bourgeois ethos.

Achebe records the ways in which the economic ethos of modern Nigeria transforms a wide range of traditional Igbo practices and conventions. For example, while the payment of bride price always required some financial negotiation between Igbo families, in *Things Fall Apart* that custom was carefully distinguished from the kind of haggling that characterized behavior in the marketplace (p. 51). By contrast, in the Nigeria of *No Longer at Ease,* the practice has become a serious business pursued openly for the financial benefits it brings to the family of the bride; efforts of the Nigerian government to control the practice have merely pushed up the already exorbitant price of marriage (p. 45). As opposed to the older folk songs and elaborate customs that governed the courtship of couples in the village, the new music of the dance clubs of Lagos celebrates the city's much freer sexual relationships based increasingly on material incentives:

Nylon dress is a lovely dress,
Nylon dress is a country dress,
If you want to make your baby happy
Nylon is good for her. (P. 108)

While a market economy has made Nigeria more prosperous and provided increasing numbers of people like Obi, and his intimate friends, Clara, Joseph, and Christopher, a wider range of experiences and personal opportunities than would have been possible in the village, it further erodes the traditional importance of kinship ties. The mere existence of the U.P.U. indicates the degree to which the association of village and clan no longer holds true in modern Nigeria. For Okonkwo, no meaningful distinction exists between Umuofia as a place and Umuofia as a clan. But as more and more of its inhabitants go abroad to study or settle in Lagos for the economic opportunities it provides, tribal identity becomes an ever more amorphous and attenuated concept. When Obi returns to Iguedo on vacation, he is struck by the isolation of his parents; only his sister Eunice remains at home to care for the aging couple:

> That was what the world had come to. Children left their old parents at home and scattered in all directions in search of money. It was hard on an old woman with eight children. It was like having a river and yet washing one's hands with spittle. (P. 128)

Given his financial means, Obi faces no practical difficulties in returning home for his mother's funeral. By the same token, his absence from the ceremony in Iguedo only becomes comprehensible in a new Nigeria in which the bonds of village and clan have given way to the more mobile and individualistic way of life of a younger generation. Although a market economy supplies the means for Obi to return home if he wishes, it also allows him the freedom to do otherwise.

For Achebe the greatest difficulty posed by a market economy is the inability of this new form of commercial life to supply the political foundations for a postcolonial *national* identity. In point of fact, a completely free market is theoretically and practically possible without nationalism. Indeed, advocates of market economies argue that the "wealth of nations" requires a rejection of nationalized markets and protective trade barriers that stunt economic growth. By contrast, Achebe seems to fear that the antinationalistic bias of a market economy promises to accelerate the dissolution of traditional tribal cultures without supplying the necessary basis for a new

Nigerian culture. For insofar as hometown societies like the U.P.U. look to a corrupt centralized national government for political largesse and special economic advantages, the vestigial tribal elements in Nigerian culture that do survive work to obstruct the full development of a market economy. This in turn keeps Nigerians from enjoying what positive material benefits true economic liberalization could offer. The net effect is political and economic arrested development; traditional cultural and social values are severely compromised in the new Nigeria without its citizens having gained the full advantages of a market economy.[52]

VII

At the heart of *No Longer at Ease* is the problem of political corruption in the new Nigeria. Obi's conviction for accepting bribes while an official of the government distills the greater tragedy of an emerging nation that Achebe represents as politically and economically unjust. Bribery, graft ("dash"), electoral fraud, and influence peddling are endemic in the Africa of *No Longer at Ease, A Man of the People,* and *Anthills of the Savannah*. In his overtly political works such as *The Trouble with Nigeria,* Achebe insists that political corruption does not reveal an inherent deficiency in African peoples, but rather a failure of their national leadership that ultimately affects all levels of society. Achebe states in his political pamphlet that an enduring and significant obstacle for the postcolonial African nation is its persistent attachment to tribalism.[53] Achebe defends the "competitive individualism and the adventurous spirit" of the Igbo people and paradoxically attempts to explain their clannishness (as well as their entrepreneurial success) as an extension of their traditional respect for individual initiative. Achebe argues that Nigeria will never successfully modernize unless it manages to encourage the entrepreneurial individualism of its citizens regardless of their tribal identities and affiliations.[54]

Though the "hybridization" of culture is currently seen by many as a cure-all for both First and Third World nations, a way of overcoming the divisions and tensions between different forms of social, political, and religious life, in Achebe's novels the volatile mixture of African and European, traditional and modern cultures is the source of many of the most difficult problems facing the new Nigeria. Corruption in *No Longer at Ease* is a product precisely of cultural hybridization. In particular, the widespread practice of political graft is largely the result of an unfortunate mixing of traditional and modern ways of life. For a great many Nigerians, including Obi's Igbo friend Christopher (educated at the London School of Economics), bribery is merely the modern equivalent of "kola" (pp. 86, 157).

The gradual transition from the giving of kola nuts as an Igbo ritual that provides a ceremonial means to encourage neighborly relations among clan members to "kola" as the popular term for bribery is one key to what is happening in *No Longer at Ease*.[55] Traditionally, the offering of a kola nut by a guest to his host, or vice versa, functions as a gesture of mutual respect. It establishes the proper context for all types of discussion among villagers in Umuofia. Moreover, it is a religious ritual, a sacrifice in honor of the gods of the clan who are called upon to bless the gathering and lend their aid to the peace and prosperity of the assembled group. Significantly, Obi's father, Isaac (Nwoye), discourages the practice of "kola" in his Christian household. On important occasions he allows the ritual to take place, even offers kola nuts to his guests, though with the important proviso that "kola nut is eaten here, but not sacrificed to idols" (p. 54). Already in Issac's Christianized generation, kola is stripped of its traditional religious connotations, though its "civic" or social dimension is preserved. For the following generation, however, the offering of a token of respect has become completely commodified; it means to offer a bribe to a public official in return for a political favor.

This transformation of "kola" works by way of a metaphoric substitution. Traditionally, the ceremony literally involved the giving of kola nuts. While they were valued items—a food supplying refreshment and energy—the accumulation of these perishables in massive numbers was neither practicable nor desirable. There were in effect natural limits to the number of kola nuts an individual could consume or save. By contrast, once "kola" comes to mean money, the desire for it and capacity to save it become endless. In Okonkwo's time, "bribing" a man with kola nuts would be absurd, not to say impossible. In Obi's day, the accumulation of "kola" is the mark of the great man who has made it in the new Nigeria. The greater the bribe he can command, the greater the respect his people have for him. While the U.P.U. officially opposes graft, their cynical attitude towards the practice is revealed in the proverbial witticism offered by one of its members who comments upon Obi's conviction: "If you want to eat a toad you should look for a fat and juicy one" (p. 13). The U.P.U is less upset by Obi's willingness to accept bribes than by his risking his career for such "small kola."

The corruption of "kola" may serve as a synecdoche for the modern tragedy of Obi and the new Nigeria. Economic modernization helps to transform a set of dignified and culturally beneficial practices into a source of contemporary political and social injustice. At the same time, residual tribal mores and clan prejudices greatly exacerbate the problem of bribery (a form of political corruption known in modern as well as premodern regimes throughout the world). The U.P.U. accepts, indeed implicitly encourages bribery and graft precisely because they promote "the greatness" of the clan: access to public officials facilitates governmental favoritism and thereby enriches members of the clan at the expense of the Nigerian public as a whole. Moreover, the U.P.U. celebrates the excessive and extravagant lifestyles of public officials like Obi, which they see as an outward mark of the clan's prestige (pp. 96, 119–20). The U.P.U. thus lends moral legitimacy to the lavish and wasteful behavior of government officials that makes bribery and graft all the more likely, even necessary. A market economy unleashes the acquisitiveness already inherent in traditional Igbo culture; the vestigial elements of tribal culture in turn undermine the modern legal and moral imperatives that serve to regulate and channel acquisitiveness so that truly free markets, unhampered by governmental interference or economic privilege, might flourish.[56]

Traditional tribal society has its own internal checks that tend to discourage the kind of political corruption we find in *No Longer at Ease*. Its chief means of doing so is by artificially restricting economic growth and personal freedom. As we have seen, the taking of titles— an aristocratic element of precolonial Igbo culture—effectively redistributes wealth among the clan and thereby prevents "excessive" accumulation of capital by any one individual. The clan remains politically hierarchical and economically stagnant. The possibilities for individual economic advancement are further restricted by an aggressive identification with one's clan that militates against the development of free trade. In *Things Fall Apart* tribal warfare is generated chiefly by the struggle among clans to protect their trade monopolies and closed markets.

By comparison, a fully rational market economy strives to eliminate all forms of economic protectionism and governmental interference in order to spur economic growth. Consequently, laws against graft, bribery, and governmental intervention on behalf of special interests—whether they be economic classes, trade organizations, specific businesses, or particular ethnic groups—become essential. A set of ground rules—legal and moral—must remain firmly in place if fair market competition is to be preserved among individuals. The tragic situation of the new Nigeria is that it lacks the strict ground rules of either the traditional or the modern forms of social and economic life. The intermixing of old and new, aristocratic and bourgeois, African and European, produces a hybrid that legitimates the corruption of an entire political and economic system.

Obi's personal tragedy embodies the contradictions of his society. He might have avoided his conviction for bribery were he either more completely traditional or more consistently modern in his behavior. Many critics have found him to be an unheroic figure, lacking in moral courage, intellectual penetration, and political prudence.[57] No doubt Obi is a weaker character than his grandfather, more given to hesitation, self-justification, and moral ambivalence. Unlike Okonkwo, he never faces the demanding and often brutal social conditions that toughened his ancestor and helped to foster the hardness, inflexibility, and determination that modern critics also find hard to stomach. Both Obi's greater affability and his fecklessness are nurtured by the more tolerant, less violent, and more prosperous social environment of the new Nigeria.

To be sure, social conditions only contribute to Obi's tragedy; they do not determine the specific personal choices that lead to his eventual disgrace. Were Obi to repudiate categorically all aspects of the new society, he might never have run afoul of the law. Nothing compels him to leave Iguedo in search of an English education or a career in the new Nigerian administration. Like his sister Eunice, he might have stayed at home to care for his parents and farm the "bad bush" between Umuofia and Mbanta. By the same token, nothing prevents him from repudiating all vestigial ties to the old way of life. Legally he has no obligation to assume financial responsibility for his parents or to pay for his brother's education. He might have accepted a present of 50 pounds from his less well-off girlfriend Clara in disregard of the traditional principle that it is demeaning for a man to receive financial assistance from a woman or for a richer member of the clan to accept a loan from a poorer member. In either case, his indebtedness would have been considerably reduced, thereby minimizing the need for him to accept a bribe in order to meet his financial obligations. But of course, to take either of these two courses of action would tend to diminish Obi in the eyes of the reader. The neotraditional alternative would demonstrate more amply what his critics charge him with—lack of initiative, timidity, passivity. The hypermodern alternative would just as likely displease his critics; it would illustrate a mean-spirited acquisitiveness untempered by respect for traditional obligations and communal responsibilities, rather than great resolve or moral courage.

Obi's sexual behavior underscores the conflicting cultural demands he faces. His willingness to pursue a long-term relationship with Clara, despite her being *osu,* wins the plaudits of modern critics, who view the social prejudices of the clan as irrational and unjust.[58] From a modern perspective, Obi's love for Clara reflects the positive aspects of the progressive rationalization of human relationships; it expresses concretely a desire both for the universal recognition of human dignity and for greater sexual and personal autonomy. By the same token, one must sympathize with Obi's reluctance to offend his parents—particularly his mother, who threatens suicide if Obi marries an *osu.* (From her perspective, Obi could just as easily marry someone who will not bring shame upon her family in the eyes of the clan). This is not an easy moral choice. Were Obi more completely bound by the traditional limits of Okonkwo's world, he might never have found himself in London, where the mixing of freeborn and *osu* takes place without tribal consent or parental approval. Were he more insistently modern, he might have severed his ties with his family in order to marry Clara. In practice, he vacillates between the two, inclining toward a hybrid mixture of sexual practices that Obi's friend, Christopher, recommends: semidiscreet pursuit of multiple sexual partners before and after a respectable marriage that meets with the approval of clan and family. Like bribery, sexual promiscuity serves as a modern substitute for a traditional practice, polygamy. It offers the African male a wide range of sexual experiences, leaving undisturbed the social and cultural authority of men in the new Nigeria. As Obi's problematic sexual life illustrates, the attempt to synthesize traditional and modern practices, far from resolving the tensions between them, creates new sources of conflict and hence a new potential for tragedy.

VIII

Achebe includes in *No Longer at Ease* a brief episode that vividly illustrates the rage that the common people, even prior to full national independence, already feel toward the new Nigerian elite. Incensed by Obi's insistence on receiving special consideration from a doctor, a poor woman waiting to be seen in a clinic where Obi has jumped the queue shouts: "Beast of no nation!" (p. 143) The happy synthesis of different cultural values often defended in principle by many contemporary critics in this instance proves to be chimerical in a double sense. It is chimerical insofar as it remains an elusive goal in the new Nigeria of the late 1950s, and chimerical because it produces hybrid monsters that defy powers of critical classification. Achebe's deep sympathy for the aspirations of the emerging nations of Africa allows him to treat this phenomenon of cultural hybridity, which his justly outraged character sees as monstrous, as the proper subject for a modern tragedy. "Modern" in the Hegelian sense, precisely because Obi's personal calamity, however emblematic of a national and political situation, has few concrete or widespread repercussions for the society as a whole. And "modern" because Obi, unlike his grandfather Okonkwo, *internalizes* the moral conflict of his age so that it becomes a decidedly more *subjective* collision. Okonkwo is closer to Hegel's model of the classical tragic hero because he embodies a single ethical substantive and acts upon it resolutely. He struggles against an objective foe that represents a moral alternative to his aristocratic conception of traditional Igbo life. By contrast, Obi is by no means a pure moral "type"; he embodies a subjective struggle to resolve the tensions between incompatible ethical and political ends, a struggle that reflects the crosscurrents of a society at the moment of transition from a colonial to postcolonial existence. The diminished significance of his fall by comparison with that of his grandfather and the general lack of critical enthusiasm for his character registers the absence of epic struggle and the disappearance of traditional heroism in the new modernizing Africa on the eve of independence.

In 1960, when *No Longer at Ease* first appeared, Achebe could plausibly view the immediate future of Africa with considerable optimism, even while his melioristic outlook was colored by a deep sense of what the new Africa had lost and what more it was likely to lose on the path of modernization. On the eve of Nigerian independence, Achebe could see the process of African modernization in Hegelian terms, even though he would have repudiated in the strongest possible sense Hegel's characterization of the African past. Even up to 1966, when *A Man of the People* appeared, Achebe's often critical perspective on the new Nigeria was consistent with the view that the tragedy of modernization would remain a subjective and perhaps unseemly affair, but one which would ultimately be resolved in favor of a more just and comprehensively modern nation. After a series of electoral crises, military coups, dictatorships, and the catastrophic events of the Biafran war, Achebe might well have questioned whether the tragedy of modernizing Africa would assume only a "subjective" and diminished form.

In fact, even in *No Longer at Ease,* Obi contemplates the possibility that enlightened dictatorship might be required to overcome the "corruption and ignorance" that retards Nigeria's progress towards modernity (p. 47). Nearly thirty years later, when *Anthills of the Savannah* appeared, Obi's prophecy had been confirmed throughout a good deal of Africa—though not in the enlightened and progressive fashion that Achebe's character had anticipated. In fact Achebe suggests in his most recent work of fiction that the history of Africa has by no means reached its happy Hegelian end and that the conflicts generated by the process of modernization are not, even at this late date in world history, necessarily of the subjective and private variety. *Anthills of the Savannah* dramatizes how the increasingly brutal dictatorship of the Head of State of Kangan (a regime modeled upon Nigeria and other postcolonial African nations) grows out of the cultural and social impasse that Achebe earlier depicted in *No Longer at Ease.*

Sam, the Head of State, increasingly justifies his despotic rule as a return to traditional African political institutions—the practice of chieftaincy, for example. Like the dictator of Henri Lopes's *The Laughing Cry* or his many historical counterparts such as Mobutu of Zaire, Achebe's Head of State makes use of the regalia of a traditional African tribal leader as a means of legitimating his increasingly authoritarian rule. Both those characters who flatter the pseudotraditional pretensions of the tyrant (such as Christopher) and those determined to criticize his rule (such as Ikem) are ultimately crushed in the ensuing political disasters that befall his regime. Sensitive to the charge that Africans are historically incapable of ruling themselves justly or democratically, Achebe is at pains to suggest that Sam's government by no means marks a genuine recovery of precolonial African political principles.[59] In fact, Sam is a product of both traditional and modern elements within postcolonial Africa. A graduate of Lord Lugard College and Sandhurst, he embodies a dangerous and highly unstable mixture of modern and traditional, African and Western elements. For Achebe the modern African dictator is a new and even more monstrous version of the "beast of no nation." As Ikem puts it, "The real danger today is from . . . all those virulent, misshapen freaks like Amin and Bokassa sired on Africa by Europe" (p. 47).

If the multiethnic group of men and women, rich and poor, Christians, Muslims, and animists who unite at the close of the novel to name the newborn daughter of Ikem and Elewa represent African aspirations for a harmonious future, the tragic deaths of Chris and Ikem serve as reminders of a harsh communal destiny "carefully programmed in advance by an alienated history" (p. 204). By improvising a new ritual for naming Amaechina (which means "May-the-path-never-close"), the resilient survivors of Sam's tyranny anticipate the creation of a new hybrid culture that will minimize the divisions represented by race, gender, class, ethnicity, and religion. In grieving for their beloved friends, the mourners wonder how great will be the sacrifice demanded of them in order to "appease an embittered history" (p. 204). Although the hopes that Achebe's characters entertain for Kangan are consistent with the Hegelian end of history, *Anthills of the Savannah* illustrates that the tragedy of modernization in postcolonial Africa has by no means reached its end. In fact, the challenge of modernization may provoke powerful countermovements, which, seen from a modern perspective, appear to be reactionary or regressive. Such a violent reaction against modernity, as it played itself out in Latin America at the turn of the century, is the subject of the novel to which we now turn, Vargas Llosa's *The War of the End of the World*.

4

Vargas Llosa:
Apocalyptic History and
the Liberal Perspective

> The war of Canudos marked an ebb, a backward flow, in our history. What we had to face here was the unlooked-for resurrection, under arms, of an old society, a dead society, galvanized into life by a madman . . . Canudos was our Vendée.
>
> Euclides da Cunha, *Rebellion in the Backlands*

I

During his unsuccessful 1990 campaign for the presidency of Peru, Mario Vargas Llosa managed to spare enough time from pressing political commitments to read the works of Karl Popper, whose *The Open Society and Its Enemies* had come to his attention in 1980.[1] In "Updating Karl Popper," Vargas Llosa rejects the teleological historicism of thinkers such as Hegel, Marx, and Comte because he feels that it has helped to legitimate authoritarian rule. Following Popper's lead, Vargas Llosa argues that an open democratic society must encourage a fluid and corrigible definition of truth. For Vargas Llosa, liberal progressive reform depends upon the continual and provisional invention of truths that prevail only so long as they are not refuted. The advance of human civilization thus depends upon rejecting the fixed and universally valid conception of historical truth that Hegel, Marx, and Comte claim to have discovered.

Vargas Llosa's essay suffers from the same theoretical inconsistencies that characterize Popper's own writings. On the one hand, Vargas Llosa argues that no universally valid truth exists and that therefore no objectively "true" account of history is possible:

History has no order, logic, sense, much less a rational direction that sociologists, economists, or ideologues can detect in advance "scientifically." History is organized by historians; they are the ones who make it coherent and intelligible, through the use of points of view and interpretations that are always partial, provisional, and, in the final analysis, as subjective as artistic constructs.[2]

On the other hand, Vargas Llosa maintains that the histories of certain disciplines, such as natural science, economics, and jurisprudence, follow an evolutionary course:

> That historical laws do not exist, however, does not mean that there are not certain patterns in human evolution. And neither does the unpredictability of the future mean that all social forecasting is impossible. In specific fields, the social sciences can establish that under certain conditions certain events will inevitably occur: the inorganic issuing of currency will always bring about inflation, for example. And there is no doubt either that in some areas, like science, international law, and civil freedom, one can trace a more or less clear line of progress up to the present.[3]

Because Vargas Llosa is confident of the truth of "certain patterns in human evolution," which are discernible in retrospect, he can assert that a free and open democratic society marks a verifiable historical advance beyond its prior illiberal alternatives:

> That truth exists is demonstrated by the progress humanity has made in many fields, scientific and technical as well as social and political. By erring, by learning from its mistakes, humankind has come gradually to know nature and itself. . . . Has humanity not progressed thus in medicine, in astronomy, in physics? Something similar can be said of social organization. Democratic culture, by means of mistakes it eventually corrected, has managed to ensure citizens in open societies better material and cultural conditions and greater opportunities for deciding their own destinies.[4]

Like Popper, Vargas Llosa attempts to minimize the tension between his confidence in the demonstrable nature of social evolution and his skepticism about teleological historicism by allowing for the possibility that historical reverses can occur:

> [It] would be imprudent to assume, even in these concrete fields [such as science, international law, and civil freedom], that this record ensures an irreversible progression in the future. Humanity can regress and fall, nullifying those advances. There were no previous collective killings of the magnitude of those produced in the two world wars. And are not the

Jewish Holocaust perpetrated by the Nazis and the extermination of millions of dissidents by Soviet communism ample proof of how barbarism can blossom anew with unwonted force in societies that seem to have attained elevated levels of civilization? Do not Islamic fundamentalism and recent events in Iran prove, perhaps, the ease with which history can transgress all dictates, follow hysterical trajectories, and experience regressions instead of advances?[5]

Vargas Llosa acknowledges that there is nothing inevitable about the historical advance of humanity towards greater personal, intellectual, economic, and political freedom, and that relapses into barbarism, intolerance, and fanaticism are possible even among the most modern and culturally advanced societies.[6] But the fact that Vargas Llosa speaks of these developments as "regressions instead of advances" shows that he still has a conception of the general direction in which history ought to proceed. Thus like Chinua Achebe, Vargas Llosa can be classified within the Hegelian tradition, broadly conceived, insofar as he believes that a generally progressive movement of universal history is visible from the privileged vantage point of the present, and that it is necessary for underdeveloped nations to pursue the path of modernization. Thus, even in the act of denouncing historicism as conducive to illiberalism and totalitarianism, Vargas Llosa implicitly endorses the idea that, despite setbacks and reverses, history proceeds melioristically towards greater social and political freedom.

It is suggestive that Vargas Llosa discovered Popper around the same time he was completing his impressive epic novel, *The War of the End of the World* (*La guerra del fin del mundo*), which was originally published in 1981. To be sure, the germination of this novel preceded Vargas Llosa's introduction to Popper by several years (it began in the early 1970s as a filmscript that never reached production).[7] Nevertheless, the difficulties that inhere in Popper's and Vargas Llosa's antihistoricist defense of the "open society" provide an important insight into the liberal democratic assumptions that enframe and inform Vargas Llosa's complex historical novel. Set in the *sertão* (backlands) of Brazil during the last years of the nineteenth century, this novel treats a major event in Latin American history that bears comparison with the Islamic revolution of the Ayatollah Khomeini.[8] Like its twentieth-century counterpart in Iran, the rebellion in the remote and underdeveloped province of Bahia was sparked by the revolutionary evangelism of a messianic figure, Antônio Vicente Mendes Maciel, known as "the Counselor" (*el Consejero*),[9] whose rebellious forces in Canudos fought the newly established Brazilian republic, a regime striving to modernize the nation along contemporary Western—specifically Comtean—lines. This violent and ultimately futile rebellion is, in the terms of Popper and Vargas Llosa, a quintessential example of a "backward" or regressive movement of history.[10] Vargas Llosa's fictional recreation of this tragic event involves a monumental narrative attempt, in the manner of Tolstoy's *War and Peace,* to define the nature of history in terms compatible with a set of liberal democratic reforms he advocates as the remedy for the immense social and political ills of Latin America in particular, and the Third World in general.

The problems Vargas Llosa poses are at once literary and political: How does one write a historical novel while eschewing a coherent theory of history? How does one explain and evaluate a significant turning point in Brazilian and Latin American history without insisting upon the "truth" of one's account or upon the transhistorical validity of the moral and political standards used to analyze and evaluate the historical events themselves? How can one dramatize a *retrograde* episode of history without implicitly acknowledging the existence of a *linear* continuum along which both regressive and progressive historical movements are charted? The richness and comprehensiveness of Vargas Llosa's novel, together with his explicit reflection on the problems of history we have been examining, give us the opportunity to expand and deepen our understanding of modernization as it is represented in the global novel. For in *The War of the End of the World* we find not only two of the historically most important kinds of premodern political communities—theocracy and feudal aristocracy—but also two of the most powerful modern challenges to liberal democracy—authoritarian dictatorship and utopian socialism. The extraordinary range of Vargas Llosa's epic novel thus provides a synoptic account of the rise and spread of modernity and a panoramic view of the political alternatives to liberal democratic society.

II

We may begin to clarify Vargas Llosa's response to the challenge of modernity by examining *The War of the End of the World* in light of Georg Lukács's illuminating theory of the historical novel. According to Lukács, the historical novel emerged as an important literary genre only after the French Revolution and the Napoleonic wars, when a growing consciousness developed among artists and intellectuals of the teleological trajectory of world history. This recognition on the part of Scott, Cooper, Manzoni, Balzac, and Tolstoy, among others, produced the distinctive generic features of the historical novel. Chief among these is the literary representation of a key event or series of events in the past that appear as the necessary historical matrix or "concrete prehistory" of the present age.[11] Lukács sharply distinguishes between authentically historical novels such as *Waverley* or *War and Peace*, and "romantic" falsely monumentalizing types such as Flaubert's *Salammbô*, which merely make use of an alien past as the exotic backdrop for an essentially domestic and contemporary narrative unconnected in any organic, causal, or meaningful way with the historical period represented.[12]

Vargas Llosa has repeatedly connected the historical subject of *The War of the End of the World*—the Canudos war—with contemporary historical and political realities in Latin America:

> I decided to write this novel because in the history of the Canudos war you could really see something that has been happening in Latin American history over the 19th and 20th centuries—the total lack of communication between two sections of a society which kill each other fighting *ghosts*, no? Fighting fictional enemies who are invented out of fanaticism, out of religious or political or economic blindness! This kind of reciprocal incapacity of understanding what you have opposing you is probably the main problem we have to overcome in Latin America if we want to civilize our countries.[13]

Vargas Llosa insists that "what happened in Brazil is still happening in the rest of Latin America."[14] The various elements of Brazilian society arrayed against one another in *The War of the End of the World* form a microcosm of the political alternatives that have confronted Latin America since its independence, ranging from feudal oligarchy and militant theocracy to utopian socialism, nationalistic military dictatorship, and progressive liberalism.

Vargas Llosa has drawn attention to the specific parallels between the religious revolution in Canudos and the fundamentalist revival sweeping much of the Islamic world, both of which he views as attempts to reject the modernizing influences of the West in order to return to the culture of the Middle Ages.[15] Vargas Llosa also suggests that his interest in the historical subject matter of Canudos is connected to his longstanding concern with political ideologies such as Marxism that have often played a decisive role in contemporary

Third World politics. He states that his disenchantment with Marxist ideology and the Cuban revolution (which followed in the wake of the Padilla affair in 1971) produced in him a "crisis" that led to his writing about the Canudos war.[16] He connects the kind of ideologically inspired revolutionary violence that swept the backlands of Brazil at the turn of the century with that which has engulfed the Andean highlands since the rise of the Maoist guerrilla organization, *Sendero Luminoso,* in the 1980s: "In Peru, for instance, we have a living Canudos in the Andes."[17] As Sara Castro-Klarén has noted, liberation theology, which emerged in the 1960s as a powerful political force in Latin America, represents a synthesis of Catholicism and revolutionary political practice analogous to the incendiary doctrine of the Counselor.[18]

At the most general level, Vargas Llosa's work represents the economic, political, and cultural realities of the underdeveloped world that make it fertile ground for instability, repression, and violence. Vargas Llosa does not present economic conditions or class conflict as the sole cause of the Canudos rebellion. In fact his work suggests that the concatenation of individual decisions that led to the revolutionary movement in Bahia often had little to do with the "class consciousness" of the followers of the Counselor, or even with their desire to improve their lives materially. Nevertheless, like Euclides da Cunha, whose historical account of the Canudos war, *Os sertões,* provides the principal literary source for *The War of the End of the World,* Vargas Llosa focuses upon the geographic, political, and economic conditions that sparked the insurrection.[19] The early chapters of the novel provide a panoramic view of Brazilian history during the last quarter of the nineteenth century: the series of droughts, culminating in that of 1877, that devasted the *sertão,* destroying crops and depopulating the region; the abolition of slavery in 1888, which set free an immense number of unskilled laborers unable to find employment; the rapid rise of the coffee industry in southern Brazil and the rubber industry in the north, which undermined the economic viability of feudal *fazendas* (country estates) in Bahia; and the collapse of the Brazilian Empire of Pedro II and the establishment of a federal republic in 1889, which shifted political power from the former capital of Salvador in Bahia to the new national capital in Rio de Janeiro.

While events in the novel necessarily reflect the specific history of Brazil, *The War of the End of the World* presents in broad outline the political and historical developments that characterize much of the

Third World: extreme poverty and widespread unemployment, a highly stratified and unequal distribution of wealth, the economic dislocations brought about by a nation's attempt to modernize its economy and integrate itself into a global market, the increasingly incompatible coexistence of premodern and modern forms of political life—lingering elements of slavery and feudalism alongside centralized parliamentary government and the persistent popular adherence to religious beliefs and conventions inconsistent with the secular ambitions of technocratic government. In short, whatever his reservations about Marxist interpretations of history, Vargas Llosa faithfully represents the concrete social conditions that for Lukács form the necessary context in which the narrative action of the historical novel must be understood.

Lukács calls the historical novel the "bourgeois epic"; its formal aim is the literary representation of the "totality of objects" that make up the modern world.[20] Its capacious structure serves to capture the "comprehensive totality" of life, "the capillary interplay of the great and small, the significant and the insignificant."[21] Vargas Llosa is widely known as a critic for his own theory of the "totalizing novel," a conception that bears a close resemblance to that of Lukács' "bourgeois epic" with its "totality of objects."[22] Vargas Llosa's conception of the "totalizing novel" is in many respects most fully realized in *The War of the End of the World,* a work that its author has characterized as his attempt to write an "epic" novel in the manner of *War and Peace* or *Moby-Dick.*[23] As such, the work constitutes an effort to represent the total social hierarchy of Brazil at the turn of the century. At the upper end of the social pyramid we find the surviving remnants of the old aristocracy, the Baron de Canabrava, his wife Estela, and Adalberto de Gumúcio. Competing with the *fazendeiros* (wealthy ranchers) for political and economic power are members of the new haute bourgeoisie (allied with the republican forces in the federal capital), such as Epaminondas Gonçalves, editor of the *Jornal de Notícias* and leader of the Progressivist Republican Party of Bahia. Military leaders such as Colonel Moreira César and General Artur Oscar complete the list of those types who struggle for preeminence in the new regime. Below this group are a great many characters who compose the middle class, ranging from relatively prosperous professionals like Dr. José Batista de Sá Oliveira and the lawyer Lélis Piedades to itinerant backlands traders, the Vilanova brothers. This group includes many federal army officers such as Lieutenant Pires Ferreira and clerics such as João Evangelista de Monte Marciano.

Lower down the social scale we find skilled craftsmen and laborers such as the tracker and guide, Rufino, enlisted men such as Sergeant Frutuoso Medrado, and various renegade priests of the backlands such as Father Joaquim, who support the Canudos rebellion. Those who fall beneath even this rudimentary level of economic existence include most of the *jagunços*[24] who follow the Counselor—former *cangaceiros* (bandits) such as Abbot João (João Abade), ex-slaves from the coastal plantations such as Big João (João Grande), the physically deformed such as the Lion of Natuba (León de Natuba), orphans and social outcasts such as Maria Quadrado and the Little Blessed One (el Beatito), and the nameless blacks and Indians who settle their own neighborhoods of Mocambo and Mirandela in Canudos.

The War of the the End of the World captures not only the hierarchic class structure of Brazilian society, but also provides an encyclopedic account of the varied regional identities, races, professions, political institutions, social organizations, religious groups, gender roles, and psychosexual practices of late nineteenth-century Brazil. The war in Canudos brings together gauchos from the southern plains, soldiers from the great cities of the coast, and the impoverished *sertanejos* of the northeastern interior of the country. All principal racial groups in Brazil are represented: Africans, Europeans, and Amerindians, and all possible ethnic intermixtures. The major social and cultural institutions of Brazil—the church, army, police, judiciary, federal and provincial legislatures and executive branches, business and industry, the media, the legal and medical professions—all play a signficant role in the narrative. And like *War and Peace*, Vargas Llosa's novel moves easily between the often separate worlds of men and women. Many of the most compelling characters in the novel—Jurema, Estela, Maria Quadrado—are female, and their experiences, however limited by nineteenth-century Brazilian social conventions, become lenses through which the great movements of Latin American history are viewed. Vargas Llosa also makes a pointed effort to present a broad spectrum of sexual practices and experiences in his novel: conventional heterosexual marriage, homosexual relationships, ascetic sexual abstinence, brutal and sadistic rapes, prostitution, homicidal sexual jealousy, dangerously repressed erotic drives, voyeurism, infantile sexual dependency, masochism, fetishism, and forms of spiritualized eroticism that seem to transcend physical need. The odd or gratuitous scenes that appear to disrupt the architectonic structure of the novel—the rape of Sebastiana, the revenge-murder of Sergeant Medrado—ultimately serve an epic objective: History is dispersed and preserved in a multitude of characters, events, subplots, and episodes in order that its total movement can be registered in the most comprehensive and individualized manner possible.

As a neo-Hegelian critic, Lukács insists upon the central role played by the "world historical individual" in the great movements of history. Nevertheless, he argues that in the historical novel, as opposed to the tragic drama, the great man of history typically does not occupy center stage, but instead remains "a minor figure."[25] The world-historical individual appears only briefly, in order to fulfill his historical mission, and otherwise remains in the background.[26] Critics of *The War of the End of the World* have noted the peculiarly laconic and distant character of the Counselor and the almost total occlusion of his varied and lengthy life prior to the founding of Canudos. This strikes many critics as especially odd given the abundance of contemporary information about the life of Antônio Mendes Maciel (a large body of his meditations and sermons have been preserved, as have several letters he wrote to Brazilian newspapers criticizing the new republican government in Rio de Janeiro).[27] Although the relative absence of direct discourse on the part of the Counselor is explained to some extent by Vargas Llosa's efforts to solve a technical problem—how to render into contemporary Spanish the distinctive Brazilian dialect of the nineteenth-century *sertanejos*—the literary portrait of a remote and enigmatic figure also accords neatly with the generic conventions of the historical novel. Vargas Llosa explains that for him to approach the Counselor too closely would dissipate the mythic aura that surrounds him.[28] By suppressing any detailed account of his early life, by preserving his silence, by generally keeping him in the background of the story, Vargas Llosa succeeds in representing the Counselor as a monumental figure, the personification of a wider historical movement affecting all levels of Brazilian society. His dignity and historical stature suffer no diminishment as a result of an intrusively intimate and overly detailed representation of his personal life.[29]

The circumscribed representation of the world-historical individual makes possible and necessary the central narrative role of historically "minor" figures. Just as in the novels of Walter Scott, characters who possess relatively little or no political authority occupy the narrative center of *The War of the End of the World*. Vargas Llosa speaks of his novel as a kind of counter-history, as an attempt to supplement the official view of the past with one written from the perspective of the vanquished.[30] Consequently, many of the characters who play pivotal roles in the story—Big João, Abbot João, Galileo Gall, Maria Quadrado, the Little Blessed One, the Lion of Natuba, the Dwarf (el Enano), Rufino, Jurema—are based upon historical figures about whom almost nothing is known or are created entirely out of the author's imagination. Although direct dialogue among these characters is infrequent, their thoughts, feelings, words, and actions are presented by Vargas Llosa with great dramatic force. His extended and detailed literary treatment of "minor" historical figures allows them to emerge from the obscurity of official histories to become heroic figures, capable of impressive acts of physical courage, self-sacrifice, administrative genius, and civic devotion that astonish even themselves. The Counselor thereby appears all the more remarkable in his remoteness as the ultimate cause of these extraordinary transformations that turn ordinary, wretched, and even vicious or contemptible men and women into a cohesive and disciplined political, religious, and ethical community capable of challenging the power of the modern Brazilian republic.

Lukács dismisses the tragic novel as a distinctive sub-genre, but makes full allowance for what he calls "the tragic atmosphere" that permeates the historical novel. Following Hegel's lead, Lukács argues that the "complex interaction of concrete historical circumstances in their process of transformation" provides the basis for a tragic conflict that defines an age.[31] *The War of the End of the World* vividly illustrates that the decisive engine of political upheaval and transformation in the modern world is often an *idea* or *theory* of history. The antagonists in the Canudos war share a common belief that history is on their side; they fight to the death in a struggle over which of the mutually exclusive versions of the "end" of history will prevail.

The power of the Counselor over his followers depends in part upon the vivid and compelling story of human history his messianic prophecy conveys:

The end was near—it could be seen as clearly as Canudos from the heights of A Favela. The Republic would keep on sending hordes with uniforms and rifles to try to capture him, . . . but no matter how much blood he might cause to flow, the Dog would not bite Jesus. There would be a flood and then an earthquake. An eclipse would plunge the world into total darkness. . . . But when the mists dispersed, one bright clear dawn, the men and women would see the army of Dom Sebastião all round them on the hills and slopes of Canudos. The great

King would have defeated the Can's bands, would have cleansed the
world for the Lord. (Pp. 49–50)

This eschatological version of human history ennobles the impoverished inhabitants of Canudos, providing them for the first time in
their lives with an exalted, indeed critical role in fufilling God's plan
for the world. It makes them capable of extraordinary heroism and
self-sacrifice as well as of appalling cruelty and savagery.

Although both Galileo Gall and Moreira César are aggressively
atheistic, displaying a sovereign contempt for the religious mysticism
of the masses, they too harken to teleological philosophies that fuel
their political ambitions. In a letter to his fellow anarchists intended
for publication, Gall, a follower of Marx, Bakunin, and Proudhon,
dismisses the sermons of the Counselor as mystical superstition, but
nevertheless insists that they contain an esoteric historical truth in
accord with his own materialist creed:

> Are religious, mythical, dynastic symbols the only ones capable of
> rousing from their inertia masses subjected for centuries to the super-
> stitious tyranny of the Church, and is this the reason why the Counselor
> makes use of them? . . . We know, comrades, that there is no such
> thing as chance in history, that however fortuitous its course may seem,
> there is always a rationality lying hidden behind even the most puzzling
> outward appearances. (P. 83)

Colonel Moreira César's historicist faith is no less deeply engraved
than that of the Counselor or Galileo Gall. A Jacobin progressive
under the influence of Auguste Comte, the colonel believes absolutely
in the "irreversible" progress of history (p. 173). For the colonel, the
army, rather than the Christian faithful or the revolutionary masses,
must assume the task of carrying out the iron law of history. During a
heated exchange with the Baron de Canabrava, Moreira César expresses his utter contempt for the hopelessly anachronistic representative of the *ancien régime* and for all other remnants of the past that
hinder the work of Brazilian modernization:

> That's what the army is for. To bring about national unity, to bring
> progress, to establish equality among all Brazilians, to create a strong,
> modern country. We are going to remove the obstacles in the way, I
> promise you: Canudos, you, the English merchants, whoever blocks our
> path. . . . You belong to the past, you are someone who is looking
> backward. Don't you realize how ridiculous it is to be a baron when
> in just four years it will be the beginning of the twentieth century?
> (P. 217)

The tragic events of *The War of the End of the World* thus clearly emerge out of what its characters perceive to be the linear movement of history. But for Vargas Llosa, the violent conflicts that result from the emergent historical consciousness of "the people" do not demonstrate the validity of historicism. The tragedy of Canudos, which leads to the violent deaths of twenty-five to thirty thousand *sertanejos* and two to three thousand federal soldiers,[32] suggests rather that historicism is itself a form of fanaticism and a principal source of cataclysmic political violence in the modern world. For Vargas Llosa, the tragedy of Canudos is historically "necessary" only in the sense that the participants in this human catastrophe are all utterly convinced of the absolute validity of their particular understandings of "the end of history" and incapable of mediating their ideological disagreements through any means other than total war.

By arguing that Vargas Llosa writes an antihistoricist historical novel, I do not mean to suggest that he tries to evade history in favor of some apolitical or purely aesthetic alternative. His repudiation of Marxism and his subsequent endorsement of democratic liberalism has not led him to ignore politics in his fiction. But it has forced him to consider the possibility of reconceiving politics on a non-Hegelian and nonhistoricist basis. *The War of the End of the World* provides Vargas Llosa with an opportunity to compare very different regimes, which coexisted simultaneously (though not peacefully) in spite of the fact that they seem to belong to different historical epochs. Vargas Llosa focuses on a suggestive era of Latin American history when the varied possibilities for organizing human society were less restricted than they appear to be today, an historical "window of opportunity" when radically different notions of social organization competed with one another, each claiming to represent the best regime and the brightest future for humanity.

At least four, and possibly five, different conceptions of the well-organized political community are represented in Vargas Llosa's novel. The Baron de Canabrava, along with Estela, Rufino, and Jurema, exemplify, at least early in the novel, a feudal and aristocratic order that had survived in Brazil for centuries. Colonel Moreira César and Epaminondas Gonçalves are the most prominent spokesmen for an alternative modern Jacobin republic organized along rigidly secular and positivist lines. The anarchist Galileo Gall embodies the hope for an even more radically utopian socialist regime that dispenses with both parliamentary institutions and military oligarchies in favor of classless egalitarian socialism. The Counselor rejects both the aristocratic feudalism of the Baron and the radical progressivism of César, Gonçalves, and Gall in favor of a theocratic regime organized according to his own peculiarly messianic and syncretistic version of the Catholic faith. Finally, the very remote figure of President Prudente de Moraes represents a moderate bourgeois parliamentarianism that remains ill-defined, a vaguely liberal-centrist alternative to the other more fully developed political possibilities in the novel. To the extent that any prominent character may be said to speak for the values of this social alternative, it is the anonymous nearsighted journalist (modeled on Euclides da Cunha), who embodies the peculiarly fragmented vision of liberal individualism. As diverse as all these political possibilities are, they may be roughly grouped according to their supporters into the liberal and socialist partisans of modernity on the one hand and the aristocratic and theocratic opponents of modernity on the other. Thus, the story of Canudos enables Vargas Llosa to explore in depth the issue of modernization, with a comprehensive view of the full range of alternatives to modernity. As the fundamental dramatic conflicts of the novel arise from the political struggle for power and legitimacy among these competing visions, I will examine each in detail as embodying a distinctive and mutually exclusive idea of the just society.

III

As its most eloquent defender, the Baron de Canabrava argues that the aristocratic and feudal order is "rooted in tranquillity" (p. 215). For the better part of three centuries that span the Portuguese and Brazilian empires, the feudal landowners in cooperation with the crown and church have aimed at a form of social stability based upon a strict political hierarchy. The psychological or ideological basis of this rule is chiefly a conservative desire for order and the complementary cultivation of obedience, duty, paternalism, and personal honor as the principal civic virtues. Falsely accused of abetting the rebels as part of a neomonarchist and English-backed plot to restore the Brazilian Empire, the baron perceives the rebellion in the backlands as the culminating threat to his continued rule:

> Those people don't steal or murder or set fires when they feel that order reigns, when they see that the world is organized, because nobody has more respect for hierarchy than they. . . . But the Republic destroyed our system through unrealistic laws, substituting unwarranted enthusiasms for the principle of obedience. (P. 215)

The baron responds to the charges of the Jacobins by pointing out that he and his kind in Bahia have more to lose personally and politically from the rebellion than any other social class. From the baron's perspective, the rebellion appears as a particularly disastrous if unintended effect of progressive changes instituted by the new republic, to which the old aristocracy was opposed. The republicans and Jacobins correctly perceive the rebellion as a *reaction* to their rule, but it is not the result of a *reactionary* plot hatched by the old aristocracy.

In fact, the rebellion spells the final collapse of the traditional system of semifeudal relationships, a patriarchal order premised upon a mutual if unequal set of social responsibilities. In exchange for their obedience and labor, the peasantry of the *fazendas* receives the financial and moral assistance of the baron (p. 91). He is renowned, if not universally respected, for his magnanimity. Chiefly responsible for the establishment of "roads, railways, bridges, charity hospitals, schools, and a multitude of public works" in Bahia (p. 130), the baron also prides himself on having freed his slaves some five years before the empire (not the republic) issued an emancipation decree (p. 214). Moreover, he is the godfather of most of his laborers and their families, and he assumes personal responsibility for the moral and social well-being of his charges, who include Rufino and Jurema. His frustrated attempt to resist the burning of his estate, Calumbi, is not motivated entirely out of economic self-interest or aristocratic pride. Unlike the *sertanejos,* who leave for Canudos, the baron and his wife possess other estates and financial resources that would enable them to go on with their lives without any significant decline in the luxuriousness of their existence. The baron's conversation with Pajeú reveals his loyalty, however paternalistic, to his "own" workers:

> Doesn't [the Counselor] see that haciendas burned down mean hunger and death for hundreds of families? . . . I will not allow you to raze the hacienda. . . . Not only on my account, but on account of the hundreds of people whose survival depends on this land. (P. 246)

By and large, Vargas Llosa draws an idealized and highly sympathetic portrait of this representative of the ancient regime.[33] The baron not only displays the virtues of noblesse oblige, aristocratic magnanimity, and civic devotion to what he understands as the common good of his people, but also exemplifies for most of the novel an enlightened devotion to reason and an accompanying suspicion of dangerous and potentially violent "enthusiasms" of all varieties.

Moreover, he and his wife appear as virtually the sole representatives in the novel of the cosmopolitan cultivation of arts, letters, and manners (the nearsighted journalist being the only other example). Vargas Llosa does not disguise the fact that their devotion to high culture depends upon their secure financial position. Their economic security within the old order allows the baron and his wife a certain freedom from material need, enabling them to view with measured contempt the single-minded devotion to money and power exemplified by the bourgeois arriviste, Epaminondas Gonçalves. Their great wealth provides the means for their extensive European travels and expensive worldly tastes that mitigate against the narrow chauvinism and extreme nationalism exemplified by Colonel Moreira César. Throughout his life, the baron views his political and financial power as something of a burden, one which serves to frustrate a longstanding desire to devote himself to intellectual and scientific pursuits rather than to the oppressive responsibilities and Machiavellian demands of politics (p. 533). As aristocratic patrons of arts and letters, the baron and his wife Estela stand as the isolated touchstones of a refined way of life that *The War of the End of the World* implicitly endorses and celebrates as an *aesthetic* phenomenon.

But the baron's aristocratic existence, with its obligations and privileges, appears increasingly anachronistic and futile by the close of the novel. The subplots involving the baron, Estela, Rufino, and his wife Jurema culminate in the final destruction of a feudal order swept away by historical change. Although the immediate threat to the old system of *fazendas* is the emergence of an antimodern and deeply conservative religious movement in Bahia, the net effect of this counterhistorical messianism is an acceleration of Brazilian modernization. Whereas the baron had long managed a mutually beneficial arrangement with the Counselor and the marauding bands of *cangaceiros,* the war in Canudos destroys an alliance that served to restrain the modernizing inroads of the new republic. Bending to the necessities of what he views as the new amoral politics, the baron refuses to turn over Gall (who has raped Jurema) to Rufino, thereby failing to honor his moral and social obligations to his godson and servant (p. 243). Rufino's subsequent repudiation of the moral authority of his patron signals the dissolution of the kind of traditional loyalty that maintained the aristocratic order (p. 243). The razing of Calumbi follows close upon the mass defection of the baron's servants and laborers, who leave the *fazenda* to fight for the Counselor. Left to wander amidst the chaos of the civil war after Rufino's death,

Jurema exemplifies the "masterless" *sertaneja* who no longer believes in the old moral codes and social institutions that formerly defined her place in the world (p. 307).

The destruction of Calumbi, Estela's descent into madness, the emasculation of the Autonomist Party, and the baron's retirement from active political life all spell the end of the old feudal order and its ethical universe. The baron assesses his declining fortunes without sentimentality:

> "I believe that we've seen the end of a style, of a certain way of conducting politics. . . . I admit that I've become obsolete. I functioned better in the old system, when it was a question of getting people to follow established customs and practices, of negotiating, persuading, using diplomacy and politesse. That's all over and done with today, of course." (P. 347)

The baron's world-weary characterization of Bahia's (and Brazil's) future foreshadows his political and moral collapse. His rape of Sebastiana, and his insistence upon a sinister ménage à trois with the terrified servant and the virtually incoherent Estela, signal the effective end of the old nobility as a viable moral or political alternative to modernity. Vargas Llosa's self-professed interest in sexuality and eroticism, fully in evidence in his recent novel, *In Praise of the Stepmother* (*Elogio de la madrastra*), here serves to illustrate the aristocracy in its late decadent phase. As with Stendhal's post-Napoleonic aristocrats, Vargas Llosa's postapocalyptic nobles must play out their political ambitions within the confines of the boudoir, with Sadean permutations as the predictable result.

The war in Canudos is the decisive event that spells the end of the feudal world; and yet, long before the Counselor takes up arms against the republic, numerous signs portend the coming dissolution of the aristocratic order. The very liberalism of the baron—his easy tolerance of the "intimate" relationship between Estela and her maid (p. 310), his aggressive support for progressive economic development in Bahia, his early emancipation of his slaves, his enlightened view of religious matters, his cosmopolitan distance from his own fatherland and its provincial ways—suggest that the Baron de Canabrava has himself been a (perhaps unwitting) agent in the destruction of the feudal way of life. In many ways, the Baron seems a perfect embodiment of the European liberalism that animated the last Brazilian Emperor, Pedro II, which both his contemporaries and modern historians argue greatly contributed to the weakening of monarchic

authority and the eventual demise of the Brazilian Empire.[34] Like the
French aristocracy in the eighteenth century, the baron subverts the
social hierarchy he aims to preserve by virtue of his innovative and
forward-looking impetuosity—another victim of the Hegelian "ruse
of reason." His scrupulously self-critical bent, his very sensitivity to
the deficiences of the old order—its dependency upon slave labor, its
extremely limited distribution of wealth and economic privilege, its
ethical inflexibility, its willingness to treat men and women as subhu-
man creatures—contributes to his loss of political authority and to
his ultimate historical obsolescence. The baron introduces to Bahia
many individual features of modern political life without recognizing
that such innovations cannot ultimately be separated from a new and
comprehensive historicist ideology that requires the political annihilation of the outmoded feudal order. The baron and his kind are
swept away by history, at least in part, because the aristocratic system they represent has no *idea* of history, no effective ideology with
which to resist the progressive appeal that characterizes the political
demand for modernity or the reactionary call for a return to a divinely sanctioned social order. Offering no alternative to competing
versions of the end of history, the aristocracy can only decay, since its
existence ultimately depends upon an uncritical appeal to tradition
and "tranquillity" that seems increasingly absurd in the face of violent revolution, messianic enthusiasm, and historical "fate."

IV

By contrast to the moribund aristocracy, the Jacobins of the novel
identify their conception of the virtuous republic with modernity. In
his commentary upon *The War of the End of the World,* Vargas
Llosa argues that the principal source of Brazilian Jacobinism was the
positivist philosophy of Auguste Comte, whose ideas became influential through Benjamin Constant Botelholde Magalhães, an intellectual, mathematician, and engineer who held a teaching position at a
military school in Rio de Janeiro and became minister of war after the
proclamation of the republic.[35] Vargas Llosa notes that positivism,
while influential throughout much of Latin America, was especially
so in Brazil:

> In Brazil, positivism had much more influence than in France itself. I
> think that Brazil was the only place in the world where these temples of
> reason that Comte suggested were actually built, temples that should be
> oriented toward Paris as the mosques are oriented toward Mecca. In

Brazil, some temples were built with this orientation. Benjamin Constant, in the military school in Rio de Janeiro, taught the young officers that the only way for Brazil to become a modern country, a progressive society, was to become a republic, substitute this old-fashioned, obsolete system of monarchy with a republic.[36]

Through an unusual alliance with civilian politicians and the urban intelligentsia of Brazil, the military succeeded in establishing the new republic in 1889.[37] Colonel Moreira César, a protégé of the second president of the Brazilian republic, Marshal Floriano Peixoto, represented the ultimate political aspirations of the Jacobin forces, whose supporters in Vargas Llosa's novel include Epaminondas Gonçalves, the leader of the Bahian Progressivist Party.

Although Comtean positivism lies behind Colonel César's infatuation with science and technology, his faith in inevitable historical progress, and his rational contempt for religion, it does not fully explain César's insistence that the army provide the institutional basis of a "Dictatorial Republic." To be sure, Brazilian intellectuals under the influence of Comte understood positivism to be consistent with the existence of dictatorship. They argued that only authoritarian rule was capable of preserving the first term in the Brazilian positivist credo, "Order and Progress."[38] In fact, many Brazilian positivists regarded the lack of firm authoritarian rule as the chief deficiency of the old monarchy under Emperor Pedro II. And at least some positivists such as Constant and Demétrio Ribeiro sought to strengthen the executive and central government as the necessary prerequisites for bringing about real social progress in the nation.[39] But whatever the specifically Comtean roots of Moreira César's authoritarianism, his ideology, insofar as Vargas Llosa represents it, consists of an eclectic mix of Brazilian Comteanism, Latin American militarism, "Third World" nationalism, and French revolutionary Jacobinism. Vargas Llosa identifies Colonel César with a specifically modern kind of political autocrat, the "nasserista," a nationalistic and militaristic leader of the Third World whose historical prototype is the Egyptian ruler, Gamal Abdel Nasser.[40] Explicitly compared in the novel with Robespierre (p. 247), César belongs to a long line of radically progressive and potentially dictatorial figures that stretches from the French Revolution to the emergence of contemporary postcolonial nation-states. The left-wing military junta under the command of General Juan Velasco Alvarado that ruled Peru from 1968 until 1975, a junta openly welcomed by the Castro regime but vehemently opposed by Vargas Llosa, provides one of the more immediate analogues of César's "Dictatorial Republic."[41]

Moreira César and the Jacobins look not only to France but also to the United States as models for the new Brazilian republic. Unlike the Nassers and Velasco Alvarados who come later, the Brazilian Comteans were not openly hostile to the United States and its market-oriented approach to the challenge of material progress.[42] Although opposed to the presence of English merchants, who in their view have historically exploited the poor of Brazil, César and his adherents are anxious to welcome North American business interests into the country as a source of the technical assistance and financial capital that the republic needs to accelerate the pace of modernization (p. 214).[43] That France and the United States at the turn of the century should appear to the Brazilian Jacobins as imitable models of progressive change only serves to underscore the common liberal republican heritage of the French, American, and Brazilian revolutions, all premised upon the rejection of premodern European forms of monarchic, theocratic, or aristocratic rule.

Nevertheless, the Jacobin admiration for the United States and cultivation of North American investments in Brazil, coupled with an equally fervent hatred of British political and economic intervention, hint at an unresolved tension at the heart of César's political ideology. The colonel combines an intensely nationalistic perspective with a deep respect for certain foreign ideas and ways of life. César's ideal of progress is derived from Europe—French positivism—while his pursuit of a strong centralized national government is aimed in part at ridding Brazil of unwanted foreign (specifically British) influence. The concept of "the nation" and the specific rhetoric of nationalism have often posed intractable theoretical and practical difficulties for many progressive political movements.[44] Against the traditional background of a feudal order that depends on regional identity and local attachments (to lord, estate, guild, or town), nationalism might well appear as a progressive alternative. The Jacobins desire that the *sertanejos* cease to conceive of themselves as the godchildren of feudal overlords or as the citizens of the *sertão* or even of Bahia; they are to become *Brazilians*.[45] Colonel César's army, drawn from many different regions of Brazil, represents the forcible attempt to constitute a national cultural identity appropriate to a centralized nation-state. Thus, "nationalization" serves an integrative function that appears fully compatible with progress and modernization. However, given the necessarily *limited* and *sovereign* conception of the nation, a modern Brazil must be defined in contrast to other nation-states—such as Britain—that threaten the integrity of Brazilian national identity by the very fact that they possess the autonomy and strength the Jacobin nationalists envy.[46] The colonel's insistence that Brazil be brought into the twentieth century as a *"modern* nation" carries with it the express desire to become like other modern nation-states, while his demand that Brazil be a *"strong* modern nation" underlines his fear that in the process his country might be subsumed into or dominated by another political entity or global system. Although he fights against what he believes to be foreign interference in and political and economic domination of Brazil, he necessarily relies upon French rifles, German cannons, American capital, and European military tactics and political ideologies to imagine and thereby create a new and specifically Brazilian national identity (p. 213). Like all "nasseristas," Colonel Moreira César makes use of a rhetoric of national autonomy and identity that exemplifies the intermediate and contradictory role that nationalism plays in the process of global modernization.

Positivism teaches César that the loyalty of the *sertanejos* to their regional customs, religious beliefs, and feudal ideology is necessarily mystical and rationally ungrounded. However, Colonel César refuses to submit his own faith in Brazilian nationalism to a comparable rational critique. Presumably, "the fatherland" possesses a privileged status for him, though it is not at all evident why this should be so. Defenders of both liberalism and Marxism have argued against the irrationality of economic or political nationalism, the former because it disrupts the free flow of goods and peoples in a global market, the latter because it violates the international unity of the world proletariat. In actual practice, however, neither liberal democratic nor socialist regimes have seen fit to jettison the nation-state, thereby drawing back from Kojève's conclusion that the inevitable and logical conclusion to the process of modernization is the universal homogeneous state. In César's case, the nationalistic aims of the Jacobins would seem to be simultaneously consistent with and opposed to the ultimate aim of integrating Brazil into the modern world.

César is neither a political coward nor a moral hypocrite. His fusion of ardent nationalism and political progressivism may ultimately be philosophically incoherent, but it does not impugn the authenticity of his political convictions or the sincerity of his moral commitments. Like Robespierre, César is incorruptible, courageous, idealistic, and committed to improving, at any cost and by every means, the lives of the common people, from whose ranks he has risen. The contradiction Moreira César embodies is not principally that between progressive idealism and recalcitrant political reality, but between the historical means and ends of modernization. That contradiction manifests itself in and through the tragic events it foments. Like Robespierre's Committee for Public Safety, the Brazilian army serves the Jacobins as the essential but violent means for bringing about historical progress. As the colonel sees it, democratic procedures, representative institutions, civilian government, and the rule of law are mere obstacles to the great leap forward. César envisions a "Dictatorial Republic, without a parliament, without political parties, in which the army, like the Church in the past, would be the nerve center of a secular society frantically pursuing henceforth the goal of scientific progress" (p. 145). The "Dictatorial Republic" finds its philosophic antecedent in Rousseau's *The Social Contract*. For the Brazilian Jacobins, a hierarchically ordered and centrally administered regime governed by a professional modern army provides the closest contemporary analogue of Rousseau's neo-Spartan polity; the head of the army fulfills the role of Rousseau's "legislator," who embodies and executes the "general will." Although Comte's own variant of the supreme leader, the "positivist superman," is not specifically mentioned in the novel, it provides another philosophic source for the dictatorial rule of the colonel.[47] In any case, for Moreira César, the distinction between military authority and civilian rule must be abolished in favor of the former; Brazil should be run as a large and efficiently organized machine under the direct command of the highest ranking military officer.

The modern scientific basis of the dictatorial republic provides the ground for Colonel César's claim that the Jacobin regime signals a progressive advance beyond earlier forms of government. But the strictly authoritarian management of scientific, economic, and technological progress embraced by the colonel in no way ensures the establishment of a democratic, much less a liberal government. Like a host of Marxist intellectuals, including Lenin and Lukács, who argued in favor of concentrating power in the hands of an intellectual vanguard, the Party, the Jacobin colonel sees no necessary connection between the material progress of Brazilian society and the progressive expansion of individual rights or the extension of democratic suffrage. The policies of the "nasserista" thus highlight two different strands of modernization that Fukuyama has identified and analyzed. Technoscientific progress proceeds in a linear historical manner and forms one of the principal engines of modernization; however, scientific and technological progress, typically driven by the demands of military competition, does not guarantee liberal democratic progress.[48] The at best tenuous relationship between the linear history of modern scientific technology and the progressive history of liberal democratic reform is in fact better dramatized in Vargas Llosa's epic historical novel than it is in his essay devoted to Karl Popper. For as we have noted, in the latter, Vargas Llosa takes for granted that the progress "in medicine, in astronomy, [and] in physics" is somehow connected with a "similar" development in "social organization," namely "democratic culture." However, he fails to identify the link between the two developments, which remain at best homologous, but essentially distinct in *The War of the End of the World*.

Inevitably, the hierarchical and disciplinary character of military rule contravenes many liberal notions of human freedom. César's iron-fisted control over his troops, exemplified by the numerous punishments and executions arbitrarily meted out to deserters and malefactors, suggests the ways in which the Jacobin desire for freedom and equality easily passes over into cruelty, the subversion of the rule of law, the neglect of civil and juridical rights, and the rigid maintenance of a rank order that controverts democratic processes. Although César understands Jacobin rule to be the opposite of the anachronistic feudal system of the Baron de Canabrava, it is difficult to find much evidence for his claim to bring liberty, dignity, and prosperity to the masses of Brazil, who suffer continual hardship and even death under his command.

The dangers of Brazilian Jacobinism include the often violent and repressive measures employed by the armed forces against the rest of society. Despite the origins of his positivist credo in the principles of the Enlightenment, Colonel César harbors a deep distrust of all artists and intellectuals. He addresses the nearsighted journalist with scorn: "All intellectuals are dangerous. . . . Weak, sentimental, capable of making use of the best of ideas to justify the worst mischief. The country needs them, but they must be handled like animals that can't be trusted" (p. 213). César's words ominously suggest the inherent tendency of military juntas and dictatorial governments—from Pinochet and Odría to Velasco Alvarado and Castro—to censor their critics, control the media, and curtail artistic and intellectual freedom. For the Jacobin colonel, the very principles of intellectual freedom, essential to the flowering of enlightenment, must be subordinated to the immediate political needs of the military elite. Journalists and intellectuals are to be the servants and tamed pets of the dictatorial republic, promulgators of official propaganda, rather than independent critics of the government (p. 147).

Were the colonel's hostility toward civilian society limited to aristocrats and bourgeois intellectuals, one might at least make the case that his illiberal actions are nevertheless consistent with his progressive desire to promote the material welfare of the poor. But Vargas Llosa suggests that the colonel's Jacobinism is a form of ideological fanaticism that eventually devours the very people whose interests it was intended to defend and promote. César's brutal torture and execution of the townsfolk of Monte Santo, whom he regards as collaborators of the Counselor, is a foretaste of the atrocities that the army, in the name of the Brazilian republic, will commit on a colossal scale once it takes Canudos (pp. 221–22). The events in Bahia thus look forward to those in the Peruvian Andes, in which the native populations have become the victims of both the military and the *Sendero Luminoso,* who attempt to convert the peasantry to their respective causes through violent intimidation.

But perhaps the most suggestive historical parallel is once again the French Revolution. The Committee of Public Safety provides the first historical example of ideological violence of a distinctly post-enlightenment variety: the mass executions of "the Terror" and the genocidal war against the Breton peasants in the Vendée. With far less justification than Robespierre had in his situation, Moreira César views the *sertanejos* as servants "of a retrograde caste whose interest it is to keep Brazil in a backward state the better to exploit it" (p. 221). The colonel fails to comprehend the nature of the rebellion that he attempts to crush. He insists that behind the Counselor are the forces of the old aristocracy and the English Crown. He does not believe that the *jagunços* could actually be fighting out of a legitimate dissatisfaction with and implacable hatred for the modern secular values that the republic represents. The uncompromising antimodernism and religious conservatism of the Counselor's followers upset his most deeply held belief that the Brazilian people *must* ultimately be on the side of the Jacobin cause and historical progress. Inevitably, the colonel is forced to conceive of the Canudos uprising as another Vendée, which, despite the claims of the *sertanejos,* really serves the interests of monarchists, aristocrats, and foreign powers.[49] The colonel consistently looks "behind" or "beyond" the actual *sertanejos* in order to discern the dim outlines of ideological enemies who exploit the "authentic" Brazilian masses for whom he claims to fight. Confronted with individual flesh and blood peasants who have suffered humiliating and brutal treatment, such as the deformed albino girl raped by the colonel's troops, César posits for the news media an idealized theoretical version of the oppressed Brazilian people in order to justify the actions of the army. Inevitably the individual victim and her particular story fail to sustain the interest of the colonel, who forgets the girl as soon as he has punished her assailants (p. 223).

The particular failures of César's military tactics, based as they are on specifically modern European models of warfare quite unsuited to the realities of guerrilla warfare in the *sertão,* mirror the larger debacle of César's political campaign. Just as he fails to understand the *sertanejos,* he fails to comprehend the military significance of the topography and the climate of their region. The tragic irony of César's position is that the *sertanejos* who follow the Counselor come to view the colonel as the consummate *foreign* tyrant. From their perspective, César, the Jacobins, and the Brazilian army are all agents of an external and utterly alien satanic power. Vargas Llosa summarizes the point in his commentary on his novel:

> What is extraordinary is that the people followed Conselheiro and accepted his ideas. They followed because they could understand what Conselheiro was telling them. Conselheiro was a charismatic figure; he had a way of reading the minds and hearts of very simple people like the peasants. On the other hand they could not understand the positivist ideas that were behind the republic, this abstract institution of the republic, these representative bodies. All such abstractions were totally remote from their daily lives. . . . When these foreigners arrived (and these military troops were foreigners, for the peasants had never seen people from Rio or São Paulo), they felt their culture was threatened. They had a culture of their own, a culture made up of primitive things, primitive customs, dogmatic religious ideas, but a culture that gave them a feeling of belonging to something that was shared by all of them. They had nothing to share with these foreigners, who arrived there with Moreira César talking about the republic and positivist ideas. These foreigners were even atheists, like César, who considered religion an obstacle to progress and modernization. For these peasants his beliefs confirmed that the republic was the antichrist.[50]

The liberator thus becomes the oppressor, the Brazilian nationalist the hated agent of a "foreign" power, the enlightened and progressive Jacobin the barbaric and hated "Throat Slitter."

V

Galileo Gall's political ideology is an improvised and inconsistent concoction of Pierre Joseph Proudhon's scientific socialism (which was to inspire French syndicalism well into this century) and Mikhail Alexandrovich Bakunin's anarchism (pp. 55–56, 81, 122). Like another revolutionary manqué who appears in Vargas Llosa's later fiction, the Trotskyite Alejandro Mayta, Gall is characterized by a certain ideological distance from orthodox—that is Marxian— socialism. While both Proudhon and Bakunin were extremely active in the First International, they were also criticized by and critical of Marx. In particular, both opposed what they perceived as Marx's endorsement of a centralized political authority responsible for the administration of all economic and social life, and both attempted to offer alternatives to Marx's etatism, which they argued promised to be oppressive.[51] Gall would therefore appear to represent a deviation from the kind of Marxian socialism that dominated the Soviet Union and Eastern Europe from 1917 until the collapse of communism in 1991 and that, in spite of (or perhaps because of) Castro's Soviet-style regime, had become increasingly suspect in Latin America by the mid-1970s. In effect, Vargas Llosa projects into an earlier era a late twentieth-century representative of revisionary (neo-) Marxism, a figure whose ideas appear to mark an advance beyond the impasse posed by the depressing legacy of totalitarian Soviet rule. By return- ing to a historical period before the establishment of official state socialism, when a more fluid sense existed of what constitutes pro- gressive revolutionary thinking, Vargas Llosa can create a credible character whose radical ideas will seem to the New Left of Europe and the Americas to be more avant garde than those of Marx.

Both as a political activist who has participated in unsuccess- ful revolutionary uprisings in Europe, the Middle East, and the Americas, and as an intellectual attuned to the most recent develop- ments in social theory and psychology, Gall has much in common with the radical left of the 1960s and 1970s. Vargas Llosa himself compares Gall, a veteran of the Paris Commune of 1870, to those twentieth-century *"revolucionarios europeos"* who were to follow in his footsteps, radicals who looked to the Third World in general, and Latin America in particular, for the resurrection of their grand revo- lutionary ideas and hopes, after they had been defeated in Europe.[52] Vargas Llosa's political essays from the late 1970s repeatedly turn to a consideration of influential neo-Marxist intellectuals who endorsed revolutionary violence in the Third World and terrorism in Europe.[53] In many respects, Galileo Gall's ideas, however much they may owe to the nineteenth-century writings of Proudhon and Bakunin, reso- nate with a good deal of neo-Marxist thinking in this century. His explanation of criminality and mental illness among the poor as products of the structural violence of capitalist society "echoes" the thinking of Frantz Fanon or the German psychiatrist Wolfgang Hu- ber, who advocated revolutionary terrorism as a form of psychiatric therapy; Gall's assumption that sexual and political liberation are inextricably linked anticipates Herbert Marcuse's synthesis of Freud and Marx; and his insistence that real political equality must neces- sarily include the equality of the sexes finds its analogue in the work of Sartre and Beauvoir. To be sure, Gall's utopian vision of the new society in Canudos, "a libertarian citadel, without money, without masters, without politics, without priests, without bankers, without landowners, a world built with the faith and the blood of the poorest of the poor" (p. 226), reflects not so much a consistent and detailed social philosophy as it does the antibourgeois and anticapitalist ro- manticism of the radical student movements of the 1960s and 1970s. A deep disaffection for all forms of political and religious authority, a comprehensive hatred of social hierarchies and formalities, a longing for total sexual freedom—all are elements of a sweeping antinomian project with its ultimate source in Rousseau that seeks to return human life to an unregulated state of nature. Vargas Llosa draws upon historical accounts of a group of nineteenth-century Catalan anarchists operating in Barcelona for his portrait of Gall; he supple- ments his characterization with a number of particulars based on the Scottish anarchist, journalist, and essayist Cunninghame Graham.[54] Nevertheless, both Gall's ideas and his fate distantly mirror those of more renowned revolutionary heroes of the left-wing student move- ments of the 60s and 70s, such as Che Guevara, Andreas Baader, and Ulrike Meinhof, figures whose political careers and personal lives, like that of Gall, ultimately ended in disaster.

   Galileo Gall therefore represents the hopes and potential not of an actually existing community, but of a utopia based on an imaginative blueprint imbued with the most up-to-date and radical social and political theories of his time. What Vargas Llosa found most intrigu- ing about the historical Catalan anarchists upon whom he based Gall's character was their avid interest in phrenology, a pseudo- science created by Franz Joseph Gall, "according to which the bones of the head were considered the materialization of the soul, of the moral and psychological characteristics of an individual."[55] Gall's devotion to phrenology, as well as to other fashionable pseudosciences, such as Cesare Lombroso's craniometry and mid-century theories of biologically based racial determinism (pp. 31–32), should be understood not as the idiosyncratic attachment of a progressive and otherwise rational theorist to his private hobbyhorses, but as a representative instance of the groundless claims to scientific truth made on the part of modern materialist political philosophies. Vargas Llosa suggests that the scientific basis of socialism—whether that of Proudhon (who coined the term "scientific socialism") or that of Marx—is ultimately no less chimerical than that of long-discredited disciplines such as phrenology and craniometry. Nor is the complete confidence Gall has in phrenology so very different from that which Marcuse, Fanon, or Adorno had in Freudian psychology.

In Vargas Llosa's novel the false science of phrenology illustrates the way in which the radical intellectual can dangerously misconstrue the realities of premodern political existence. Beginning with the assumption that political history and social life are ultimately derived from the material conditions of existence, Gall presumes to understand the rebellion in the *sertão* better than the *jagunços* themselves do. Gall employs in the social and political sphere the same interpretive strategies that he utilizes when confronting the psychophysical realm of human existence. One cannot deny that each individual has a skull with an individuated topography, or that certain shapes tend to repeat themselves among a sufficiently large number of cases. However, onto this neutral "landscape" of the skull, Gall projects an interpretive schema that allows him to reduce all spiritual, moral, intellectual, artistic, and social distinctions to a rudimentary set of classifiable physical features. The idea of transforming political philosophy into a social science on the model of modern natural science dates back at least as far as Hobbes's *Leviathan* (1651), if not Bacon's *The Advancement of Learning* (1605). However, for Vargas Llosa it is chiefly the materialist philosophies of thinkers such as Marx, Comte, Bakunin, Proudhon, and Lenin that have taken the dangerous and ultimately destructive step of assuming that they have succeeded in this enterprise.

Galileo Gall's interpretation of the revolt in Canudos displays in magnified form all the shortcomings of his "anarchophrenological" method. Gall insists on understanding a genuinely conservative, antimodern religious revolution as a progressive secular rebellion along the lines of the Paris Commune of 1870:

[Religion] could serve to rouse the victims of society from their passivity and incite them to revolutionary action, in the course of which rational, scientific truths would gradually take the place of irrational myths and fetishes. . . . It was of little moment that instead of speaking of justice and injustice, freedom and oppression, classless society and class society, they talked in terms of God and the Devil. He thought that when he arrived in Canudos he would see something he'd seen as an adolescent in Paris: a people bubbling over with revolutionary fervor. (Pp. 264–65)

Gall's analysis of the Canudos rebellion is wrong in almost every particular. Far from being the Machiavellian leader hiding his radical views behind the "façade of religion for a tactical reason" (p. 48) whom Gall imagines him to be, the Counselor is a genuinely religious leader, one in fact, profoundly devoted to the "conservative morality" Galileo detests. The reason the Counselor and the *jagunços* speak of God and the Devil is that they actually believe in these supernatural beings and assume they are active participants in the civil war in Bahia. If the rebels were to succeed in defeating the republic, which they call "the Antichrist" and the "Can" ("dog"), the irrational myths and fetishes Gall detests would become the foundational truths of a new theocratic regime, rather than "fade away" as he assumes (p. 226).

Gall does not completely lack access to the real facts about the Canudos uprising. Although he never sets foot in the city, he is privy to a great deal of first-hand testimony about the actual conditions there and even meets a number of the *jagunços*. His misunderstandings stem from his dogmatic interpretation of the facts according to a rigidly materialist and historicist ideology. When informed that the followers of the Counselor reject civil marriage, which they understand as a sacrilegious interference on the part of the republic with the holy rite of matrimony, Gall jumps to the conclusion that the rebels of Canudos have instituted "free love," "communal sex," and "free paternity" (pp. 45, 48). Gall's view bears no relation to the conditions in Canudos, in which the sanctity of marriage and family is honored only slightly less than that of ascetic chastity. In a similar vein, Gall understands the rejection of republican currency as heralding the abolition of money and private property and as paving the way for the establishment of communal property (pp. 48, 83). The reality of the situation is that the *jangunços* reject the coins of the republic because they are minted with what they regard as the image of the Antichrist on their face; coins with the effigies of the

Emperor Dom Pedro and Princess Isabel continue to circulate. Though the pilgrims in Canudos willingly surrender their goods for the glory of God and volunteer their labor for the building of the Temple of the Blessed Jesus, they view these acts as devotional forms of tithing and not as attempts to abolish personal property and eliminate the money economy.

Economic life in Canudos is rather strictly controlled by means of a number of interventionist and even socialistic measures. But the Vilanova brothers, who oversee the economic functioning of the community, are themselves merchants, whose chief responsibilities in Canudos prior to the war are to distribute goods to new arrivals and then to guarantee that the property rights of all individuals are observed. The redistribution of wealth in Canudos exists side by side with private property, entrepreneurial activity, and a small and rudimentary barter economy. But the most important feature of Canudos to which Gall is oblivious is that financial and material concerns are not the central focus of the community. The principal goal of the Counselor is not the abolition of the division of labor, the redistribution of income, the elimination of a money economy, or the communal ownership of the means of production; the highest aim of the Counselor, for whom all political and economic measures are merely instruments, is the worship of God and Jesus Christ. For those who seek their joy in heaven, the material cares of this world are of secondary importance, if not altogether irrelevant. The basic premise of Gall's social philosophy, the fundamental importance of material conditions for human happiness, is rejected by the ascetic and messianic Catholicism of a leader whose highest task is the spiritual salvation of the soul, not the care of the body.

Gall's insistence that religious beliefs are merely the superstructural effects of more basic material forces blinds him to the real power and unpredictable nature of the irrational elements of life. His rape of Jurema not only takes the poor peasant woman by surprise, it also shocks Gall himself. This highly idealistic revolutionary believes that he can simply channel his sexual desires into more productive political activities. Unfortunately for the oppressed and impoverished woman for whose sake Gall ostensibly agitates, his sophistical theoretical explanation of the relation between erotic and political activity proves to be seriously flawed. Especially deplorable is the refusal of this self-righteous theorist to admit that something is fundamentally wrong with his thinking or with his ethical commitments.

Gall rationalizes the rape as a historically farsighted act of political and sexual liberation: "Perhaps she'll be roused from her lethargy now and discover injustice. . . . Perhaps you've done her a service" (p. 104). Vargas Llosa's satire of radical left theorizing is merciless; the self-proclaimed liberator refuses to acknowledge the oppressive consequences of his own actions, contenting himself with a minor revision of his ideological paradigm.

Gall's failure to comprehend the real desires and beliefs of the Counselor and his followers, his inability to transcend the limitations of his own political ideology or to take seriously religious convictions, philosophic ideas, and political opinions alien to him, lead directly to his pathetic failure as a would-be revolutionary leader. One cannot doubt his commitment to the anarchist cause, his extraordinary courage, or even his martial skill as a guerrilla fighter. But these qualities prove insufficient for his ultimate task: to reach Canudos and fight (even die) for his anarchist ideals. The corollary to Gall's inability to understand the *sertanejos* on their own terms is his incapacity to make himself understood in terms comprehensible to them. Although a man of action, Gall suffers from an odd propensity that Vargas Llosa finds endemic among intellectuals on the radical left; Gall often retreats into a realm of theoretical preoccupations remote from political reality, where he finds himself as isolated from the masses he claims to represent as were Catholic scholastics from the laity in the Middle Ages.[56] In Gall's case, that isolation takes the specific form of linguistic estrangement. He plans to play a leading role in the rebellion in Canudos despite the fact that he lacks full command of the local dialect of Portuguese. At moments of crisis, when Gall most urgently needs to make himself clear to the *sertanejos,* he inevitably finds himself speaking broken Portuguese or even English—mere gibberish as far as the bewildered peasants are concerned. His linguistic misadventures form part of a larger pattern of miscommunication: Gall never manages to convey his political ideas and ambitions to those he would lead. To both the circus performers with whom he travels and their audience, Gall appears as some sort of eccentric magician or sideshow performer who can read the fortunes of an individual by feeling his skull (p. 201). To Pajeú and the *jangunços* who refuse to bring him to Canudos, Gall appears as merely a pathetic curiosity, a raving soul overwhelmed by the fear of "the dogs" who fight for the Antichrist (pp. 293–94). And to Jurema, Caifás, and Rufino, Gall remains a criminal rapist—a contemptible and dangerous man completely lacking in the virtues of honesty, fidelity, and above all honor, a monster who violates all the most revered ethical norms of the *sertanejos*.

Gall earnestly desires to help those whom he regards as poor and oppressed. But just as his attempts to lecture the downtrodden audiences of the circus troop only serve further to bore and depress them, his efforts to fight for the liberation of the *sertanejos* lead him to inflict further acts of cruelty upon them: the rape of Jurema and the murder of Rufino. Like the Jacobin general Moreira César, another idealist, Gall becomes the very thing he most detests, an oppressor of the masses. In both cases, the reversal of positions emerges dialectically out of a modern and progressive political ideology, ostensibly based on a scientific understanding of humanity and society that thinks of itself as an expression of the inevitable march of history. And yet it is that historical anachronism, the Baron de Canabrava, who proves most prescient when it comes to foretelling the fate of Gall: "The one thing he really wants to do is go die like a dog among people who don't understand him and whom he doesn't understand. He thinks that he's going to die like a hero, and the truth is that he's going to die exactly as he fears he will: like an idiot" (pp. 250–51).

VI

To suggest that the Counselor consciously rejects the movement of history or the consequences of dialectical materialism risks misrepresenting his religious beliefs. The Counselor's vision of God's divine plan for humanity does not even contain the notions of "modernization" or "secularization." These processes are understood by the Counselor only in terms of more fundamental ethical and religious categories: they are *evil*, the work of the Antichrist. The battle between Canudos and the republic is merely the most recent, and according to the Counselor, the final act in the cosmic struggle between God and the Devil. To be sure, the Counselor believes in the linear history of humanity, or to be more precise in a divine eschatology. The imminent end of the world, which the Counselor confidently prophesies, will complete a theological history that began with God's creation of the universe. Nevertheless, this Christian eschatology, even if retrospectively seen as an anticipation of philosophic historicism, remains distinct from it.[57] The Counselor does not acknowledge the existence of the most basic conceptual categories—modernization, secularization, historical progress, science, enlightenment, freedom, economic equality—that form the basis of the political philosophies of Moreira César and Galileo Gall.

The political community that the Counselor founds at Canudos is a theocracy. The legitimacy of the Counselor's rule is not based on a rational appeal to natural rights, the will of the people, the laws of historical development, or the benefits of enlightened self-interest. In Canudos divine authority supersedes all claims of unassisted human reason. The Counselor rules because he is God's prophet, because he makes known to the *jangunços* the Word of God. One of the greatest virtues of Vargas Llosa's novel is his largely successful attempt to capture life under theocratic rule as seen from inside the community. What he provides is not merely a sociological analysis of religious messianism from the perspective of a modern skeptic; he also makes every effort to render the psychological and social nuances of life in a nonmodern community as experienced by those who avidly embrace its beliefs and fully participate in its customs. In so doing, Vargas Llosa helps to dramatize for his modern readers how such irrational and even retrograde movements as those of Khomeini and the Counselor are both historically possible and politically popular.

Vargas Llosa has a considerable advantage over many traditional sociologists and historians who have attempted to account for outbreaks of messianism. As a novelist he does not offer a general theory of mass movements or religious hysteria, but instead individualized presentations of many quite different characters who follow the Counselor. Vargas Llosa presents the *jangunços* as something more than a faceless mass that has discovered its "class consciousness" or acknowledged its "common humanity"; they form a collectivity, but one made up of strikingly distinct and psychologically complex individuals, whose particular fears, hopes, and personal histories remain distinguishable from but ultimately related to one another in a cohesive manner.

One cannot say of the followers of the Counselor that they have been uniformly poor or powerless or ignorant. Nor have they all suffered from the same forms of social and political injustice. Despite repeated economic disasters, the Vilanova brothers are well on their way to becoming relatively prosperous merchants when they decide to follow the Counselor. Father Joaquim, though relatively poor, is well educated by local standards and has long possessed in the Church an avenue of social and economic advancement, though one he has declined to follow with any ardor. By joining the Counselor, this country priest stands to sacrifice his easygoing sexual pursuits, financial comforts, and any hope of rising within the Catholic hierarchy. As the most fearsome *cangaceiro* in the backlands, Satan João ignores bourgeois social mores and exercises arbitrary power over the *sertanejos* that in many ways rivals that of a local feudal lord like Adalberto de Gumúcio. His conversion to the cause of the Counselor cannot be explained as a desire for greater material prosperity, since he will have less in Canudos, or for greater liberty from the oppressive moral constraints of civil society, since he effectively prostrates himself before the authority of the religious leader. More generally, one cannot say that those who flock to Canudos do so because they believe that the material conditions of their lives will be improved or because their civil and political rights will be better secured. To the degree that characters as diverse as the Vilanova brothers, Big João, Maria Quadrado, Abbot João, the Little Blessed One, and the Lion of Natuba hunger for the same thing, it is for some intangible spiritual sustenance that only the Counselor seems able to provide.

One must, of course, remember that Vargas Llosa is not a religious writer, but a modern secular novelist, who portrays the impact of religious impulses on his characters. He makes palpable their spiritual cravings by dramatizing those psychological needs that are not fulfilled or only incompletely satisfied within modern secular societies. No amount of wealth, no extension of civil or human rights can ever alter the fact that the Lion of Natuba is irremediably deformed. No general change in economic or political conditions can provide the kind of dignity, respect, and, above all, intimate love that the Counselor gives him. Neither economic empowerment nor the public recognition of their social victimization could ever assuage the guilt and self-hatred that Maria Quadrado, Abbot João, and Big João harbor within themselves. What the Counselor alone can grant is something beyond the power of any secular political institution to deliver: a subjective feeling of peace and contentment in his presence, a confidence in having been truly forgiven one's crimes and misdeeds, a belief that one has been granted life anew, a sense of *blessedness*.

Of course, Canudos is finally more than an aggregate of individual psychological destinies. It is a political community centered around a strictly regulated set of religious practices and beliefs: "The life of the community was devoted to spiritual activities: prayers, funerals, fasts, processions, the building of the Temple of the Blessed Jesus, and above all the evening counsels that often lasted until far into the night. During those everything else in Canudos came to a halt" (p. 52). In this community there is no separation of church and state.

The Counselor's vehement objections to civil marriage, municipal burial, taxes, the census, and the metric system—all introduced under the republic—are an attack on the demarcation between the spiritual and temporal spheres of life characteristic of modern secular government. Even the Counselor's opposition to the census, which seems motivated by the secular fear that the republic will use it to reinstitute slavery, may be traced to a biblical source: 2 Samuel 24, wherein God punishes David for taking a census of his people.

While the Counselor's vision remains fixed on transmundane matters, his concrete efforts to realize on earth the holy life of a truly Catholic people signals a return to the universal claims of the Catholic Church to temporal authority during the European Middle Ages. (In Vargas Llosa's novel, one of the most characteristic impressions of foreign visitors to the *sertão* is that life in these parts—with its troubadours, religious mendicants, feudal estates, and messianic movements—closely resembles that of medieval Europe.) Although the Catholic hierarchy of Brazil officially condemns him for heresy, the Counselor remains steadfastly loyal to the Holy Catholic Church. As a mere *beato* (lay preacher), the Counselor depends upon official clerics such as Father Joaquim to perform holy rites for the people of Canudos. Moreover, the Counselor's claims to temporal authority are moderated by his loyalty to the old Brazilian Empire of Pedro II and its feudal order.[58]

However, with the fall of the empire and his growing political isolation during the Bahian civil war, the Counselor increasingly presumes to speak for the Church and the empire. His prophecy that the sixteenth-century Portuguese King, Dom Sebastião, will return from the bottom of the sea to lead the faithful of Canudos to victory over the republic suggests the degree to which fidelity to outside political and ecclesiastical authorities has been subsumed under the mantle of the Counselor's personal prophetic authority. The old empires, Portuguese and Brazilian, will serve the Counselor, rather than he them.

As Canudos loses all support from the Catholic Church and the landed barons, the Counselor's regime seems increasingly to take on the character of the Christian Church during its infancy in the first century A.D. While the Counselor never claims to be anything more than a prophet, his followers increasingly treat him as if he were divine, as if his word and the Word of God were one and the same. Vargas Llosa returns us via the modern secular era of nineteenth-century Brazil and the European Middle Ages to the epoch of primitive Christianity in the Near East. Canudos *is* Jerusalem, its streets and topography correspond to those of the holy city at the time of Christ (p. 106). For the Counselor and his followers, "history" is synchronous. The past age of Jesus remains immanent within the present moment that promises his return.

The apocalyptic faith of the inhabitants of Canudos provides a crucial ideological support of the Counselor's regime. The material inadequacies of life in Canudos, the extreme sacrifices required of its citizens, their blind submission to the Counselor's religious rituals and theological-political dogma, are all made acceptable by the fundamental communal belief that the end of the world and the Second Coming of Christ are at hand. The Counselor overcomes each believer's fear of death not by making life more secure, comfortable, equitable, or free, but by promising his followers eternal life: "Believers too might die, but three months and a day later, they would be back, their bodies whole and their souls purified by the brush of angels' wings and the breath of the Blessed Jesus" (p. 225). The willingness and even enthusiasm with which a poor, ill-equipped, untrained, and unsophisticated people fights against a modern army, the eagerness with which tens of thousands rush to embrace almost certain martyrdom, flow from their unshakable conviction that in dying for the Counselor they gain an everlasting life in heaven. From the perspective of the republic, the rebellion in Canudos is another Vendée, but from that of the Counselor's true believers, it is a holy war.

If at the center of Canudos we find a charismatic figure, a prophet, perhaps even a god, such a leader nonetheless requires a formal system of government in order to guarantee that the community he founds survives and prospers. The apocalyptic prophecies, the theological-political orthodoxies, the religious rituals and exhortations, provide an ideology and a set of mores.

But the political organization of the community remains an essential task once the Counselor abandons his mendicant and nomadic existence and decides to settle in Canudos. The disorganized and ragtag life of his early days is incompatible with the demands of founding a city. Not all aspects of life in the New Jerusalem are planned in advance, but gradually a governmental structure and a socioreligious hierarchy emerges. Immediately surrounding the charismatic figure of the Counselor is the inner circle of disciples who assume the principal administrative functions of government. Maria Quadrado heads the Sacred Choir, the group that attends to the daily personal needs of the Counselor. Big João assumes command of the

Catholic Guard, who serve as the praetorian force protecting the divine leader. As Street Commander, Abbot João is responsible for organizing and directing all military enterprises and defending the city. The Lion of Natuba serves as scribe and historian, the Little Blessed One as the highest ranking administrator of all religious functions. Finally, the Vilanova brothers direct the economic and civil affairs of the community, supervising everything from the distribution of farm land and the manufacture of armaments to the establishment of facilities for the care of the sick, aged, and orphaned.

In the end Canudos is annihilated, and Vargas Llosa implicitly challenges his reader to judge the ultimate success or failure of the Counselor's radical political alternative to the modern secular state. Despite his own liberal sympathies and his outspoken hostility toward the tradition of religious fanaticism he sees lurking behind contemporary forms of political intolerance in Latin America,[59] Vargas Llosa suggests that the *happiness* of those in Canudos remains a subjective possibility unassailable by reference to the material deprivations or ideological excesses of its inhabitants. Father Joaquim calls them "the happiest people I've ever seen, sir. It's difficult to grant that, even for me. But it's true, absolutely true. He's given them a peace of mind, a resigned acceptance of privations, of suffering, that is simply miraculous" (p. 254). But if it is finally impossible to refute the bliss of martyrdom (for what kind of rational argument can deny the existence of what is an admittedly subjective state?), Vargas Llosa can nevertheless point to the defects and failings of the Counselor's theocracy that are evident to those who remain outside the mystical circle of the elect.

To a defender of modernity, whether liberal democratic or Marxist, the economic conditions in Canudos are appallingly primitive, even well before the outbreak of the civil war. To be sure, a kind of rough economic egalitarianism reigns, but only by virtue of the fact that its inhabitants are equally impoverished, malnourished, sickly, and ill-housed. Because of the Counselor's success in converting the great bandits of the *sertão* to his cause, the security of life and property is greater than before, though almost any governmental system would mark an advance beyond the political chaos that has plagued the backlands since the decline of the empire. In short, on material or utilitarian grounds there is no reason to prefer life in Canudos to that in any modern industrialized state.

Moreover, while the community strictly enforces a moral code, the religious principles of Canudos are not compatible with civil liberties.

Freedom of religion, of the press, of opinion, of assembly cannot be said to have been actively suppressed in Canudos if only because rigid orthodoxy is the raison d'être of the community. All prospective members of the community must swear allegiance to the Counselor's peculiar faith or be turned away from the city (p. 105). Obviously a range of personal choices concerning sexual activity is out of the question in Canudos. Nor are men and women left to decide for themselves the occupations and pursuits for which they are best suited; as among the Igbos of *Things Fall Apart,* the division of labor in Canudos corresponds to strictly defined gender roles. Women prepare food, tend the sick, elderly, and young, and in general, assume all domestic chores. Even the most exalted of women in Canudos, the "magdalenes" who belong to the Sacred Choir, must be content with looking after the Counselor's personal domestic needs.

The ascetic religious life of Canudos makes extremely difficult, if not impossible, the cultivation of the arts and sciences. The economic penury and the religious morality of Canudos fail to provide fertile ground for the growth of literature, painting, sculpture, philosophy, architecture, or drama. And while Canudos has need of certain practical arts—the making of weapons, the cultivation of crops—it has no place for the pursuit of pure science.[60] It is of course not impossible that if left in peace, Canudos might one day have given birth to a cultural renaissance. However, such a development, like that of Muslim Spain under the Almohads and Almoravids, would from the Counselor's perspective have signalled the onset of degeneracy and corruption, a failure of the community to remain focused upon the worship of God and the necessary preparations for the Last Judgment.

While racial harmony and domestic peace characterize life in Canudos, its powerful sense of communal identity and religious brotherhood fosters fierce intolerance of and violent hostility towards the outside world. The Counselor founds his community as an escape from what he regards as the persecution of the republic. But domestic peace in Canudos is purchased at the price of constant war with foreign enemies. Machiavelli would know how to appreciate the Counselor's "miraculous" conversion of murderous and rapacious *cangaceiros* into the pious Catholic Guard and defense forces of Canudos. The Counselor succeeds in taming the cruelty of Big João, Abbot João, and Pajeú by directing their aggression outward, towards the forces of the Antichrist. No religious restrictions or moral scruples apply to the massacre, torture, and mutilation of republican soldiers by the faithful of Canudos. Although the pious hope of the Counselor is for universal peace, the practical result of his policies is fanatical violence and perpetual war. The apocalyptic strain in the Counselor's sermons, his tireless spiritual struggle against the "Can," suggest that Canudos depends for its unity upon the existence of an omnipresent and eternal enemy with whom no negotiation or compromise is possible.

The ultimate destruction of Canudos is no mere historical accident; it grows out of the inherent weaknesses and limitations of life in this community. Long before the final annihilation of Canudos, strains appear in the social fabric that threaten the communal spirit. The happiness of individuals is, as we have noted, dependent upon their personal relationship with the Counselor. But as the community continues to grow in size, the Counselor becomes an ever more remote and elusive figure. Even the disciples closest to the religious leader increasingly lose touch with him and in the waning days of Canudos find themselves once again troubled by anxieties, fears, and self-doubts. Lest we assume that it is only the demands of war that threaten to rob the community of its spiritual vitality, Vargas Llosa makes clear that Canudos has never really considered what might happen to it once its spiritual leader dies. Like Lord Jim's regime in Patusan, Canudos ultimately depends for its survival on the Counselor's personal magnetism. When he dies, the only recourse for Abbot João and the other leaders of the city is to conceal this fact from the citizens of the city. Had Canudos managed to withstand the assaults of the republican armies, no rational (or even irrational) mechanism existed for designating the Counselor's successor and for the peaceful transfer of power.

This striking deficiency grows directly out of the particular religious teachings of the Counselor. Since he sincerely believes in the imminent end of the world and Second Coming of Jesus, the Counselor cannot very well make long-range plans for the preservation and maintenance of his regime. The Counselor would ultimately face the same grave difficulty that confronts all messianic movements, including that of the earliest Christians: how to explain to the faithful why the apocalypse never arrives. The Counselor and his followers are spared this dilemma, since the republic supplies a secular version of the apocalypse that makes the absence of the divine original a moot point.

In any case, the collapse of Canudos stems directly from the nature of the regime and not simply from any particular failures in political or military judgment on the part of the Counselor and his disciples. Vargas Llosa seems especially impressed with the courage and ferocity of those who fought to defend Canudos. Moreover, as both the novelist and da Cunha suggest, the military tactics and strategy of the city's leaders in most respects were better adapted to the local environment of the *sertão* than those of Moreira César and the professionally trained officers of the republican armies. As in the nearly contemporary Boer War in South Africa and the later conflicts in Vietnam, the war in Canudos featured the astonishing successes of guerrilla fighters who managed to hold off much larger and better equipped modern armies, whose training and methods were based on the inappropriate model of European warfare. Possessing a vastly superior knowledge of local terrain and climate, as well as a fanatical devotion to their own beliefs and homeland, the rebels of Canudos comprised a formidable fighting force. Nevertheless, in Vargas Llosa's novel there is never any question that, as long as the republic is willing to pursue the war relentlessly, Canudos is doomed. Ultimately, no amount of fanatical courage or tactical supremacy can overcome the technological advantages of the republic's armies. Eventually Canudos runs out of bullets, supplies, food, water, soldiers, and defensible positions. By contrast, the republic, although its military and economic resources are strained, fields ever larger and better equipped armies to crush the rebellion.

The military superiority of the republic is of course not an accident; it derives from the political and technological organization of a modern nation-state. As Fukuyama points out, one of the two engines of progressive history is the unilinear character of modern science. Drawing upon the insights of Machiavelli, Fukuyama notes that competition among states, the necessity for military preparedness, eventually forces all regimes to modernize their armies. And this in turn means that they must accept modern natural science as a necessary basis of their existence. Fukuyama persuasively argues that successful military modernization depends in turn upon economic modernization, a process rapidly accelerated by the liberalization of market forces. Without an enormous increase in capital, no regime can hope to afford the ever rising costs of military preparedness.[61]

The survival of Canudos would therefore ultimately depend on relaxing the exclusive claims of religious faith in order to make way for the pursuits of modern natural science and the development of a modern economy. Any regime that rejects even the metric system as a manifestation of evil cannot begin to withstand the more corrosive long-term effects of the pursuit of scientific truth unfettered by religious dogma. For a time, Abbot João and his lieutenants manage to defend Canudos by stealing the arms and supplies of the republican armies. But such "borrowings" from modernity are only stop-gap measures. To defend Canudos successfully would ultimately require the regime to compromise its unquestioned trust in God's favor and devote itself to more secular enterprises. The Counselor's irrational belief that Dom Sebastião will rise from the ocean with his legions to defend Canudos is not an effective counter to the republic's political and economic capacity to field a vast modern army equipped with technologically sophisticated weapons.

As we saw in varying ways in Hardy's Casterbridge, Conrad's Patusan, and Achebe's Igboland, ultimately the very insularity of Canudos, its distance from the modern world in moral, political, and scientific terms, both provides it with its attractive character and dooms it to extinction once it comes in conflict with modernity. However sympathetic Vargas Llosa's treatment of the subjective joys of life in Canudos, his novel illustrates that the objective character of the regime breeds an ignorant and violent fanaticism that necessarily culminates in its complete destruction. For all his misgivings concerning the dangers of historicism, Vargas Llosa never seriously challenges the historical inevitability of the demise of Canudos.

VII

The War of the End of the World seems to lack any single character who fully embodies and forcefully articulates the liberal democratic alternative to the antiliberal and antimodern ideologies that dominate the novel. The civilian leader of the Brazilian republic, President de Moraes, who might be thought to represent the path of liberal reform, remains a shadowy figure, who never makes a direct appearance in the work. The closest that Vargas Llosa comes to creating a mouthpiece for his own liberal democratic and reformist convictions is the anonymous journalist, based on Euclides da Cunha, who witnesses many of the dramatic events of the Canudos war.[62] The interpolated narratives of the journalist provide a fuller sense of what the Baron de Canabrava, Moreira César, Galileo Gall, and the Counselor represent ideologically and politically. But the journalist seems unwilling or unable to offer a clear statement of his own political and moral convictions. It is, in fact, very difficult to see the journalist (as opposed to the historical da Cunha) as an advocate of any clearly articulated ideological position; at most he seems a pessimistic critic of the folly and ideological extremism of his contemporaries. Moreover, his authoritative status within the novel seems inconsistent with his virtual blindness. His view of Canudos and his understanding of its historical significance depend finally on little more than secondhand reports and on his own rather vague, confused, and clouded perceptions. And yet we are left with Vargas Llosa's dedication, presumably not ironic, to "Euclides da Cunha in the other world," suggesting that the novelist implicitly endorses the ostensibly limited perspective of the journalist.

This notable absence of any character who can be said to speak for the values of a liberal democratic future for Latin America explains why Gerald Martin ultimately finds Vargas Llosa's novel wanting:

> [The novel] runs out of steam at the climactic moment because its internal logic requires the kind of ideological coherence which Vargas Llosa himself had so consistently rejected in earlier days—all the more irrational, this, since the conclusion of the work emphasizes the illusory nature of ideologies. The classical transparency which Vargas Llosa achieves, now that his ideology has moved to the right, here produces a kind of conceptual paralysis.[63]

In contrast to *War and Peace,* Vargas Llosa's historical novel must seem strangely inconclusive. Nothing in *The War of the End of the World* corresponds to the famous "Second Epilogue" with which Tolstoy rounds off his epic novel. Whereas Tolstoy offers an elaborate theory of the meaning and movement of universal history, Vargas Llosa appears to offer little more than the smoking ruins of a vanished community and the superstitious ravings of an aged survivor of Canudos who speaks of the Counselor's ascension to heaven.

While not especially evident in the dialogue or narrative content of the novel, Vargas Llosa's adherence to liberal democratic reformism is reflected in the formal and structural features of his work. In particular he employs modernist techniques to infuse his work with a skeptical liberal perspectivism. The fragmentary and confused reports of the half-blind journalist, the constantly shifting authorial perspective which moves rapidly from the viewpoint of one character to that of another, the conflicting versions of the same historical events, the piecemeal assemblage of history from a variety of unreliable records, letters, speeches, and eyewitness accounts, the eventual emergence of a linear narrative out of a multitude of apparently disconnected episodes presented in achronological order—all these techniques serve two different, but ultimately related aims. First, they form the pieces of a grand epic that represents in a realistic manner a significant and comprehensible historical movement. Second, they impose upon the reader a skeptical attitude towards the reliability of all historical eyewitnesses and the infallibility of all parties involved in the Canudos war. Vargas Llosa thus offers a more or less coherent and comprehensive account of the historical events in Bahia that emerges out of a chaos of untrustworthy, partial, and biased accounts.[64] The political and epistemological effect of the novel is to disabuse its readers of their faith in all who presume to possess certain knowledge of the nature of an ideal human society; all ideologies—religious and political—have at best a relative claim on the allegiance of the reader, but no absolute claim to truth.

Although in his essay on Popper Vargas Llosa explicitly rejects the historicism of Hegel, his novel embodies a central feature of philosophic historicism: the emergence of a comprehensible history out of a seemingly disordered series of events. From the perspective of individual participants, the Canudos war seems merely incomprehensible, senseless, and terrifying. The ultimate significance of the event becomes evident only retrospectively and does not generally accord with the immediate intentions or ambitions of particular historical agents. As the end product of a historical cataclysm in which all antiliberal alternatives have violently cancelled each other out, the modern republic of President Moraes triumphs by virtue of the relative military and political weaknesses of its opponents, rather than because it persuades its antagonists of the moral superiority of liberal democracy. The values of tolerance, moderation, and pluralism do not win over the rational allegiance of their historical antagonists so much as they emerge as the inevitable end products of a decisive struggle in which unyielding attachment to illiberal and uncompromising political ideologies proves self-destructive. In *The War of the End of the World,* the historical meaning of the Canudos war, the triumph of the nascent liberal democratic state in Brazil, is thus made manifest by a "ruse of reason," the product of the "invisible hand" that produces a modern rational outcome out of a violent and seemingly irrational struggle. The objective and demonstrable superiority of the modern liberal state, its decisive advantage over premodern and nonliberal or antiliberal alternatives, is thus proved by and through historical events that are necessarily violent. Despite Vargas Llosa's claims to the contrary, his novel seems to point towards the

Hegelian conclusion that what is rational is actual and what is actual is rational.

Gerald Martin's demand for "ideological coherence" is at least partially met in the novel not by the presence of a character who speaks cogently and powerfully for the liberal democratic state, but rather by the formal structure of the work as a whole. The radical perspectivism of the novel should be understood not as an evasion of politics and ideology, but as the structural embodiment of the political principles of democratic pluralism. That is, the aesthetic form of the modernist novel serves as the literary equivalent of a liberal political system in which all ideological disagreements are arbitrated and resolved by means of purely formal procedures. The perspectivism of the novel allows characters of all political stripes to speak out, to participate in the action of the plot; but none of these characters is allowed to occupy a privileged position or to attain any kind of unquestioned narrative, epistemological, moral, or political authority. The apparent exception to this formal principle, the one character who seems to speak for Vargas Llosa, the journalist, is accordingly not presented as an ideologue, but as a skeptic who offers a pragmatic critique of the destructiveness of ideological extremism let loose in political life and who merely establishes in some limited sense the narrative form in which this political struggle takes place. The only significant intervention made by the journalist at the close of the novel is to marry Jurema and accept the ailing dwarf as an adopted member of his family. Like Alejandro Mayta, the protagonist of Vargas Llosa's next novel, who ends up modestly running a small business after a career as a failed Marxist revolutionary, the journalist effectively abandons the world of great ideological struggles in favor of immersing himself in local, domestic, and personal concerns. In short, by appearing as a "neutral" witness to the great historical events of the novel and by retreating into the ostensibly apolitical world of private bourgeois life, the journalist finally occupies a mediating position between the premodern and the modern, the nonliberal and the liberal worlds. His very reluctance to articulate explicitly the values of the modern liberal democratic order therefore serves a strategic end: it allows Vargas Llosa to present the modern secular state of the bourgeois as somehow beyond or above ideology, a merely pragmatic result of the movement of history.

Thus the generic perspectivism of Vargas Llosa's novel, its *modernism,* can be described as the formal embodiment of liberal democratic *modernity.* The skeptical undercutting of all nondemocratic ideologies, the interplay between different antiliberal perspectives that effectively cancel out one another, and the fictive staging of political disputes lead to a domestication of political life in which, paradoxically, only the modest, the humble, and the temperate survive. The liberal democratic society that begins to emerge at the close of *The War of the End of the World* is not represented by a passionate and charismatic ideologue because Vargas Llosa understands that the pluralism, and therefore the peace and prosperity of a liberal democratic society, depend on the disappearence of all strongly held ideologies and all charismatic and uncompromising ideologies. The virtues of such a society are defined negatively or by implication: a pluralistic society avoids the political violence and historical tragedy of Canudos by abandoning the search for the kind of utopia embodied in antiliberal alternatives. By relativizing all claims to truth, attachments to dangerous political ideas that demand violent action are greatly moderated, if not completely neutralized. In place of a tragic clash among incompatible claims concerning the nature of *the* political truth, modern liberal pluralism substitutes a formalized exchange of different points of view that constantly reinforces the relative and contingent nature of political preferences.

While the aesthetic form of Vargas Llosa's modernist novel is perfectly consistent with and illustrative of his liberal democratic politics and thereby provides a response to the charge that his work lacks ideological coherence, Martin's criticism nonetheless points up a difficulty that haunts many contemporary defenders of the open society who claim to reject all absolute or final definitions of the political good, while implicitly embracing human freedom and equality as the fundamental basis of political life. The attempt to arbitrate all ideological disputes by means of value-neutral formal procedures—popular elections, representative government, due process, majority rule, to name only a few of the preferred methods—only makes sense within an ideological context in which the political alternatives to liberal democratic rule have already been effectively excluded. The attempt to transcend ideology by virtue of the "impartiality" of liberal institutions ultimately rests on the tacit assumption that nondemocratic and premodern regimes could never be preferred to modern democratic ones; if they were, impartiality would be recognized as no more (and no less) than the politically interested ideology of liberal democracy. The neutrality of the latter cannot be pushed beyond certain limits without threatening the regime that guarantees a level playing field for its citizens and unqualified toleration for different political points of view. By the same token, if even the essential feature of the open society, its openness, can be questioned—and theoretically rejected—then the reemergence of a closed society must remain a viable historical possibility.

This difficulty points to a significant difference between Hegel and Popper. While both thinkers ultimately endorse human freedom, Hegel insists that freedom emerges as the complete and final truth of human history—properly speaking, it is the *end* of history. By contrast, Popper argues that freedom is the means by which the truth emerges and that whatever truth arises is always corrigible and revisable. But of course, if history is endless, and the truth endlessly revisable, then human freedom may itself prove to be nothing more than a fiction to be dispensed with at the next unpredictable turn of history. If then Vargas Llosa's novel exemplifies a kind of ideological incoherence, it is not due to an inconsistency of aesthetic form and political commitment, but rather it is the product of a modern liberal perspective that at one and the same time *knows* itself to be superior to all historical alternatives and yet, because of its commitment to the principles of political tolerance and epistemological skepticism, cannot bring itself to acknowledge that what it knows is finally, absolutely, and definitively *true*.

Epilogue

There in the tomb stand the dead upright,
But winds come up from the shore:
They shake when the winds roar,
Old bones upon the mountain shake.

W. B. Yeats, "The Black Tower"

At the end of 1993, I attended the North American premiere of *Paixão e Guerra no Sertão de Canudos,* a documentary about the Bahian civil war directed by the Brazilian filmmaker, Antonio Olavo. An image from Olavo's film continues to haunt me, a master shot of what was once the site of the holy city of Canudos—today completely submerged under water. That site that more than one hundred years ago witnessed the apocalyptic end of the Counselor's antimodern vision now lies below the surface of an immense reservoir that supplies the Bahian *sertão* with water. After the screening of his film, Olavo made clear to his Durham audience that the decision of the central Brazilian government to flood the valley in which the Canudos war was fought flowed as much from political as economic objectives. As a popular rallying place for disaffected groups protesting the policies of the modern Brazilian government, this obscure locale, with its tragic legacy of civil strife and religious fanaticism, had become an embarrassing symbol of regional resistance to centralized government authority. For me too, the image of that serene body of water was a source of personal (and petty) frustration: I had, after all, come to see Canudos, or at any rate, what was left of it. And yet I came away feeling that Olavo's panoramic shots of the reservoir at sunset were nevertheless an appropriate coda for the historical catastrophe that was Canudos. For this ambitious engineering project, representative of the transformative powers of technological and political modernization, has at once obliterated the premodern past and prevented the return of the periodic droughts that formerly devastated the *sertão* and impoverished its inhabitants. In more than one respect, the reservoir, with its apparent calm disguising an immense and seemingly irresistible force, is a fitting image of modernity.

But can I, or anyone else, conclude on the basis of a few novels, or a documentary film, that the end of history has arrived, that the modernization of the world and the globalization of culture have become irreversible and permanent features of human existence? As I write these concluding lines in the early days of 1994, I am struck by how far off Kant's "perpetual peace" now seems. Only this week a worldwide audience has been witness to the astounding televised images of a major armed rebellion in Chiapas, Mexico, carried out by the revolutionary Zapatista Army of National Liberation. Just weeks after the passage of NAFTA, which promised the complete political and economic integration of modern Mexico with the rest of North America, pundits around the world are stunned by the sudden emergence of a secret army whose existence seemed unthinkable only yesterday. The initial successes of the Mexican federal forces in suppressing the rebellion and the attendant controversy that has arisen as to whether they have, in the process, committed gross abuses of human rights, has not dulled the shock of this amazing eruption of political violence in our midst.

Nor is the Chiapas rebellion, this weirdly postmodern revisitation of the Mexican revolution, complete with vacationing tourists trapped in their luxury hotels by the fighting and the reemergence of Emiliano Zapata as inspirational godfather of the rebels, an isolated and unique event in the post–Cold War era. From Mogadishu to Sarajevo, Port-au-Prince to Stepanakert, Ayodha to Tblisi, Algiers to Kigali, the world finds itself plunged in a new and powerful surge of political violence, religious strife, and ethnic conflict. This unexpected worldwide development has led one thoughtful political analyst, Patrick Glynn, to suggest that we have entered "the Age of Balkanization." Positing a turn in the cycles of world history, Glynn suggests that the great ideological conflicts of the recent past have ended not in some final Hegelian resolution, but instead in a new form of global fragmentation:

> Today a fundamental change is under way in the character of global political life. A new era is in the making. Gone or fading are the great bipolar conflicts—between democracy and fascism, between democracy and Communism, and even perhaps between Left and Right—that shaped war and peace in the 20th century. In their place a new political struggle is emerging—more complex, more diffuse, but nonetheless

global in character. On every continent, in almost every major nation, and in almost every walk of life the overriding political reality today is that of increasing social separatism and fragmentation—a sometimes violent splintering of humanity by ethnic group, race, religion, and even (to a less dramatic extent) such characteristics as gender or sexual orientation.[1]

Glynn's geopolitical hypothesis forces me to question once more the thesis advanced by Hegel, Kojève, and Fukuyama, among others, in light of the most recent events of world history. I am compelled to revisit the question of whether history has a telos and of whether the global process of modernization, even if it was not inevitable, is nonetheless irreversible.

Even at the end of 1992, when I completed the original draft of this book, many of the grand hopes for the "Year of Europe" already seemed faded. Despite the apparent victory of democratic universalism throughout much of the world formerly ruled by communist governments, Europe appeared in many respects to be as fragmented and divided as ever. Hopes for the total economic integration of the European Community had dimmed, a wave of anti-immigrant sentiment was sweeping many Western European nations, and most Eastern European countries were still struggling with only limited success to reform their political institutions and liberalize their economies. Not long after in the Western Hemisphere, nominally democratic governments in Peru and Haiti fell victim to new forms of dictatorial rule, while abortive revolutions took place in Venezuela and Mexico. American promises of a "New World Order" were accordingly redefined and scaled back in recognition of the numerous intractable political, ethnic, and religious conflicts that remained beyond the control of U.S. power.

Avowed critics of Hegelian thought, of course, never required such outward manifestations of the messiness of history in order to reject teleological historicism. As early as March of 1991, at the very height of democratic optimism in the West, Vargas Llosa sounded a cautionary note with regard to the rise of neo-Hegelianism:

> Should we, then, join Francis Fukuyama in claiming that communism's last gasp marks the true "end of history" in the Hegelian sense? I think we should not. On the contrary, events in the Soviet Union and Eastern Europe have unexpectedly revitalized the very notion of "history." . . . Today, we can confirm the position that Karl Popper, Friedrich Hayek, and Raymond Aron always held in opposition to thinkers like Machiavelli, Vico, Marx, Spengler, and Toynbee. The

former insisted, rightly, that history is never "written" before it happens; it does not proceed according to some script determined by God, nature, reason, or the class struggle and the means of production. History is rather a continuous and variable creation that can move through the most unexpected turns, evolutions, involutions, and contradictions. Its complexity always threatens to sweep away those who attempt to predict and explain it. We are right to be thrilled by current trends. . . . But none of this was "written." No hidden force, waiting in the catacombs of obscurantism and terror that impoverished and humiliated entire peoples, led to the fall of Ceauşescu, the triumph of Solidarity, or the demolition of the wall that divided Berlin. . . . The victory of freedom over totalitarianism has been overwhelming, but it is far from fully secured.[2]

And yet. And yet, I am not fully persuaded that any of the events that have occurred since Vargas Llosa presented his address in Managua in the spring of 1991, and that would seem to confirm his view, demonstrate a fundamental reversal of global modernization and the worldwide homogenization of political and social life. From the Olympian perspective that Hegel or Kojève presumed to occupy, these events can be understood to confirm rather than refute the validity of their historical conclusions. For after all, none of these above-mentioned conflicts and catastrophes presage the return to a premodern form of existence. To take the example of the Chiapas rebellion: the demands of the Zapatista Army, of the indigenous peoples who have supported them, and of Mexican-American groups who protest the abuses of human rights perpetrated by the Mexican armed forces, collectively amount to a call for accelerating the pace of modernization in Mexico. First and foremost among the objectives of the Zapatista leadership is free and fair democratic elections in Mexico monitored by international observers. The supporters of the rebels, both domestic and foreign, have advocated the universal recognition of the political and personal liberties of individuals belonging to an oppressed minority, the scrupulous observation of international standards of human rights by the Mexican government, and the full extension of greater economic prosperity to all of Mexico's citizens. In a similar manner, the initial condemnation of the military junta in Haiti, the worldwide outcry against the atrocities committed by Rwandan forces, and the continuing U.N. boycott of the Serbian government, while failing to effect any material change in the policies of these regimes, were nevertheless perfectly consistent with an ideological commitment to the fundamental principles of political modernity. In short, these conflagrations represent either a popular (and sometimes frustrated) wish to accelerate the pace of modernization—as in Chiapas—or they have called forth the opposition of an international community that still remains firmly committed to the universal establishment of the moral, political, and social standards of modernity—as in Haiti, Rwanda, or the former Yugoslavia.

What is particularly telling is how infrequently even the most reactionary forces have managed to articulate a coherent or persuasive ideological position, much less one that in a fundamental way questions the desirability and legitimacy of modern political life. The rise of figures like Zhirinovsky, Milosevic, and Tudjman in Eastern Europe, while threatening the peace and stability of their own, as well as of surrounding countries, does not promise the eclipse of the modern project: these leaders do not, for example, advocate a return to monarchy or theocracy, to slavery or feudalism. Despite their failures to grasp the dynamic potential of market economies, they desperately seek the economic advancement and modernization of their countries. And though they all manifest to varying degrees authoritarian, imperialist, and chauvinist proclivities, they derive what limited legitimacy they do possess from their status as popularly elected representatives. Finally, none of these figures contemplate dispensing with the secular and technological underpinnings of modern geopolitics; their capacity to gather intelligence and employ military force, both now and in the future, necessitates the ongoing development of modern natural science.

I would agree with Glynn that revivified nationalism, ethnic particularism, and, most importantly, religious fundamentalism appear to impede the global homogenization of culture insofar as each depends upon the idea (or unstated assumption) that a nation, people, or religion is a discrete and unassimilable entity that must retain and continually reassert its distinct identity. Moreover, I recognize that all these movements have the potential to spark political and sectarian violence. But at the same time, I continue to wonder, a là Kojève, whether these disruptive and manifestly antiuniversalist movements nevertheless suggest that the modernization of the globe is inexorably advancing. For even if the Azeris and Armenians of Nagorno-Karabakh, and the Serbs, Croats, and Muslims of Bosnia ultimately inhabit ethnically "cleansed" societies, will they have established premodern, nonmodern, or antimodern regimes? Will the societies they inhabit differ from one another in ways comparable to those that distinguish a feudal society from an industrial one, or a monarchy from a democracy, or will these differences consist primarily of linguistic and ethnic attributes? More importantly, can these efforts at cultural essentialism actually resist, over the long run, the global economic and political forces that erode the "sovereign" borders constructed by even the most brutal regimes?

Perhaps what we see in Eastern Europe and the former Soviet Union is best understood as only the most recent example of modern decolonization, a process set in motion by the collapse of the Soviet Empire. An initial surge of stultifying nationalism, cultural essentialism, and ethnic particularism now characterizes the first phase of postcolonial life. However, this explosion of cultural protectionism and national fervor will gradually give way when it confronts global economic and political realities. Short of isolating itself from the outside world, in the manner of Communist Albania, postcolonial Paraguay, or Tokugawa Japan, no regime can insure its cultural "purity." Not suprisingly, postcolonial societies in this century have typically followed a trajectory towards cultural hybridity. But even if certain exceptions to this pattern were to emerge, and a few post–Cold War societies were to maintain their political isolation and cultural hermeticism, the existence of these societies would hardly constitute a significant challenge to the global spread of modernity. Because such regimes cut themselves off from the rest of the world, they renounce all efforts to influence the course of modernization around the world, resorting to a rearguard action that only temporarily and tenuously holds modernity at bay. Moreover, the techniques whereby ethnic or cultural nationalism are promoted and maintained depend paradoxically upon a concurrent modernization of even the most insular society. Without a modern educational system and modern media, the construction of a homogeneous cultural identity cannot be attempted. In any case, given that the nation-state is itself a modern political phenomenon, the contemporary multiplication of nation-states, even if they remain for long periods cut off from or hostile to one another, can be seen as an acceleration if not a fulfillment of political modernization.[3]

The rise of multiculturalism in the United States is only the most obvious example of how ethnic particularism, even when vehemently expressed, can turn out to be consistent with a more basic adherence to the principles of modern political life. Contemporary American enthusiasm for ethnic and cultural diversity in actual practice amounts largely to an embrace of different and constantly changing styles in cuisine, music, literature, art, and dress, a commitment that gains its moral authority as the cultural outgrowth of a more basic commitment to democratic pluralism, recognition of individual rights and freedoms, and confident belief in the basic equality of all human beings. Which is to say that multiculturalism, despite the rhetoric sometimes used to characterize it, does not represent a fundamental alternative to Western modernity, but rather its latest—postmodern—incarnation.

Were it not for the threatening rise of religious fundamentalism in many places in the world—India, North Africa, the Middle East—I would be tempted to describe even the most disturbing post–Cold War developments as promoting the marginal cultural differentiation of regimes which in all other crucial respects are similarly committed to economic, political, and technological modernization. But a movement such as resurgent Islam (especially in its Iranian, Sudanese, or Algerian manifestations) would seem to offer a significant and politically active challenge to global modernity. The government in Tehran deviates from the path of modernity most obviously in its insistence that the revealed word of Allah should dictate the organization of political life and that such an organization is incompatible with the freedoms of religion, association, and speech and with the fundamental equality of all individuals (men and women being assigned unequal roles in society). But if Islamic extremism calls into question the legitimacy of the modern age, the question remains whether it can actually roll back or even substantially hinder the global process of modernization. As Fukuyama has pointed out, the temptations of Islamic extremism do not extend to regions of the globe that were not already part of the Muslim world before the rise of Western modernity.[4] Moreover, by comparison with the antimodernism of Canudos, Islamic fundamentalism, even in its most extreme forms, seems already to have made significant, perhaps even decisive compromises with the modernity it purports to resist. As Salman Rushdie suggests in his allegorical novel, *The Satanic Verses,* the very success of the Iranian Revolution initially depended upon Khomeini's use of modern technology, especially the media of radio, television, print, and tape-recorded messages, as well as upon the political protection and de facto logistical support the West provided the imam in exile. The current regime in Tehran, for all its rhetorical posturing that it has reversed the course of westernization, and its implacable *fatwa* against Rushdie, nevertheless observes many of the outward forms of modern democratic life (multiparty elections, parliamentary rule); publicly proclaims its commitment to international law and the principles of the United Nations Charter; and pursues a policy of technological, military, and economic modernization, however inefficiently and incompetently. Though one must not ignore the selective indifference and even hostility of the Iranian government to international standards of human rights, the ideological animus of the regime towards "Western" modernity cannot completely disguise its pragmatic acceptance of many of the most fundamental features of modern political life. As the example of Canudos suggests, it is by no means certain that a theocratic regime can long endure in an economically and politically competitive global environment without compromising the coherence and distinctiveness of its ostensibly antimodern ideology.

For resurgent religious movements to pose a decisive historical challenge to modernity, the desecularization of the world must become more than the fanciful hypothesis of science fiction writers or the longed-for utopia of conservative mullahs, Branch Davidians, and Hindu communalists. The visions of contemporary Counselors promise an apocalyptic end only for the faithful few unless it becomes possible to conceive of the global return of religion as an inevitable outgrowth or dialectical product of modernity itself. It is no accident that many works of modern science fiction that envision a return to a religious worldview are premised upon the literary convention of a global technological catastrophe. No doubt concerns have been and continue to be raised about the technological viability of modernity: apocalyptic scenarios range from nuclear annihilation to more contemporary and fashionable worries over global warming and environmental degradation. But those who raise such grim possibilities typically turn to modernity themselves, to its technological, political, and ideological powers (revolutionary methods of production, new international agreements, alternative energy sources) in order to stave off the feared catastrophe. What is at issue for these people is not the worth or desirability of modernity, but whether the logic of development will produce new (and more powerful) techniques, strategies, and tools quickly enough to cope with the unintended consequences of modernization.

While such apocalyptic narratives cannot be dismissed out of hand, the more serious (and obscure) challenge to modernity consists in the potential collapse of its fundamental ideological premises. Nietzsche and Heidegger are foremost among those who initiated a philosophic critique of Hegelian thought that rejects the reasonableness or logic of history and questions the validity of universal reason itself. Contemporary assaults on reason, direct descendants of this Nietzschean and Heideggerian critique, threaten, at least in theory, to subvert the modern project from within, by conceiving of it as merely the narrow historical prejudice of the West. By undermining all claims for the superiority of reason, these contemporary critiques of modernity risk effacing the distinction between the rational and the irrational, the secular and the sacred. Such a repudiation of the universal claims of reason potentially opens the way for desecularization, for the re-mystification of the world, for the return of the gods. To be sure, most contemporary academic Nietzscheans and Heideggerians represent themselves and their ideas as liberal, tolerant, pragmatic, secular, progressive, and modern. And I, for one, do not doubt their sincere attachment to the basic ideals of modernity. But the inner core of the thought of Nietzsche and Heidegger—what one might call their radical nihilism—has the potential to relativize the philosophic claims of modernity, rendering the modern project as only one among many equally legitimate modes of historical existence, rather than as the proper end of history per se. As Nietzsche understood it, nihilism, even radical nihilism, is compatible with democratic pluralism; it is in fact the philosophic expression of the leveling of all hierarchies of value, a phenomenon that takes the political form of modern democratic culture. But a relativistic democratic ideology, having undermined the claims of absolute reason, can no longer articulate a reason for resisting the resurgence of nondemocratic or antimodern forms of life that make no claim to be based on human reason.

It is not possible here to do justice to the complexity of Nietzsche's and Heidegger's thought or to the philosophic responses their work has engendered. But one might begin to suggest what is at stake by raising, however belatedly, a fundamental question their writings pose: is modernity fundamentally satisfying?[5] If the answer to this question is yes, as Hegel and Kojève believed it to be, then the global disturbances and political violence of the post–Cold War era might more easily be understood as evidence of the accelerated pace of modernization. What we are witnessing today would then signal not a reversal of history's linear movement, but as Kojève put it, "the elimination of numerous more or less anachronistic sequels" to the premodern past. Kojève might have underestimated how long the globalization of culture would take, but his central insight would remain valid. If, however, modernity is in some basic way unsatisfying, if some ineradicable human desire is inherently frustrated in the modern world, or if the modern world produces new desires among its inhabitants that it cannot quench, then a powerful engine for fundamental historical change would remain.

If my analysis of the modern global novel has often granted the Hegelian view of history a privileged status, it has, I hope, also raised serious concerns about the power of modernity to satisfy human desire completely and definitively. By focusing on particular human figures—the individual characters who inhabit the world of literature—I have attempted to avoid the tendency of modern philosophy to lose sight of the heterogeneous nature of human existence in a general, abstract, and universal definition of the subject. Given its concreteness, literature helps us to see that the forms of human satisfaction are various and incompatible. The fictional lives of Julien Sorel and Michael Henchard, Okonkwo and Jim, the Baron de Canabrava and the Counselor, though they may be made to conform to a Hegelian conception of history, nevertheless offer vistas on worlds not our own, if only because these characters seek after forms of satisfaction unavailable in modernity. In their tragedies one may yet see a ghostly intimation of a way of life alien to the global posthistorical present, a spectral suggestion of a fundamentally different past, if not of a radically new future.

Notes

Preface

1. I am aware that the terms "Third World" and "Third World literature," like the terms "postcolonial" and "postcolonial literature," are controversial and imprecise. I have many reservations concerning the way their use tends to obscure or even eliminate political and literary distinctions that are of considerable importance. I have nevertheless used these terms as a kind of shorthand, attempting to refine and specify their meaning whenever it seemed necessary. I take some reassurance from the fact that many writers and intellectuals from so-called Third World and postcolonial societies make use of these terms themselves. For a recent discussion of the political problems and theoretical deficiencies that characterize the deployment of these terms, see Anne McClintock, "The Angel of Progress: Pitfalls of the Term 'Postcolonialism,'" *Social Text* 31/32 (1992): 84–97.

2. This is not a book on Hegel. To do justice to the complexity of his highly controversial theory of history would indeed require an entire book, one quite different from the one I have written. I focus on the broad outlines of the debate about the end of history and do not involve myself directly in the detailed disputes of Hegel scholarship, such as the relation between his *Phenomenology of Spirit* and the lectures published as *The Philosophy of History* and the possibility that Hegel's view of the end of history changed during his career. My concern is not with Hegel's direct influence on the novelists I discuss, but with analyzing their works in terms of the general ideas of linear history and modernization that Hegel was among the first to articulate.

3. J. E. Wiredu, "How Not to Compare African Thought with Western Thought," in *African Philosophy: An Introduction,* ed. Richard Wright (Washington, D.C.: University Press of America, 1979), 172–73.

4. Georg Lukács, *The Historical Novel,* trans. Hannah and Stanley Mitchell (London: Merlin Press, 1962), 139. Lukács borrows the phrase, "totality of objects," from Hegel, who originally used it to describe the representational aim of the epic.

5. I wish to emphasize that my use of the terms "premodern" and "traditional" is *not* meant to imply that these societies are all alike. In fact, one of my principal aims in this book has been to discriminate among quite different kinds of societies and regimes that from the perspective of modernity are understood to be "premodern."

Introduction

1. For Kojève's interpretation of Hegel's *The Phenomenology of Spirit,* see Alexander Kojève, *Introduction to the Reading of Hegel,* trans. James H. Nichols, Jr. (Ithaca, N.Y.: Cornell University Press, 1969). For Kojève's discussion of the end of history as the prerequisite for a consistent philosophic historicism, see especially 31–66 and 159–68. Also see Kojève's "Tyranny and Wisdom," in Leo Strauss, *On Tyranny* (Ithaca: Cornell University Press, 1963), 178.

2. I hasten to add that many of these historicist thinkers, especially Sartre, Adorno, and Habermas, are themselves often critical of Hegelian master narratives, though they remain in some fashion committed to a modified version of objective or developmental history. It is of course possible to trace the roots of philosophic historicism back beyond the work of Hegel, at least as far as the thought of Vico, Lessing, Herder, Burke, and Kant.

3. Kojève, *Introduction to the Reading of Hegel,* 68–69, 162, 237. Also see, Kojève, "Tyranny and Wisdom," 155–56 and 178.

4. For the moment, I have set aside the apparent exception posed by resurgent Islamic fundamentalism, a subject to which I return in the chapter on Vargas Llosa.

5. See Francis Fukuyama, *The End of History and the Last Man* (New York: The Free Press, 1992), 199–208. For the relevant material in Kojève, see his *Introduction to the Reading of Hegel,* 3–74 and 235–37.

6. Kojève, *Introduction to the Reading of Hegel,* 160–61.

7. Georg Wilhelm Friedrich Hegel, *The Philosophy of History,* trans. J. Sibree (New York: Dover, 1956), 21.

8. For a lucid commentary on this aspect of Hegel's aesthetics, and a further elaboration of Hegel's fundamental insight, see Lukács, *The Historical Novel,* 92–102, especially 97.

9. Hegel, *The Philosophy of History,* 33.

10. Alexis de Tocqueville, *Democracy in America,* trans. George Lawrence (New York: Harper & Row, 1969), 11–12.

11. See also Stendhal, *Life of Napoleon,* 61, 84, 92, 114.

12. See Stendhal, *Racine and Shakespeare,* trans. Guy Daniels (New York: Crowell–Collier, 1962), 188–90.

13. Stendhal, "Letter to Vicenzo Salvagnoli," quoted in Gita May, *Stendhal and the Age of Napoleon* (New York: Columbia University Press, 1977), 230–31. For the original, see Stendhal, *Correspondence,* ed. Henri Martineau and Victor del Litto (Paris: Bibliothèque de la Pléiade, 1962–68), II, 484–85.

14. Stendhal, *Racine and Shakespeare,* 42.

15. This is Stendhal's argument in "La comédie est impossible en 1836."

16. See Stendhal, "Letter to Vincenzo Salvagnoli," 231; *Racine and Shakespeare,* 17, 44, 150; "Sir Walter Scott and *La Princesse de Clèves,"* in *Racine and Shakespeare,* 213–14; and *Life of Napoleon,* 110.

17. See Victor Brombert, *Stendhal: Fiction and the Themes of Freedom* (New York: Random House, 1968), 35.

18. Erich Auerbach describes Julien as "a man born too late who tries in vain to realize the form of life of a past period." See *Mimesis: The Representation of Reality in Western Literature,* trans. Wilard Trask (Princeton, N.J.: Princeton University Press, 1968), 465.

19. René Girard, *Deceit, Desire, and the Novel,* trans. Yvonne Freccero (Baltimore: Johns Hopkins University Press, 1966), 113–38.

20. Girard, *Deceit, Desire, and the Novel,* 131–33. See also Robert M. Adams, "France in 1830: The Facts of Life," in *Red and Black,* 417.

21. In 1793, an uprising of Catholic peasants in the Vendée, led principally by disenchanted clergy and aristocrats, attempted to restore the French monarchy. Following an extremely brutal and violent civil war, the French revolutionary government succeeded in putting down the rebellion. For a recent account of the counterrevolution in the Vendée, see Simon Schama, *Citizens: A Chronicle of the French Revolution* (New York: Alfred A. Knopf, 1989), 690–706, 760–66, 786–92.

22. Kojève, *Introduction to the Reading of Hegel,* 161.

23. Kojève, *Introduction to the Reading of Hegel,* 161–62.

24. On the mediated or triangulated nature of desire in Stendhal's novel, see Girard, *Deceit, Desire, and the Novel,* 11–24, 113–24. For Girard's discussion of social vanity and its relation to democratic social conditions of the Bourbon Restoration, see 116–32.

25. See Friedrich Nietzsche, section 257, *Beyond Good and Evil,* trans. Walter Kaufmann (New York: Vintage, 1966), 201; and the First Essay, section 2, *On the Genealogy of Morals,* trans. Walter Kaufmann (New York: Vintage, 1969), 26.

26. Stendhal, *The Charterhouse of Parma,* trans. Margaret R. B. Shaw (Harmondsworth: Penguin, 1958), 181.

27. See Kojève, "Tyranny and Wisdom," 167. On the potential dissatisfactions at the end of history, see also Strauss, *On Tyranny,* 222–26, and Fukuyama, 300–339.

Chapter 1

1. The events of *Things Fall Apart* take place between 1875 and 1910. The missionaries of the Church Missionary Society were active in the interior of Igboland beginning in 1890. Hardy twice significantly revised the 1886 edition of *The Mayor of Casterbridge,* for reissue in 1895 and 1912.

2. For a general account of these political and economic reforms, see G. M. Trevelyan, *History of England,* vol. 3 (Garden City, N.Y.: Doubleday Anchor, 1953), 157–207, 232–83.

3. See Michael Millgate, *Thomas Hardy: A Biography* (New York: Random House, 1982), 276–77.

4. Like contemporary postcolonial African writers such as Ngugi and Achebe, Hardy was especially concerned with the homogenizing effects that a centralized modern educational system was having upon regional speech, like the "Wessex" or Dorset dialect. Hardy clearly saw his own works and the verse of contemporaries such as the regional poet William Barnes as a last–ditch attempt to preserve an oral tradition and spoken dialect in written form. Hardy acknowledges that such efforts of preservation necessarily altered these original and distinct linguistic forms to make them comprehensible to a modern British readership. Preservation is thus an act of linguistic translation and presumptive cultural transformation: "It must, of course, be always a matter for regret that, in order to be understood, writers should be obliged thus slightingly to treat varieties of English which are intrinsically as genuine, grammatical, and worthy of the royal title as is the all–prevailing competitor which bears it; whose only fault was that they happened not to be central, and therefore were worsted in the struggle for existence, when a uniform tongue became a necessity among the advanced classes of the population." See Thomas Hardy, "Papers of the Manchester Literary Club," in *Thomas Hardy's Personal Writings,* ed. Harold Orel (New York: St. Martin's Press, 1966), 92–93. Also see in this same volume, Hardy's "Preface to Select Poems of William Barnes," 76–81, and "The Dorchester Labourer," 170. In the latter article, Hardy specifically singles out the system of national schools as the principal cause of this linguistic homogenization. Also see Laurence Lerner, *Thomas Hardy's* The Mayor of Casterbridge: *Tragedy or Social History?* (London: Sussex University Press, 1975), 96–97.

5. Thomas Hardy, "General Preface to the Wessex Edition of 1912," in *The Mayor of Casterbridge* (London: Macmillan, 1974), 379. For a suggestive comparison of Hardy's regionalism with Scott's, see Lerner, 88–89. For a comparative analysis of Hardy's novels and Achebe's, see Steven Jervis, "Tradition and Change in Hardy and Achebe," *Black Orpheus* 2 (1971): 31–38.

6. At the time Hardy was composing his novel, a number of Roman graves were accidently unearthed on the outskirts of Dorchester, on the very site where the novelist was building his new home of Max Gate. The findings

of this archaeological discovery made their way into an essay that Hardy presented to the Dorset Natural History and Antiquarian Field Club in 1884, of which he was a member, and also provided material for Hardy's narrative description of Casterbridge's Roman character. See Thomas Hardy, "Some Romano–British Relics Found at Max Gate, Dorchester," in Orel, *Thomas Hardy's Personal Writings*, 191–95. Hardy wrote a number of other short pieces dealing with local archaeological discoveries and appears to have been reading about the archaeology of the locality during the period he was working on *The Mayor of Casterbridge;* see Michael Millgate, *Thomas Hardy: A Biography*, 244–46. On the subject of Hardy's archaeological narrative propensities, see Lerner, 97–98.

7. Hardy, "General Preface to the Wessex Edition of 1912," 378.

8. See for example, Hardy's "Memories of Church Restoration," in Orel, *Thomas Hardy's Personal Writings*, 203–17. Hardy objects in particular to attempts to unify the style of a restored church by removing all features of earlier or later historical styles. Hardy's own design for his home, Max Gate, displays a "postmodern" penchant for mixing the architechtural styles of distinct historical periods: the Gothic, neoclassical, and the Saxon; see Millgate, *Thomas Hardy: A Biography*, 259.

9. For a different account of Casterbridge as a "primitive hierarchic society," see John Paterson, *"The Mayor of Casterbridge* as Tragedy," *Victorian Studies* 3 (1959): 162–63. For an analysis of Casterbridge in terms of Ferdinand Tönnies' sociological categories of *Gemeinschaft* and *Gesellschaft*, see Lerner, 89–94, and Noorul Hasan, *Thomas Hardy: The Sociological Imagination* (London: Macmillan, 1982), 68–72. Hasan concludes that Casterbridge is in fact closer to a *Gesellschaft* (a modern, artificial society) than to a *Gemeinschaft* (a traditional organic community).

10. For the classical definition of the polis, see Aristotle, *Politics*, 1253a–b. For the distinction between the ancient city and the modern state, see Harry Jaffa, "Aristotle," in *History of Political Philosophy*, ed. Leo Strauss and Joseph Cropsey (Chicago: Rand McNally, 1972), especially 65–67.

11. There were large cities in the ancient world, such as Rome in the late republican and imperial eras. However, it is arguable that Rome ceased to be a polis, in any meaningful sense, at precisely that point in its history at which it became the large cosmopolitan capital of a vast empire.

12. For a similar view, see Ian Gregor, "Introduction" to *The Mayor of Casterbridge* (London: Macmillan, 1974), 15.

13. Ian Watt, *The Rise of the Novel* (London: Chatto & Windus, 1957), 185, 198.

14. For the view that Henchard is a public speaker in a kind of "city–state," see Earl Ingersoll, "Writing and Memory in *The Mayor of Casterbridge,*" *English Literature in Transition* 33 (1990): 299–309, especially 300.

15. M. M. Bakhtin, *The Dialogic Imagination,* trans. Caryl Emerson and Michael Holquist (Austin: University of Texas, 1981), 132.

16. Bakhtin, 131–36.

17. For a similar view, see Irving Howe, *Thomas Hardy* (New York: Macmillan, 1967), 94–95.

18. See Michael Millgate, *Thomas Hardy: His Career as a Novelist* (New York: Random House, 1971), 223–24; Hasan, 71; and Lerner, 79.

19. For Hardy's discussion of how from the Middle Ages until the middle of the nineteenth century the English system of leaseholds worked to bind even many free laborers to particular plots of ground, see "The Dorchester Labourer," 168–90.

20. See Howe, 93.

21. Many of these aristocratic privileges were abolished in England by the seventeenth century, far in advance of events elsewhere on the European continent. At the time of the French Revolution, the specifically feudal character of Britain was thus far less in evidence than that of France or Germany. For a discussion of this point, see Alexis de Tocqueville, *The Old Regime and the French Revolution,* trans. Stuart Gilbert (New York: Anchor, 1955), 14–19.

22. See D. A. Dike, " A Modern Oedipus: *The Mayor of Casterbridge,*" *Essays in Criticism* 2 (1952): 172.

23. For a general history of this development, see Albert O. Hirschman, *The Passions and the Interests: Political Arguments for Capitalism before Its Triumph* (Princeton, N.J.: Princeton University Press, 1977). See also Leo Strauss, *The Political Philosophy of Hobbes* (Chicago: University of Chicago Press, 1952), 113–22, 125–26, and Leo Strauss, *What Is Political Philosophy?* (New York: Free Press, 1959), 48–50. For the philosophical foundations of this trend of thought, see in particular the discussion of "the passions that incline men to peace" at the end of chapter 13 of Thomas Hobbes, *Leviathan* (Oxford: Clarendon Press, 1965), 98. See also Adam Smith's contrast of the education of the modern laborer with that of the traditional warrior in *The Wealth of Nations* (New York: Random House, 1937), 734–35.

24. See Dike, 177.

25. See Robert Heilman, "Introduction" to *The Mayor of Casterbridge* (Boston: Houghton Mifflin, 1962), xxiii. Heilman argues that Hardy "anticipates" the "Horatio Alger myth."

26. See Heilman, vii, and Lerner, 93.

27. See Dike, 172.

28. For this latter suggestion, see Millgate, *Thomas Hardy: His Career as a Novelist,* 227.

29. For readings of the Faust motif in the novel, see Paterson, 153, 159, and Lawrence Starzyk, "Hardy's *Mayor:* The Antitraditional Basis of Tragedy," *Studies in the Novel* 4 (1972): 597–98.

30. For a discussion of Henchard's ambivalence toward Farfrae's intro-

duction of writing and bookkeeping as modern tools of business, see Ingersoll, 301–2.

31. For a good discussion of the contrast between Henchard and Farfrae, see Lerner, 77–78.

32. I have been among those critics making such claims. See Michael Valdez Moses, "Agon in the Marketplace: *The Mayor of Casterbridge* as Bourgeois Tragedy," *SAQ* 87 (1988): 234. For a detailed discussion of the way in which Henchard reduces his family and friends to the level of commodities, see Juliet Grindle, "Compulsion and Choice in *The Mayor of Casterbridge*," in *The Novels of Thomas Hardy*, ed. Anne Smith (London: Vision Press, 1979): 93–95.

33. On the chattel status of wives and children under Roman law, see Hegel, *The Philosophy of History*, 286.

34. For further analysis of the wife sale as pointing to the theme of incomplete modernization, see Leonora Epstein, "Sale and Sacrament: The Wife Auction in *The Mayor of Casterbridge*," *English Language Notes* 24 (1987): 50–56.

35. For a feminist interpretation of the clash between the materialistic patriarchal values represented by Henchard and the spiritual domestic values represented by Elizabeth-Jane (and Farfrae), see Elaine Showalter, "The Unmanning of the Mayor of Casterbridge," in *Critical Approaches to the Fiction of Thomas Hardy*, ed. Dale Kramer (London: Macmillan, 1979): 99–115.

36. Alexander Kojève, *Introduction to the Reading of Hegel*, trans. James H. Nichols, Jr. (Ithaca, N.Y.: Cornell University Press, 1969), 62.

37. For a feminist interpretation of how this domestic sphere comes into being, see Showalter, 113.

38. For the suggestion that Farfrae may be intended as a parodic rendering of one of Scott's heroes, see Patrick Joseph Glynn, "The Conflict Between Pagan and Modern Values in Thomas Hardy's Major Fiction," Ph.D. diss. Harvard University, 1979. See especially the chapter entitled, "The Taming of Heroic Man."

39. For a provocative discussion of the paradoxical, if not contradictory relationship between economic and technological modernization and the commercial production of literary regionalism, see David Lloyd, *Anomalous States: Irish Writing and the Post–Colonial Moment* (Durham, N.C.: Duke University Press, 1993), 37, 147.

40. A recent and spectacular example of this phenomenon is "The Lost City"—a $300 million theme park built by the South African entrepreneur and developer, Sol Kerzer, located in what used to be the Bantustan of Bophuthatswana. The Lost City represents one of the most commercially sophisticated and elaborate attempts yet to "recover" an archaic or primitive African past—as represented in the novels of H. Rider Haggard—in a marketable form.

41. For the suggestion that Hardy deliberately set about marketing the Wessex name in order to increase the sales of his novels, see Millgate, *Thomas Hardy: A Biography*, 249. Writing to one of his publishers, Hardy asks: "Could you, whenever advertising my books, use the words 'Wessex Novels' at the head of the list? . . . I find that the name *Wessex*, wh. I was the first to use in fiction, is getting to be taken up everywhere: & it would be a pity for us to lose the right to it for want of asserting it."

42. See Hardy, "The Dorchester Labourer," 181–83.

43. Hardy, "The Dorchester Labourer," 183.

44. For a succinct summation and critical discussion of these arguments, see Lerner, 74–88.

45. See Lerner, 87–88.

46. See G. M. Trevelyan, *History of England*, vol. 3 (Garden City, N.Y.: Anchor Books, 1953), 188–90.

47. See Thomas Hardy, *The Life and Work of Thomas Hardy*, ed. Michael Millgate (Athens, Ga.: University of Georgia Press, 1985), 335. The passage comes from a letter to H. Rider Haggard published in the latter's book, *Rural England*, and then reprinted in a modified form in Florence Hardy's biography of Hardy, a work ghostwritten by Hardy himself.

48. Hardy, "The Dorchester Labourer," 182.

49. Hardy, "The Dorchester Labourer," 183–84.

50. Norman Friedman, "Criticism and the Novel," *Antioch Review* 18 (1958): 348–52; and Howe, 98–99.

51. Howe, 99.

52. Heilman (xix) notes that Hardy dismisses Casterbridge's reaction to the furmity woman's revelation in a single cursory paragraph. It would appear that Hardy has little interest in working out the public ramifications of Henchard's earlier domestic misdeeds.

53. Hardy seems to have realized that his novel suffered from an overabundance of narrative episodes and incredible coincidences of plot. See Hardy, *The Life and Work of Thomas Hardy*, 183, 185.

54. For examples of critics who view Hardy's novel on the model of Greek and Shakespearean tragedy, see Dike, 169–79; Paterson, 151–72; Heilman, v–xxxviii; Millgate, *Thomas Hardy: His Career as a Novelist*, 232–34; Lerner, 59–72; Frederick Karl, "*The Mayor of Casterbridge*: A New Fiction Defined," *Modern Fiction Studies* 6 (1960): 195–213; Duane Edwards, "*The Mayor of Casterbridge* as Aeschylean Tragedy," *Studies in the Novel* 4 (1972): 608–18; and Jeanette King, *Tragedy in the Victorian Novel* (Cambridge: Cambridge University Press, 1978): 21–26, 41–42, 97–102, 107–12.

55. For a feminist evaluation of Henchard's life after his abortive suicide attempt, see Showalter, 112–14. Showalter argues that Henchard's life becomes "a humbling, and yet educative and ennobling apprenticeship in human sensitivity" (113).

56. See Carl J. Weber, *Hardy of Wessex* (London: Routledge & Kegan Paul, 1965), 151–53.

57. To be sure, a magistrate in Casterbridge does have the power to transport a criminal to Australia, as Hardy notes in passing (348). However, in this capacity, the magistrate acts as a representative of the national, rather than the local city government. In any case, none of Henchard's actions would make him subject to such punishment.

58. For an analysis of Henchard's anachronistic status, see Hasan, 61–63.

59. Thomas Hardy, *Jude the Obscure* (London: Macmillan, 1974), 419.

60. For the view that Tess and Jude are compromisers who long for a fully democratized modernity, whereas Henchard is Hardy's closest approximation to a classical tragic hero, see Dale Kramer, *Thomas Hardy: Tess of the d'Urbervilles* (Cambridge: Cambridge University Press, 1991), especially 73–78. Kramer points out that the story of Tess's personal loss lacks the social significance that would make it a traditional tragedy.

61. Hardy, *The Life and Work of Thomas Hardy*, 185.

62. Thomas Hardy, letter to Edward Wright, 2 June 1907, *The Collected Letters of Thomas Hardy*, ed. Richard L. Purdy and Michael Millgate, vol. 3 (Oxford: Clarendon Press, 1982): 255.

63. Thomas Hardy, *The Dynasts* (London: Macmillan, 1977), xxv.

64. Hardy, *The Dynasts*, xxi–xxiii.

65. Hardy, "General Preface to the Wessex Edition of 1912," 380.

66. Hardy, *The Life and Work of Thomas Hardy*, 241.

Chapter 2

1. For the view that Conrad's novels cover over the contradictions of modern industrial capitalism and Western imperialism and thus serve to legitimate their influence, see Fredric Jameson, *The Political Unconscious* (Ithaca, N.Y.: Cornell University Press, 1981), 206–80; Jacques Darras, *Conrad and the West: Signs of Empire* (Totowa, N.J.: Barnes & Noble, 1982); Benita Parry, *Conrad and Imperialism* (London: Macmillan, 1983), 1–19, 76–98; and Mark Conroy, *Modernism and Authority: Strategies of Legitimation in Flaubert and Conrad* (Baltimore: Johns Hopkins University Press, 1985), 99–117. For the view that Conrad's works are racist, see D.C.R.A. Goonetileke, *Developing Countries in British Fiction* (London: Macmillan, 1977); and Chinua Achebe, "An Image of Africa: Racism in Conrad's *Heart of Darkness,*" in *Hopes and Impediments* (New York: Doubleday, 1989), 1–20. Those few critics who argue that Conrad takes an equivocal or critical view of Western imperialism include Avrom Fleishman, *Conrad's Politics: Community and Anarchy in the Fiction of Joseph Conrad* (Baltimore: Johns Hopkins University Press, 1967), 79–126; Stephen Zelnick, "Conrad's *Lord Jim:* Meditations on the Other Hemisphere," *The Minnesota Review,* 11

(1978): 73–89; John A. McClure, *Kipling and Conrad: The Colonial Fiction* (Cambridge, Mass.: Harvard University Press, 1981), 82–167; and Bruce Henrikson, *Nomadic Voices: Conrad and the Subject of Narrative* (Champaign: University of Illinois Press, 1992), 10, 16, 102–7.

2. For the view that Conrad both invokes and undermines a Spencerian sociological view of the progressive character of modern European civilization, see Brian W. Shaffer, "'Rebarbarizing Civilization': Conrad's African Fiction and Spencerian Sociology," *PMLA* 108 (1993): 45–58.

3. Joseph Conrad, "Autocracy and War," in *Notes on Life and Letters* (London: J. M. Dent & Sons, 1921), 118. For a treatment of Conrad as a displaced author, see Asher Z. Milbauer, *Transcending Exile: Conrad Nabokov I. B. Singer* (Miami: Florida International University Press, 1985), 1–26.

4. See Joseph Conrad, "An Observer in Malaya," in *Notes on Life and Letters,* 80. Also see Conrad's preface to *The Rescue,* in which he offers oblique praise of James Brooke, 3–4. Finally, see Conrad's private letter to Aniela Zagorska, of 25 December 1898, quoted in Zdzislaw Najder, *Conrad's Polish Background* (London: Oxford University Press, 1962), 232.

5. See Joseph Conrad, "The Crime of Partition" and "A Note on the Polish Problem" in *Notes on Life and Letters,* 153–77, 179–87.

6. See Parry, 1–19.

7. See Conrad, *Notes on Life and Letters,* 141–42.

8. See for example, J. Hillis Miller, *Fiction and Repetition* (Cambridge, Mass.: Harvard University Press, 1982), 30; and Jameson, 206–80.

9. Arnold E. Davidson, *Conrad's Endings: A Study of the Five Major Novels* (Ann Arbor, Mich.: UMI Research Press, 1984), 29.

10. Even an earlier generation of critics who basically regarded Jim as an estimable figure found the Patusan episodes inferior to the first half of the novel. See F. R. Leavis, *The Great Tradition* (London: Chatto & Windus, 1948), 189–90; Albert J. Guerard, *Conrad the Novelist* (Cambridge, Mass.: Harvard University Press, 1958), 168; David Daiches, *The Novel and the Modern World* (Chicago: University of Chicago Press, 1960), 35–36; and Ian Watt, *Conrad in the Nineteenth Century* (Berkeley: University of California Press, 1979), 308. However, for a recent defense of the formal integrity and aesthetic coherence of Conrad's novel, see Ralph W. Rader, *"Lord Jim* and the Formal Development of the English Novel," in *Reading Narrative: Form, Ethics, Ideology,* ed. James Phelan (Columbus: Ohio State University Press, 1989), 220–35.

11. Jameson, 255–56. For a further development of Jameson's thesis, see Michael Sprinker, "Fiction and Ideology: *Lord Jim* and the Problem of Literary History," in Phelan, *Reading Narrative,* 236–49.

12. Darras, 28.

13. Conrad's indebtedness to a number of contemporary accounts of James Brooke's career was long ago acknowledged by scholars, though few

have made much of this fact. Recent critics have almost completely neglected the historical basis for Jim's life, first noted by John Dozier Gordan, *Joseph Conrad: The Making of a Novelist* (Cambridge, Mass.: Harvard University Press, 1940), 64–73. Only Fleishman has made a signficant attempt to integrate this material into a wider consideration of Conrad's fiction. See Fleishman, 97–104. Most recently, Andrea White has discussed the importance of Brooke for Conrad, though surprisingly she does not treat *Lord Jim* in any detail. See her *Joseph Conrad and the Adventure Tradition: Constructing and deconstructing the imperial subject* (Cambridge: Cambridge University Press, 1993), 24–28, 103–4. For White's discussion of Conrad in relation to postcolonial literature, see 199–203.

14. Stephen K. Land, *Paradox and Polarity in the Fiction of Joseph Conrad* (New York: St. Martin's Press, 1984), 80.

15. See Guerard, 167; and Davidson, 10.

16. Bakhtin's account of the prehistory of the Western European novel as the cumulative subsumption of previous literary genres offers a theoretical framework in which to understand Conrad's efforts. See, in particular, M. M. Bakhtin, "From the Prehistory of Novelistic Discourse," in *The Dialogic Imagination* (Austin: University of Texas Press, 1981), 41–83. For further discussion of the formal perspectivism of *Lord Jim* in terms of Bakhtin's theory of polyphony, see Henrikson, 104.

17. For detailed discussions of the political situation in Patusan, see Fleishman, 106–11; and Conroy, 106–13.

18. See Norman Sherry, *Conrad's Eastern World* (Cambridge: Cambridge University Press, 1966), 119–38. Sherry has collected a number of Conrad's sources for depicting Patusan in an appendix of the Norton *Lord Jim,* 344–56. Also see Jerry Allen, *The Sea Years of Joseph Conrad* (London: Methuen, 1967), 197–202; Hans Lippe, "*Lord Jim:* Some Geographic Observations," *The Conradian* 10 (1985): 135–38; Hans van Marle and Pierre Lefranc, "Ashore and Afloat: New Perspectives on Topography and Geography in *Lord Jim,*" *Conradiana* 20 (1988): 109–35; Watt, 254–356; and Gordon, 64–72. A useful map and supplemental material may be found in Joseph Conrad, *Lord Jim,* ed. Cedric Watts and Robert Hampson (New York: Viking/Penguin, 1986), 6–7, 361–63. The Berau River region is geographically distinct from Sarawak and Brunei, where the real Patusan was in fact located; the former lies off the Macassar Straits, on the opposite coast of Borneo from Sarawak, which faces the South China Sea. To make matters more complicated, Brown's route places Conrad's fictional Patusan on the northwestern coast of Sumatra, facing the Indian Ocean, around a thousand miles from the island of Borneo. All recent critics acknowledge that Conrad's Patusan is a conflation of different geographical locations.

19. My information on the history of Borneo and the reign of the Brookes is largely drawn from Stephen Runciman's *The White Rajahs: A History of Sarawak From 1841 to 1946* (Cambridge: Cambridge University Press,

1960). Other sources include S. Baring Gould and C. A. Bampfylde, *A History of Sarawak under Its Two White Rajahs* (London: Henry Sotheran, 1909); Robert Payne *The White Rajahs of Sarawak* (New York: Funk & Wagnalls, 1960); and Nicholas Tarling, *Britain, the Brookes and Brunei* (Cambridge: Cambridge University Press, 1970). Some twentieth-century historians have presented a more negative view of the Brooke dynasty than was typical of the popular Victorian accounts available to Conrad. In some cases, modern historians have uncovered facts that cast the actions of James Brooke in a less flattering light.

20. The term *Dyak* comes from the Dutch term, *Dayak,* which denotes *any* indigenous people in Borneo as distinct from the Malays or other immigrant peoples. The heterogeneous Dyaks are in fact composed of distinct ethnic groups that share many social customs. Among those known to the Dutch and English as Dyaks are the Ibans, Muruts, Bakatans, Kanowits, Kayans, Kelabits, and Kenyahs. See Runciman, 5–9. It is likely that the fishing folk under the rajah's rule are Ibans or "Sea Dyaks."

21. See Fleishman, 107–11. For a contrary view of Jim's rule, see Conroy, 108–10; and Darras, 8–29.

22. Before 1888, the Brookes maintained an extremely complex relationship with Britain and the other Western imperial powers. In the early days of his regime, James Brooke approached a number of competing European states for protection and assistance, without sacrificing the political autonomy of Sarawak. Although Brooke occasionally relied on the visits of English warships for support, he often ran afoul of the British government. At one time a special tribunal established by Parliament put Brooke on trial and on another occasion the British intervened militarily against the rajah in order to prevent him from carrying out a campaign against indigenous pirates. In many respects, Brooke's policy anticipated that of subsequent Third World leaders who maintained their limited independence by playing off global superpowers against one another, while seeking assistance and support from them as the political situation demanded.

23. James Brooke and his successor Charles were responsible for suppressing the practices of head–hunting, slavery, and piracy, which had been widely practiced throughout Borneo. They consistently tolerated a variety of religious faiths (often over the objections of Christian missionaries from Europe), going so far as to welcome Hindus to Sarawak after the Sepoy Mutiny of 1857. The judicial system they established was based on the principles of equality before the law and judicial impartiality towards the various races and ethnic groups of Sarawak. With certain exceptions, they established free trade and voluntary wage labor, economic practices at variance with the preexisting tribal and feudal societies. See Runciman, 68–91, 159–73.

24. Once again, the Brookes of Sarawak provide an interesting historical model for Jim's regime. Charles Brooke, the second rajah and Conrad's

contemporary, scandalized many in Britain by tolerating and even encouraging interracial unions among his subjects. Brooke suggested that the population needed to develop and administer Sarawak must come from a fusion of European and Asian peoples, and went quite far toward putting this policy into effect. See Runciman, 160–63. On James Brooke's respect for native customs, see White, 27.

25. Brooke was in principle opposed to chartered companies and concessions and worked actively to prevent the British Eastern Archipelago Company from intervening in the affairs of Sarawak. Nevertheless, Brooke's chronic shortage of capital eventually led him to sanction government monopolies on coal, antimony ore, and opium. His prosecution of Chinese "smugglers" of opium led in 1857 to a violent uprising of the Chinese community that nearly toppled the rajah and that was only put down with considerable bloodshed. See Runciman, 52, 82, 93, 103–5, 125–26.

26. Quoted in Runciman, 52.

27. See Francis Fukuyama, *The End of History and the Last Man* (New York: The Free Press, 1992), 134 and 241.

28. The following discussion of Jim's invention of a new national identity for Patusan is indebted to Benedict Anderson's *Imagined Communities* (London: Verso, 1991).

29. See Fleishman, who argues both for the organic character of Patusan and for its resemblance to the classical polis, 69–75.

30. For a different account of Jim's unsuccessful attempt to escape from the consequences of modernity in Patusan, see Daniel Cottom, "*Lord Jim*: Destruction through Time," *Joseph Conrad's Lord Jim*, ed. Harold Bloom (New York: Chelsea House, 1987), 117–34.

31. Joseph Conrad, *The Secret Agent* (Garden City, N.Y.: Anchor, 1953), 125.

32. For a suggestive analysis of the Nietzschean critique of the end of history, see Fukuyama, 300–312. See also Nietzsche's characterization of liberal democratic culture in sections 37 and 38 of "Skirmishes of an Untimely Man," in *Twilight of the Idols*, contained in *The Portable Nietzsche*, ed. Walter Kaufmann (New York: Viking, 1968), 540–41. It is well known that Conrad's comments on Nietzsche are negative, but this fact does not mean that their ideas do not at times converge.

33. Thomas Brassey, *British Seaman* (London: Longmans, Green, 1877), 349.

34. Brassey, 329.

35. See Conroy, 101, 103.

36. See Fukuyama, 301.

37. For the standard critical view of the maritime code, see Jameson, 265; Conroy, 103; and Parry, 89–90.

38. H. Moyse–Bartlett, *A History of The Merchant Navy* (London: Geroge G. Harrap, 1937), 266–68.

39. The specific clause that governs Jim's desertion reads as follows: "The Board of Trade may suspend or cancel the Certificate (whether of Competency or Service) of any Master or Mate in the following Cases; . . . (2) If upon any Investigation conducted under the Provisions contained in the Eighth Part of this Act, or upon any Investigation made by a Naval Court constituted as herein–after mentioned, it is reported that the Loss or Abandonment of or serious Damage to any Ship or Loss of Life has been caused by his wrongful Act or Default." The maximum fine for this offense is fixed at £50. See *The Statutes of The United Kingdom Great Britain and Ireland,* 17 & 18 Victoria, 1854, C. 104, 242, 2, p. 522.

40. See Brassey, 341.

41. See Thomas Hobbes, *Leviathan,* especially chapters 14 and 21, 99–109 and 161–71; and John Locke, *Two Treatises of Government* (New York: New American Library, 1965), especially chapters 2–5 of *The Second Treatise,* 309–44.

42. For the view that Conrad's work demonstrates the metaphysical groundlessness of political activity, see especially Royal Roussel, *The Metaphysics of Darkness* (Baltimore: Johns Hopkins University Press, 1971), 12–16. For an attempt to place Conrad's "nihilism" within a political or historical context, see Fleishman, 68, and Jameson, 261.

43. According to a contemporary account, a representative pilgrim ship on the route taken by the *Patna* carried "Turcomans, Arabo-Persians, and Bedouins." See the material collected by Sherry in *Lord Jim,* 313.

44. To be sure, the Asian pilgrims on the way to Mecca are united by their common faith in Islam; but this demonstrates only that the cohesiveness of the passengers depends upon a premodern faith that cannot sustain the more secular officers who run the *Patna.* In any case, Islam is not capable of uniting the modern empire or the global network of commercial relations of which Jim is a part.

45. One of Brassey's recommendations was to require the apprentices aboard training ships to learn foreign languages; the curriculum of the *Conway* offered only occasional and optional instruction in French and Latin for those willing to pay additional fees. See Brassey, 330, 341–42.

46. For a different interpretation of such moments, see especially Miller, 28; Roussel, 84–86; and Tony Tanner, "Butterflies and Beetles—Conrad's Two Truths," *Chicago Review,* 16 (1963): 136–38.

47. For a further development of this point, see Joseph McLaughlin, "Writing the Urban Jungle: Metropolis and Colonies in Conan Doyle, General Booth, Jack London, Conrad, and T. S. Eliot," Ph.D. diss. Duke University 1992, 170–98.

48. For an analysis of the connection between Conrad's formal techniques as versions of Bakhtin's theory of polyphony and Lyotard's notion of *petit récits* that work to subvert imperialist ideology, see Henrikson, 102–7.

49. See Mario Vargas Llosa, "Questions of Conquest: What Columbus wrought, and what he did not," *Harper's Magazine,* December 1990, 48–51.

50. García Márquez's *The General in His Labyrinth* is a notable exception; it presents a relatively favorable, nostalgic, though ultimately critical portrait of Bolívar's political career.

51. For a contrary view of this moment, see Fleishman, 107, 110; Parry, 85, 89–90; and Conroy, 112.

52. See, for example, Robert E. Kuehn, "Introduction," *Twentieth–Century Interpretations of Lord Jim* (Englewood Cliffs, N.J.: Prentice Hall, 1969), 12; and Todd G. Willy, "Measures of the Heart and of the Darkness: Conrad and the Suicides of 'New Imperialism,'" *Conradiana* 14 (1982): 193, 195.

53. Anne and Henry Paolucci, eds., *Hegel on Tragedy* (New York: Harper & Row, 1962), 102.

54. For a more critical appraisal of Jim's self–conscious efforts to affirm his own heroic, premodern ideals, see Barbara DeMille, "Cruel Illusions: Nietzsche, Conrad, Hardy and the Shadowy Ideal," *Studies in English Literature* 30 (1991): 697–714, especially 705–7.

Chapter 3

1. George Wilhelm Friedrich Hegel, *The Philosophy of History,* trans. J. Sibree (New York: Dover, 1956) 91, 99.

2. For a representative critique of Hegel's view of Africa, see Henry Olela, "The African Foundations of Greek Philosophy," in *African Philosophy: An Introduction,* ed. Richard Wright (Washington, D.C.: University Press of America, 1979) 65–82, especially 68–69. For the view that Hegel's philosophy is not relevant to the understanding of Achebe's work, see C. L. Innes, *The Devil's Own Mirror* (Washington D.C.: Three Continents Press, 1990), 87. For an attempt to contrast Achebe with Hegel, see Margaret E. Turner, "Achebe, Hegel, and the New Colonialism," in *Chinua Achebe: A Celebration,* ed. Kirsten Holst Petersen and Anna Rutherford (Oxford: Heinemann, 1991), 31–40. Ironically, in her attack on Hegel's view of history, Turner relies on a Hegelian conception of tragedy, as her talk of "conflicting sets of values" (33) in Achebe's novels reveals.

3. For a contemporary Hegelian defense of the modernization of African society, see J. E. Wiredu, "How Not to Compare African Thought with Western Thought," in *African Philosophy: An Introduction,* ed. Richard Wright, 166–84.

4. Chinua Achebe, "What Has Literature Got to Do with It?," in *Hopes and Impediments* (New York: Doubleday, 1989), 155. The essay originally appeared in 1986. For Achebe's critique of the "universalist" assumptions of Western criticism, see his "Colonialist Criticism," "Where Angels Fear to

Tread," and "Thoughts on the African Novel," in *Morning Yet on Creation Day* (New York: Anchor Books, 1976), 3–24, 61–64, 65–73.

5. Achebe, "What Has Literature Got to Do With It," 155. This statement is by no means unusual in Achebe's writing. On numerous occasions he has reiterated the necessity of "modernization." For example, see Charles H. Rowell, "An Interview with Chinua Achebe," *Callaloo* 13 (1990): 91; as well as Achebe, "Koofi Awoonor as a Novelist," in *Hopes and Impediments*, 126; and *The Trouble with Nigeria* (London and Nairobi: Heinemann, 1983), 2–3.

6. Chinua Achebe, "Preface," *The African Trilogy: Things Fall Apart, No Longer at Ease, Arrow of God* (London: Picador, 1988), x.

7. Jeffrey Meyers points out that this Hegelian characterization of African history and peoples had its advocates well into the twentieth century, and included such prominent individuals as Lord Lugard, high commissioner of Northern Nigeria, and Sir Alan Burns, Governor-General of the Gold Coast. See, "Culture and History in *Things Fall Apart*," *Critique* 11 (1968): 25–26.

8. Chinua Achebe, "An Image of Africa: Racism in Conrad's *Heart of Darkness*," in *Hopes and Impediments*, 17.

9. Chinua Achebe, "The Role of the Writer in a New Nation," in *African Writers on African Writing* ed. G. D. Killam (Evanston, Ill.: Northwestern University, 1973), 8.

10. For a pointed critique of the conceptual binarism that strictly opposes Africa to the West, see Kwame Anthony Appiah, *In My Father's House: Africa in the Philosophy of Culture* (Oxford: Oxford University Press, 1992), 138–57, especially 155–57.

11. See Rowell, "An Interview with Chinua Achebe," 97.

12. See Robert M. Wren, *Achebe's World: The Historical and Cultural Context of the Novels* (Washington, D.C.: Three Continents Press, 1980), 16–21, 116–21. For Achebe's use of historical and anthropological material in his later works, see Charles Nnolim, "A Source for *Arrow of God*," and C. L. Innes, "A Source for *Arrow of God*: A Response," both in *Critical Perspectives on Chinua Achebe*, ed. C. L. Innes and Bernth Lindfors (Washington, D.C.: Three Continents Press, 1978), 219–43, 244–45.

13. See Rowell, "An Interview with Chinua Achebe," 97. For a detailed examination of the Aristotelian dimension of *Things Fall Apart*, see Roger L. Landrum, "Chinua Achebe and the Aristotelian Concept of Tragedy," *Black Academy Review* 1 (1970): 22–30; and G. D. Killam, *The Novels of Chinua Achebe* (New York: Africana, 1969), 13–34. For a broader discussion of Achebe in relation to traditional tragedy, see Alastair Niven, "Chinua Achebe and the Possibility of Modern Tragedy," in *Chinua Achebe: A Celebration*, 41–50.

14. Achebe, "The Role of the Writer in a New Nation," 9.

15. For a discussion of Achebe's realistic and critical portrayal of traditional Igbo life, see Abdul R. JanMohammed, *Manichean Aesthetics*

(Amherst: University of Massachusetts Press, 1983), 154–56; and J. M. Waghmare, "Chinua Achebe's Vision of the Crumbling Past," in *Indian Readings in Commonwealth Literature,* ed. G. S. Amur, V. R. N. Prasad, B. V. Nemade, and N. H. Nihalani (New York: Sterling, 1985), 117–18. For the view that Achebe stresses what traditional Igbo society had in common with modern democratic society, see Diana Akers Rhoads, "Culture in Chinua Achebe's *Things Fall Apart,"* *African Studies Review* 36 (1993): 61–72.

16. Okonkwo is chastised by the clan for his attack on Ekwefi only because he violates the sanctions governing the Week of Peace; throughout most of the year his wives are not accorded this protection.

17. For a feminist analysis of Achebe's portrayal of traditional patriarchal Igbo society, see Rhonda Cobham, "Problems of Gender and History in Teaching *Things Fall Apart,"* in *Canonization and Teaching of African Literatures,* ed. Raoul Granqvist (Amsterdam: Rodopi, 1990), 25–39.

18. This episode is based on the murder and cannibalization of Dr. J. F. Stewart, a white British missionary captured by the Ahiara people near Obizi in 1905. See Wren, *Achebe's World,* 26.

19. Significantly, these practices provide the tragic subject matter of much classical Greek literature. The sacrificial offering of Iphigenia to the gods and the *sparagmos* (ritual dismemberment) of Pentheus are pivotal events referred to in Aeschylus's *Agamemnon* and Euripides's *The Bacchae.*

20. René Girard, *Violence and the Sacred,* trans. by Patrick Gregory (Baltimore: Johns Hopkins University Press, 1977), 26.

21. Girard, *Violence and the Sacred,* 258.

22. For a general discussion of the ways that "religious beliefs of traditional peoples constitute explanatory theories and that traditional religious actions are reasonable attempts to pursue goals in the light of these beliefs," see Appiah, 120–22.

23. Chinua Achebe, "Named for Victoria," in *Morning Yet on Creation Day,* 96.

24. Achebe, "The Role of the Writer in a New Nation," 9.

25. See Wiredu, 177–79; and Appiah, 94–95. Appiah, however, stresses that if philosophy, in the modern sense, is to exist within a society, it must take the form of a social organization of inquiry, rather than remain the enterprise of individual speculative thinkers (126–29).

26. Chinua Achebe, "The Truth of Fiction," in *Hopes and Impediments,* 146.

27. See Stanley Fish, "Change," in *Doing What Comes Naturally* (Durham, N.C.: Duke University Press, 1989), 141–62.

28. Rowell, "An Interview with Chinua Achebe," 88.

29. Appiah argues that those who typically object to universalism are in fact objecting to pseudo–universalism, with the paradoxical result of occluding local differences. Moreover, he notes that the danger of relativism in a

postcolonial context is its implicit endorsement of political tyranny, justified on contingent and local grounds (58, 152).

30. Wiredu, 169.

31. For general accounts of the conflict between African and European ways of life in Achebe's novels, see Killam, *The Novels of Chinua Achebe,* 13–58; Abiola Irele, "The Tragic Conflict in the Novels of Chinua Achebe"; and Lloyd W. Brown, "Cultural Norms and Modes of Perception in Achebe's Fiction," both in *Critical Perspectives on Chinua Achebe,* 10–21, 22–36; and C. L. Innes, *The Devil's Own Mirror,* 85–86.

32. For another discussion of the Christian infiltration of Umuofia, see JanMohammed, 165–67.

33. Alexander Kojève, *Introduction to the Reading of Hegel,* trans. James H. Nichols, Jr. (Ithaca, N.Y.: Cornell University Press, 1969), 5–67.

34. Wren, 35.

35. Wren, 88–89.

36. Achebe has heavily criticized the British imperial government for its failure to create a lasting "spirit of common nationality" in Nigeria during fifty years of colonial rule. See his "The African Writer and the Biafran Cause," in *Morning Yet on Creation Day,* 118.

37. Wren, 18, 91.

38. For one view of the role of trade in the destruction of traditional Igbo life, see Killam, *The Novels of Chinua Achebe,* 30.

39. Wren, 92.

40. Achebe, "The Role of the Writer in a New Nation," 11.

41. Achebe, "What Has Literature Got to Do With It?," 168. For Achebe's implicit recognition that the West possesses the "ability to provide better than anybody else for man's material needs," see "The Writer and His Community," in *Hopes and Impediments,* 51.

42. On the central importance of literacy as a modernizing force in traditional African society, see Appiah, 130–31.

43. For another account of modernization in Achebe's novel as both inevitable and tragic, see E. V. Ramkrishnan, "The Novel of Memory and the Third World Reality: Gabriel García Márquez and Chinua Achebe," in *Indian Readings in Commonwealth Literature,* 124–31.

44. See Achebe's explicit statement to this effect, "What Has Literature Got to Do with It?," 159–60. For another critique of Weber's thesis within the context of African culture and history, see Appiah, 144–47.

45. See JanMohammed, 153–60.

46. See Killam, *The Novels of Chinua Achebe,* 35.

47. For critics who see this passage as a key to understanding the generic character of Achebe's novel, see Killam, *The Novels of Chinua Achebe,* 55–56, and Francis Silbey, "Tragedy in the Novels of Chinua Achebe," *Southern Humanities Review* 9 (1975): 367.

48. See C. L. Innes, *Chinua Achebe* (Cambridge: Cambridge University Press, 1990), 50.

49. See George Eliot, *The Mill on the Floss* (Boston: Houghton Mifflin, 1961), 90, 174. For a generic analysis of *No Longer at Ease* as a topical satire formally distinct from the "epic tragedy" of *Things Fall Apart*, see C. A. Babalola, "A Reconsideration of Achebe's *No Longer at Ease*," *Phylon* 47 (1986): 139–47.

50. Wren, 166.

51. Innes, *Chinua Achebe*, 45.

52. Appiah, however, suggests that "hometown societies," or *"associations des originaires,"* like the Umuofia Progressive Union may actually provide the best and most important means for postcolonial African nations to modernize and advance materially. He points out that their private character and decentralized organization have made them far more efficient and productive than the corrupt centralized governments of most African nations. Appiah notes that in the 1970s and 1980s hometown societies increasingly took over the functions of government, providing medical, educational, and social services that would otherwise have been unavailable (169–71). Appiah's point seems valid and compatible with the argument I have advanced. For the problem that Achebe focuses on in *No Longer at Ease* is the incompatibility of a strong centralized national government and a strong traditional tribal society. The corruption of the new Nigerian regime comes about when the two are mixed; rather than operating as commercial enterprises free of governmental interference, local tribal interests attempt to coopt the national government and use its power and influence to pursue their particular private ends. If, as Appiah suggests, the hometown societies are to serve the public good by providing necessary services in a decentralized manner, then the power of the central government has to be strictly limited, and hence the goal of African *nationalism*, at least in its more potent form, abandoned. Moreover, these hometown associations, though originating in a particular clan or village, must become modern private commercial enterprises—family businesses on a large scale—and hence not clans in the traditional sense. Their distinctive ethnic character will be further eroded as they integrate themselves into a global economy.

53. Achebe, *The Trouble with Nigeria*, 1–7.

54. Achebe, *The Trouble with Nigeria*, 45–50.

55. See Wren, 45–47, 63, and especially 74–75. My argument concerning corruption is heavily indebted to Wren's discussion of "kola."

56. For the view that political corruption in Nigeria is a legacy of British colonialism, see Killam, *The Novels of Chinua Achebe*, 43.

57. See Irele, 16–17; and Roderick Wilson, "Eliot and Achebe: An Analysis of Some Formal and Philosophical Qualities of *No Longer at Ease*," in *Critical Perspectives on Chinua Achebe*, 165–66; also see Killam, *The Novels of Chinua Achebe*, 50–51.

58. See Innes, *Chinua Achebe*, 55.
59. The Igbo people, at any rate, were not ruled by kings or chiefs before the arrival of the British. Their leaders consisted jointly of men with titles, the elders of the clan, and the chief priests.

Chapter 4

1. Mario Vargas Llosa, "A Fish Out of Water," *Granta* 36 (1991): 56.
2. Mario Vargas Llosa, "Updating Karl Popper," *PMLA* 105 (1990): 1022.
3. Vargas Llosa, "Updating Karl Popper," 1023.
4. Vargas Llosa, "Updating Karl Popper," 1019.
5. Vargas Llosa, "Updating Karl Popper," 1023.
6. See Ricardo A. Setti, "Diálogo con Vargas Llosa," in Mario Vargas Llosa, *sobre la vida y la política* (Argentina: Editorial InterMundo, 1989), 139–40. Vargas Llosa remarks: "Hay cierto tipo de flagelos, distorsiones, deformaciones del espíritu humano que persiguen a la Historia a lo largo de los tiempos y que continuamente están reapareciendo. El nacionalismo, el racismo—casi no existen sociedades que estén vacunadas contra esos flagelos. Son flagelos que en un momento dado se adormecen, pasan a ser completamente secundarios, pero que en cualquier momento, dadas ciertas circunstancias, resucitan, y entonces otra vez pueden provocar toda clase de estragos." ["There are certain types of plagues, distortions, deformations of the human spirit that continuously haunt history throughout the ages and that are constantly reappearing. Nationalism, racism—virtually no society exists that could be inoculated against these plagues. These are plagues that in a given moment are dormant, that seem completely insignificant, but that at any moment, given certain circumstances, revive, and then once more can cause all manner of destruction."] Also see Mario Vargas Llosa, "El elefante y la cultura," in *Contra viento y marea* (Barcelona: Seix Barral, 1983), I, 438–39.
7. For an account of the origin of the novel, see José Miguel Oviedo, "Vargas Llosa habla de su nueva novela," in *Mario Vargas Llosa: El escritor y la crítica*, ed. José Miguel Oviedo (Madrid: Taurus, 1981), 307–8. (The interview took place in 1979). Also see Setti, "Diálogo con Vargas Llosa," 40–46.
8. It is possible that the rise of Khomeini and Islamic fundamentalism in Iran provided Vargas Llosa with a secondary historical referent for his novel. (The shah fell in 1979, at a time when Vargas Llosa was still at work on his novel). In his 1986 interview with Setti, he describes Canudos as an example of "el fenómeno del fanatismo, básicamente, de la intolerancia que pesa sobre nuestra historia." ["the phenomenon of fanaticism, basically, of intolerance that weighs heavily upon our history."] In the same interview Vargas

Llosa employs almost identical language to categorize recent events in Iran: "El fanatismo, la intolerancia, por razones ideológicas o religiosas; ya lo vemos hoy en el mundo islámico, como el fanatismo cobra de pronto un poder de arraigo, de arrastre con las masas, como en la época de la Edad Media. Y eso puede provocar situaciones como las de Irán o de Libia, sociedades donde se llega a veces a una violencia completamente insensata por intolerancia, por fanatismo." ["Fanaticism, intolerance, because of ideological or religious reasons—already we see today in the Islamic world, how fanaticism suddenly recovers its power to set down its roots in the masses and to win them over, as in the epoch of the Middle Ages. And that can lead to situations like those in Iran or in Libia, societies where at times a totally senseless violence has been brought about by intolerance, by fanaticism."] See Setti, 48, 140.

9. Upon the first appearance of the names of characters I have supplied in parenthesis the original Spanish versions unless they are identical to their English counterparts.

10. Vargas Llosa, "Updating Karl Popper," 1019, 1023.

11. Georg Lukács, *The Historical Novel,* trans. Hannah and Stanley Mitchell (London: Merlin, 1962), 296.

12. Lukács, 189–90, 199, 206.

13. "The Voice from the End of the World," *The Washington Post,* Oct. 1, 1984, B11.

14. See Raymond Leslie Williams, "The Boom Twenty Years Later: An Interview with Mario Vargas Llosa," *Latin American Literary Review* 15 (1987): 205.

15. See Setti, 48, 140; and Oviedo, 310.

16. See Dick Gerdes, *Mario Vargas Llosa* (Boston: Twayne, 1985), 188. The Castro regime had arrested the Cuban poet Herberto Padilla, imprisoned him, and forced him to confess to a long list of political crimes in a manner reminiscent of the Stalinist show trials of the 1930s. Along with such literary figures as Jean–Paul Sartre, Simone de Beauvoir, and Alberto Moravia, Vargas Llosa issued a public statement criticizing the Castro government and demanding the release of Padilla.

17. Mario Vargas Llosa, *A Writer's Reality* (Syracuse, N.Y.: Syracuse University Press, 1991), 133. See also Williams, 205.

18. Sara Castro-Klarén, *Understanding Mario Vargas Llosa* (Columbia: University of South Carolina Press, 1990), 187.

19. For the English translation of *Os sertões,* see Euclides da Cunha, *Rebellion in the Backlands,* trans. Samuel Putnam (Chicago: University of Chicago Press, 1944). For a discussion of Vargas Llosa's relation to da Cunha, see Renata R. Mautner Wasserman, "Mario Vargas Llosa, Euclides da Cunha, and the Strategy of Intertextuality," *PMLA,* 108 (1993): 460–73.

20. Lukács, 133.

21. Lukács, 126.

22. On Vargas Llosa's theory of the "totalizing novel" and its connection to neo–Hegelian Marxism, see Castro–Klarén, *Understanding Mario Vargas Llosa,* 119–20.

23. See Oviedo, 311: "Salvando las distancias del caso, siempre quise escribir una novela que fuera de algún modo lo que pudo ser, respecto a su época, digamos *La guerra y la paz* o las series históricas de Dumas o *Moby–Dick* inclusive; es decir, libros con una gran peripecia épica." ["Allowing for obvious differences, I had always wanted to write a novel that would be, with respect to its age, the same kind as, let us say, *War and Peace* or Dumas's series of historical novels or *Moby–Dick,* that is, books of grand epic adventure."] On the epic conventions of *The War of the End of the World,* see Gerdes, 181; and Alfred J. MacAdam, *Textual Confrontations: Comparative Readings in Latin American Literature* (Chicago: University of Chicago Press, 1987), 149–73.

24. Originally the Portuguese term *jagunço* meant a cowboy of the interior region of northeastern Brazil, although it also took on the connotations of bandit, ruffian, or hired thug. Da Cunha uses it as a synonym for *sertanejo* or backlands inhabitant. Vargas Llosa tends to use it in a more limited sense as a synonym for a follower of the Counselor.

25. Lukács, 127.

26. Lukács, 312.

27. On the silence of the Couselor, see Sara Castro-Klarén, "Santos and Cangaceiros: inscription without discourse in *Os sertões* and *La guerra del fin del mundo,*" *MLN* 101 (1986): 366–88.

28. See Setti, 54: "[E]l Consejero prácticamente no habla nunca, está visto desde lejos, porque me parecía que acercarme al Consejero era como romper el mito." ["The Counselor practically never speaks; he is seen from a distance because it seemed to me that approaching him too closely was to demystify him."] See also Vargas Llosa, *A Writer's Reality,* 138.

29. See Lukács, 313–14. In fact, the few instances in which Vargas Llosa does provide the intimate physical details of the Counselor's life, such as those of his fatal sickness, seem calculated to diminish the great man's heroic stature.

30. See Oviedo, 309.

31. Lukács, 58.

32. These numbers reflect the estimates of da Cunha. Modern historians of the Canudos rebellion place the number of inhabitants in Belo Monte at fifteen to twenty thousand. See, for example, Robert M. Levine, "'Mud Hut Jerusalem': Canudos Revisted," in *The Abolition of Slavery and the Aftermath of Emancipation in Brazil,* ed. Rebecca J. Scott et. al. (Durham, N.C.: Duke University Press, 1988), 121.

33. See Gerdes, 177–78.

34. See Gilberto Freyre, *Order and Progress,* trans. Rod W. Horton (Berkeley: University of California Press, 1986), 15–18.

35. Vargas Llosa, *A Writer's Reality*, 126.

36. Vargas Llosa, *A Writer's Reality*, 126.

37. See also Vargas Llosa, *A Writer's Reality*, 126–27.

38. See Freyre, 12–17.

39. See Freyre, 15–18.

40. See Oviedo, 309–10.

41. Vargas Llosa's satiric treatment of military governments is not exclusively devoted to left–wing regimes. César's "Dictatorial Republic" has strong affinities with a number of right–wing military governments, including those led by Manuel Arturo Odría (Peru), Jorge Rafael Videla (Argentina), Anastasio Somoza (Nicaragua), and Augusto Pinochet (Chile), that have been the frequent targets of Vargas Llosa's political criticism.

42. It is noteworthy, however, that during the Canudos war, rumors circulated throughout Latin America concerning a secret army of 67,000 that had been organized in the United States by monarchist sympathizers for the purposes of assisting the rebels in their fight against the Brazilian republic. Da Cunha records that this unsubstantiated claim appeared in an influential Argentine newspaper and that despite the editor's own skepticism towards the report, the rumor was widely believed in Brazil itself. See da Cunha, *Rebellion in the Backland*, 385.

43. See also Vargas Llosa, *A Writer's Reality*, 126–27.

44. For a recent and illuminating discussion of this problem, see John Tomlinson, *Cultural Imperialism* (Baltimore: Johns Hopkins University Press, 1991), 68–101.

45. Da Cunha's *Os sertões* has been called "The Bible of Brazilian nationality" and a "great national epic." Its author may be said to have intended it as a founding text or document on which the modern Brazilian nation was to be built. See, for example, Samuel Putnam's introduction to *Rebellion in the Backlands*, iii.

46. On the limited and sovereign character of the modern nation-state, see Benedict Anderson, *Imagined Communities* (London: Verso, 1991), 1–8.

47. For a discussion of Comte's doctrine of the positivist superman and its relationship to the thought of Marx and Nietzsche, see Eric Voegelin, *The New Science of Politics* (Chicago: University of Chicago Press, 1952), 80.

48. See Francis Fukuyama, *The End of History and the Last Man* (New York: The Free Press, 1992), 55–152, especially 126–39.

49. The title that da Cunha originally intended to give *Os sertões* could be translated as *"Our Vendée"*. See da Cunha, *Rebellion in the Backlands*, 162.

50. Vargas Llosa, *A Writer's Reality*, 132–33.

51. Leszek Kolakowski, *Main Currents of Marxism*, trans. P. S. Falla (Oxford: Oxford University Press, 1978), vol. 1, 203–11, 246–59.

52. Oviedo, 309.

53. See especially, Mario Vargas Llosa, "Albert Camus y la moral de los

límites," and "El homicida indelicado" in *Contra viento y marea,* 231–52 and 265–75.

54. On Gall's connection to the Catalan anarchists, see Vargas Llosa, *A Writer's Reality,* 138–89. On Gall's resemblance to Graham, see John Walker, "Canudos Revisted: Cunninghame Graham, Vargas Llosa and the Messianic Tradition," *Symposium* 41 (1987–1988): 308–16.

55. Vargas Llosa, *A Writer's Reality,* 138–39.

56. Vargas Llosa, "El homicida indelicado," 273.

57. On the transition from eschatology to the philosophy of history, see especially Gotthold Lessing, "The Education of the Human Race," in *Lessing's Theological Writings,* trans. Henry Chadwick (Stanford, Calif.: Stanford University Press, 1956), 82–98.

58. The historical Antônio Mendes Maciel was a more Machiavellian figure than Vargas Llosa sometimes represents him, a religious prophet especially adept at cooperating with the local *fazendeiros* and *coronels* whom he supplied with votes and cheap labor in exchange for political and economic support. See Ralph Della Cava, "Brazilian Messianism and National Institutions: A Reappraisal of Canudos and Joaseiro," *The Hispanic American Historical Review* 48 (1968): 411–13.

59. Oviedo, 312–14.

60. On the necessity of liberty for the initial cultivation of the arts and sciences, see David Hume, "Of the Rise and Progress of the Arts and Sciences," in *Essays, Moral, Political, and Literary.*

61. Fukuyama, 71–97.

62. As noted above, to some degree the Baron de Canabrava also serves this function, not, of course, as an advocate of liberal democracy, but as a critic of its antagonists—the Counselor, the Jacobin generals, and Galileo Gall.

63. Gerald Martin, "Mario Vargas Llosa: Errant Knight of the Liberal Imagination," in *On Modern Latin American Fiction,* ed. John King (New York: Farrar, Straus and Giroux, 1987), 222–23.

64. For a similar argument in a different context, see Wasserman, 468–69.

Epilogue

1. Patrick Glynn, "The Age of Balkanization," *Commentary* 96 (1993): 21.

2. Mario Vargas Llosa, "The Culture of Liberty," in *The Global Resurgence of Democracy,* ed. Larry Diamond and Marc F. Plattner (Baltimore: Johns Hopkins University Press, 1993), 84.

3. For a sociological analysis of the connections among modern industrial society, the rise of the nation-state, the establishment of a centralized educational system, and the homogeneity of global modernity, see Ernest

Gellner, *Nations and Nationalism* (Ithaca, N.Y.: Cornell University Press, 1983), especially 19–39, 110–122.

4. Francis Fukuyama, *The End of History and the Last Man,* (New York: The Free Press, 1992), 46.

5. In what is perhaps the most original, but underappreciated section of his book, Fukuyama offers a detailed and illuminating analysis of this question; see 287–339.

Editions Cited

Achebe, Chinua. *Anthills of the Savannah*. New York: Anchor Books, 1988.
———. *No Longer at Ease*. New York: Fawcett, 1960.
———. *Things Fall Apart*. London: Heinemann, 1958.
Conrad, Joseph. *Lord Jim*, ed. Thomas C. Moser. New York: W. W. Norton, 1968.
Hardy, Thomas. *The Mayor of Casterbridge*. London: Macmillan, 1974.
Stendhal. *A Life of Napoleon*. New York: Howard Fertig, 1977. Abbreviated as LN.
———. *The Red and the Black*, trans. and ed. Robert M. Adams. New York: W. W. Norton, 1969. Abbreviated as RB.
Vargas Llosa, Mario. *The War of the End of the World*, trans. Helen R. Lane. New York: Avon, 1984.

Index

231

DATE DUE

JUL 11 09			